DISCARD

# RACISM AND MEDIA

*Racism and Media* addresses one of the major challenges of today's world: the continuing racisms propagated, reproduced and reinforced via different genres and media in many context dependent ways. This book is an excellent, well argued, and comprehensive overview, with several in-depth case studies, which illustrate how pervasive racist attitudes, strategies, and practices have become and how they are disseminated both in formal and informal everyday interactions. A most valuable contribution to media studies, discourse studies, and political science.

**Ruth Wodak, Lancaster University**

This book is important. It builds on an astonishing array of writers on race and media to develop an original perspective on what it calls the 'debatability' of racism. Its arguments are well illustrated. It is theoretically sophisticated. It is also politically sharp. All that's left is for you to read it.

**Ghassan Hage, University of Melbourne**

As a scholar and journalist who feels rather familiar with ideas about race, I found this book refreshing and clarifying. It helped me see patterns in the fog of racial claims, to connect developments in the U.S. and Europe and to better understand how change and continuity are unfolding in mediated racial politics. Ultimately, *Racism and Media* will inform how I craft arguments about the relationship between media and race and how I think about what we are fighting for.

**Chenjerai Kumanyika, Rutgers University**

Media logics are integrated into the formation of racism which are, as Titley argues, 'simultaneously everywhere and nowhere in our public culture'. In calm and measured prose, he unpicks numerous conceptual issues around postracialism, the domopolitical and Islamophobia, using case materials about the Charlie Hebdo affair, the English Defence League and others. This is a sophisticated contribution to both understanding and acting against the re-emergence of the far Right.

**Annabelle Sreberny, SOAS**

# RACISM AND MEDIA

## GAVAN TITLEY

**◎SAGE**

Los Angeles | London | New Delhi
Singapore | Washington DC | Melbourne

Los Angeles | London | New Delhi
Singapore | Washington DC | Melbourne

SAGE Publications Ltd
1 Oliver's Yard
55 City Road
London EC1Y 1SP

SAGE Publications Inc.
2455 Teller Road
Thousand Oaks, California 91320

SAGE Publications India Pvt Ltd
B 1/I 1 Mohan Cooperative Industrial Area
Mathura Road
New Delhi 110 044

SAGE Publications Asia-Pacific Pte Ltd
3 Church Street
#10-04 Samsung Hub
Singapore 049483

Editor: Michael Ainsley
Assistant editor: John Nightingale
Production editor: Imogen Roome
Copyeditor: Aud Scriven
Proofreader: Leigh C. Smithson
Indexer: Adam Pozner
Marketing manager: Lucia Sweet
Cover design: Francis Kenney
Typeset by: C&M Digitals (P) Ltd, Chennai, India

© Gavan Titley, 2019

First published 2019

Apart from any fair dealing for the purposes of research or private study, or criticism or review, as permitted under the Copyright, Designs and Patents Act, 1988, this publication may be reproduced, stored or transmitted in any form, or by any means, only with the prior permission in writing of the publishers, or in the case of reprographic reproduction, in accordance with the terms of licences issued by the Copyright Licensing Agency. Enquiries concerning reproduction outside those terms should be sent to the publishers.

**Library of Congress Control Number: 201896465**

**British Library Cataloguing in Publication data**

A catalogue record for this book is available from the British Library

ISBN 978-1-4462-9853-4
ISBN 978-1-4462-9854-1 (pbk)

For Mary and Alan Titley

# Contents

# Preface and acknowledgements

Racism does not stay still; it changes shape, size, contours, purpose, function – with changes in the economy, the social structure, the system and, above all, the challenges, the resistance to that system. (Ambalavaner Sivanandan, 1990: 64)

In intensely mediated societies racism stays still less and less, and it is this communicative generativity, and its social and political significance, which is the subject of this book. It is shaped by the general observation that, in many contemporary societies, the extent of public debate and controversy as to what constitutes racism, and who gets to decide, is politically consequential. This is not simply confusion as to the 'correct' meaning of racism, but productive noise, a dimension of how racisms change size, contours and function. Racism, this book argues, is a subject not just of debate but also of what I term *debatability*, a constant contest as to what counts as racism and whose reality counts in this evaluation, a process that renders it a matter of opinion and speculative churn, not history, experience and power. This general observation is pulled into different shapes and directions depending on particular issues, relations and contexts, but it is based on two factors that intersect in the socio-political contexts under discussion in this book.

The first is socio-political, and can be contingently summarized as a pronounced sense of postracialism. That is, 'race' does not exist, and racism, when it does exist, is defined by its pastness and its extremism, an ignorant or ideological passion, out of time. Given the tendency to measure out international time in US presidencies, it may seem strange to talk of postracialism in a book commenced during Obama's era of 'hope' and completed during Trump's experiment in full-throated racist scapegoating (not to mention in a European conjuncture where anti-migrant and anti-Muslim racism is articulated with increasingly open enthusiasm in polities across the continent). However, as Chapter 1 discusses at length, there are many ways of understanding the question of postracialism, and one of them is congruent with the shape-shifting renewals of racism as a political force that Sivanandan insists on in the quotation above.

The second is that of networked digital media systems, and profound and still unfolding shifts in the accelerated and expanded production, distribution and circulation of information, images and artefacts. Under these conditions mediated forms of racialized provocation carry renewed political charge. Intensive media events unfolding around whether an act or a statement *actually* constitutes racism have become staple rituals of public culture. Racialized meanings and practices have historically been formed both contextually and in networks of international exchange and influence, and digital media's transnational networks of exchange intensify and complicate these dynamics, in spectacular and quotidian ways. While the book argues that these processes often result in enhanced forms of racist force, they are also contingent, and as Sivanandan reminds us, always contested and resisted, including in and through media conditions that bolster and complicate these anti-racist practices.

The title *Racism and Media* has an encompassing and authoritative ring to it, but it is not intended to signal more than the twin preoccupations of the thematic chapters that follow. There are many dimensions that this book does not do proper justice to, such as production studies and institutional analysis, or the particular complexity of racialized relations in settler colonial societies. It does attempt, however, to give an integrated weight to the discussion of racisms, and of media, and not to merely use one theme to talk about the other. In so doing it tries to avoid being a Media Studies book on the topic of racism that establishes an orienting understanding of racism before moving on to the main business, such as the study of racialized media representations. The insistence of historicity and social relationality in Sivanandan's pithy formulation implies that there can be no general theory of racism from which explorations of media products and practices depart. Instead the focus of analysis must be the historical specificity of racisms, and their contextual articulation in and through particular political ideologies, social antagonisms, national imaginaries, and forms of representation, discourse and media work.

At the same time, it strives not to be a book on the sociology of racism or race theory that includes media but solely or primarily as a structuring factor, ideological agent or discursive illustration. In this disciplinary field, my aim is to explore the ways in which media logics have become more fully integrated into the formations of racism. This attempt at a deeper integration between the fields that inform my scholarship and political commitments accounts for the choice to often delve deep into particular contextual issues and case studies, and to draw on conceptual possibilities and analytical approaches adequate to these dynamics, processes and relations (though 'text book'-like coverage of theoretical issues and relevant research on key themes is also included). The book treats certain contexts in depth while maintaining a focus on the (transnational) relationality of racisms across contexts, and while the US and the UK are amongst these contexts, the book's approach is deeply resistant to the implicit tendency to generalize about racism, and racism and media, from these Anglophone sites. That said, the irony is not lost on me that focusing primarily on the politics and polities of western Europe enacts something of the Eurocentrism so integral to historical and contemporary forms of race-making. In that regard, unless otherwise stated, all translations – and any possible loss of nuance or accent – are mine.

This book has been a while in the making, and it simply would not have been possible without advice, support and inspiration from quite a few people. At SAGE Publications I'm grateful for the editorial advice, support and patience of Mila Steele, Chris Rojek, John Nightingale and, in particular, Michael Ainsley. Several key arguments profited from the engagement and commentary of interlocutors at different institutions, so thanks to those who invited me to speak on the book over recent years: the COMET lecture series in the University of Tampere; Isabel Awad and Jiska Engelbert at Rotterdam Erasmus University; Bob Brecher and Cathy Bergin at the Centre for Applied Philosophy, Politics and Ethics (CAPPE) for their 'Thinking the Politics of "Race"' lecture series at the University of Brighton; Suvi Keskinen and Raster, the Finnish anti-racist research network; the Hrant Dink Foundation, Istanbul; Donatella della Porta at the Scuola Normale in Florence; and Gargi Bhattacharyya, Satnam Virdee and Aaron Winter for their 'Histories and Futures of Anti-Racism' seminar in the University of East London. I have presented aspects of this work at the Diaspora, Migration and Media section of the European Communication Research and Education Association, thanks also to the section teams and members.

I finished this book as a visiting researcher at the Department of Media and Communication Studies, University of Helsinki; *kiitos* Mervi Pantti and colleagues on our Academy of Finland Hybra project, *tack* and *merci* to the rooftop terrace collective at the Swedish School of Social Science. Only in Maynooth, or #OIM; I have great colleagues in the Department of Media Studies, Maynooth University, and here I'd particularly like to thank Anne O'Brien, Anne Byrne, Maria Pramaggiore and Stephanie Rains. I'm also grateful to the university for research support and a generally supportive environment. This book owes something, in some way or another, to a fantastic bunch of people; Irati Agirreazkuenaga Onaindia, Sharam Alghasi, Bolette Blaagaard, Harry Browne, Miyase Christensen, Colin Coulter, Monika Dac, Nicholas de Genova, Natalie Fenton, Priyamvada Gopal, David Hesmondhalgh, Charles Husband, Gholam Khiabany, Sarah Mazouz, Aurélien Mondon, Marie Moran, Kaarina Nikunen, Anamik Saha, Sanjay Sharma, Oula Silvennoinen, Aoife Titley, Paloma Viejo, Milly Williamson. It has been immeasurably improved by the attentive reading and generous engagement of Carolina Sanchez Boe, Michael Cronin, Des Freedman, Malcolm James, Kylie Jarrett, Olivia Umurerwa Rutazibwa, Eugenia Siapera, Jason Toynbee, and, as always, Alana Lentin. I am especially grateful for the incisive and caring attention that Sivamohan Valluvan invested in this book at key moments. It goes without saying that none of the above are responsible for the book's shortcomings (though I reserve the right to modify this stance over time).

I have learned much from activist friends and comrades in Ireland, Finland and elsewhere in Europe, not to mention on those dread platforms that shall not be named here. All author royalties from this book are pledged to the Movement of Asylum Seekers in Ireland (MASI) and their struggle for justice against the inhumanity of the deportation and detention apparatus. Päivi, Jonas-Liam and Alvar, thank you for your precious love and support, and two out of three of you get extra thanks for the relentless supply of memes. This book is dedicated to my parents, Mary and Alan Titley, *le grá agus buíochas*, with love and gratitude.

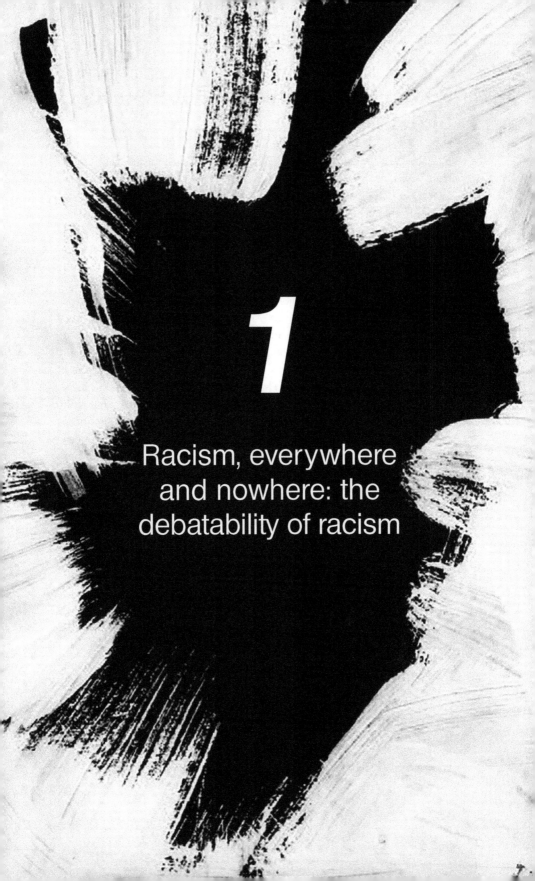

# 1

Racism, everywhere and nowhere: the debatability of racism

# Postracialism and the debatability of racism

In 2015 the Finnish newspaper *Helsingin Sanomat* reported that Laura Huhtasaari, an MP for the right-wing nationalist True Finns Party, was a member of a closed Facebook group 'The racist background of rapists that hide in bushes'. Under a banner montage of photos of unnamed men of what appear to be Somali and North African heritage, the group description outlines how it is dedicated to proving how 'Muslim immigration' had increased instances of rape in Finland and other northern European countries. As well as detailing the endless timeline entreaties to 'defend our culture', the newspaper report drew attention to several instances of overt anti-black racism in posted memes and comments. Given this unwelcome media attention, Huhtasaari sought to distance herself from it publicly, first contending that a rogue algorithm had 'liked' the page for her, and then arguing that 'I'm not racist. Maybe I could define myself for myself?' (Muraja, 2015). The Finnish politician's exquisite remix of *I'm not racist, but*, is, of course, interchangeable with countless similar attempts at racism denial from a wide range of national contexts, as such minor public scandals have become a generic dimension of political life. There is something about the plaintiveness of her plea for 'self-definition', all the same, that acutely illustrates a central dynamic explored in this chapter, and book.

Racism, in public culture, is simultaneously everywhere and nowhere. The very mention of race serves as an invitation to disprove its salience, the mention of racism as an invitation to refute its relevance. In the contemporary political context, to speak publicly about racism is to be immediately integrated into an intensive process of delineation, deflection and denial, a contest over who gets to *define* racism, when 'everyone' gets to speak about it. This incessant public contestation is shaped both by contemporary socio-political conditions and conflicts, and by the integration of complex, transnational media connectivity to the spaces of social action in which these conflicts are lived and played out. In the postcolonial, migration nations of western Europe and North America, this contestation centres on the dominant imaginary of these societies as 'postracial', socio-political spaces in which, the story goes, the divisive 'idea of race' no longer matters, and the violence of racism has been largely transcended. The public cultures of these societies are also shaped by dense transnational networks of media flow and communicative connectivity that provide unprecedented possibilities to both extend and challenge racializing discourses, images, frameworks and information. The overlap between the two produces what this book terms the *debatability* of racism, the constant contest as to what constitutes racism, as to whose 'definition' and voice counts, and as to the consequences that should stem from these fractious forms of public recognition and denial.

This is, in introduction, a very general contention. Racism in public culture may be simultaneously everywhere and nowhere, but the analysis of it cannot linger at this level of generality, for engaging everywhere is to risk ending up nowhere in particular. Racism is not a generic phenomenon or a universal category, and the study of *racisms* requires paying attention to the historical and contextual specificity of its operations and mobilizations. Context is not defined by or limited to the borders of the nation-state, for while nation-specific or comparative studies are often the main form through which historical specificity is explored, racisms have taken shape within the transnational systems of colonial and capitalist modernity (Stam and Shohat, 2012). They have taken on renewed force within the relations and networks of neoliberal globalization, through which the racialized politicization of migration has become integral to the expression of social insecurity and cultural anxiety. And through the spatial rescaling and disordering of the enduring mutations of the 'war on terror', the transnational figure of 'the Muslim' has been shaped as a malleable focus of apparently reasonable aversion. In critical social theory, consequently, the analysis of racism requires us to focus on the interplay of structural commonalities and contextual differences, historical specificities and continuities, relational linkages and exchanges across territories and terrains (Murji and Solomos, 2015). Contemporary media theory demands similarly supple coordinates, as racist practices and understandings of racism increasingly take shape within what Ingrid Volkmer (2014: 1) describes as an '… unprecedented landscape of digital connections and a new architecture of globalized communication, which we are only beginning to understand'.

The idea of debatability, therefore, is not proposed as a definitive concept. Rather, it is a conjunctural orientation. That is, it proposes, in this particular socio-political and historical moment, a mode of thinking about racism *in* the media, and racism *and* the media. That racism appears to be 'everywhere and nowhere' suggests that the prevalence of insistent, mediated contestation as to *what racism is* must be taken seriously. This is not a straightforward analytical task, for as Sanjay Sharma (2013) argues in relation to circuits of social media exchange, networked, interactive media generate a 'racialized info-overload' of 'casual racial banter, race-hate comments, "griefing", images, videos and anti-racist sentiment (that) bewilderingly intermingle, mash-up and virally circulate'. The everyday ubiquity of this 'bewildering' media productivity extends from Sharma's social media focus across an integrated media terrain, through what Andrew Chadwick (2013) describes as a 'hybrid media system' that integrates 'old' and 'new' media into a system of competing and merging media logics shaping the production of news, mediation of public opinion, flow of political information, and contest of symbolic power. On this terrain, racism is not just a focus of political contestation but also a source of fascination. Long a reliable object of public scandal and ritual repudiation, it is now also a hyperlink to data-productive controversies. The ubiquity of this confusion, fascination and contestation suggests that it must be approached analytically as saying *something* about the shape and force of contemporary racisms.

At least in part, that something suggests an apparent contradiction: the more racism is regarded as having been overcome in a 'postracial' era, the more it is discussed, defined and denied. The extent of this contradiction has expanded significantly in recent years, for as David Theo Goldberg observes in *Are We All Postracial Yet?*, 'Race today is supposed to be a thing of the past. But all we do, seemingly, is talk about it' (2015: 1). The idea of debatability recognizes that this talk is hosted and shaped in a very particular media terrain, one characterized by increased communicative participation through connective media, where 'more talk' is a socially valorized and economically prioritized pursuit (Van Dijck, 2013). It is this apparent contradiction, under these conditions, that allows an argument to be built on these opening observations, an argument that is threaded through the chapters of this book. If the meaning of racism is historical and contingent and shifting under changing social relations and through new political conditions and conflicts, then the persistent communicative work that is invested in the attention as to *what counts as racism* does more than say something of analytical value about the cultural production of contemporary racisms. It must also be approached as a generative political dimension of how racism functions in a putatively 'postracial' conjuncture. In other words, in contexts where official narratives and dominant public discourses assume the 'end of racism' even as people who experience racism attest to its renewed formations and exclusionary and humiliating force, these everyday communicative concentrations on the status, nature and extent of racism are politically consequential.

While this argument is explored throughout the book, it requires some further initial explanation, as it underpins the approach of this chapter. For some analysts, the prevalence of this 'talk' suggests a troubling inflation and relativization of public understandings of racism, where 'racism' has become politically and conceptually overloaded (Song, 2014). For others, it suggests a critical gap between racism's contemporary mutability and the 'limited conceptual understanding of "racism"' that broadly dominates in public culture (Bonilla-Silva, 2015: 57). What I have thus far referred to as 'the postracial' moment encompasses these dynamics, while also involving further considerations. These further dimensions can be explored by acknowledging, firstly, that the idea of the 'postracial' is also inevitably entangled in competing meanings, in part because of different valences between North America and Europe, but also because the 'post' implicates two very different imaginaries of a world without racism.

In the first, the *post* is future-oriented, as it gathers together a knot of theoretical engagements, social observations and political commitments focused on the abolition of *race*. Race, understood as a pseudo-scientific discourse increasingly ascendant during the late modern period of imperialism, nation-building and genocidal expansionism, imposed a hierarchical system of dehumanizing distinctions that retain a 'commonsense' explanatory purchase even in societies where biological racism has been repudiated. Thus the false category of race must ultimately be eliminated, particularly in forms of anti-racism that mobilize racial identifications, concepts and solidarities in opposition to racist violence or exclusion. As Joshua Paul argues, 'Post-racialism attempts to develop an anti-race anti-racism capable of imagining and bringing into being a world where the pernicious hierarchies of race no longer feature' (2014: 705). This aim has engendered a hugely complex debate, for as Colette Guillaumin remarks, 'race does not exist. But it does kill people' (1995: 107). In other words, the conceptual erasure of race does not necessarily impact on its socio-political and material consequences, consequences that make it *real*.

The second pronounced trajectory of the 'postracial' looks not to the future but to an image of the present, a present regarded as no longer marked by the legacies of what is held to be consigned to the past. Barnor Hesse describes this widely assumed narrative of overcoming:

> Since the ending of the US civil rights movement, the Cold War and the apartheid regime in South Africa, political discussion of the meaning of racism seems to be over in the West. Its sociality is overwhelmingly conceived as a problem that has largely been overcome. What remains is seen as residuum, consigned to pathology, a profound moral deviation from the western liberal and democratic ethos and ethnos. Racism has been declared an unacceptable form of western social behavior, committed by groups voluntarily on the political fringes of society or desperately by classes economically jettisoned to its decaying edges. (2004: 10)

Hesse points to the ways in which dominant understandings of racism in western countries tend to be over-determined through association with the still-recent histories of overtly racist regimes that have been discredited and defeated, and, as Chapter 4 examines, the far-right movements and parties that recall these pasts in ideological and iconographic terms (the *residuum*). Moreover, as the endless parade of public scandals over mediated racist outbursts such as Huhtasaari's suggests, racism is framed as an exceptional outburst and treated as an individual aberration, not only unconnected from any broader political or systemic patterns, but also often 'repudiated publicly so that the routine activities of racist statecraft may continue' (James et al., 2018). This broad mesh of assumptions constructs what Brett St Louis describes as the 'fiction' of the 'actually existing post-racial society' (2015: 118). This fiction is not simply a superficial cover story laid over an unchanged racist reality. Rather, this over-identification of racism with particular historical formations and lexicons constricts an understanding of how 'new' racisms constantly take shape and function. Alana Lentin (2016) has described this as the problem of dominant public understandings of racism being '"frozen" in relation to past events that have been sanctioned for identification as racist'.

This fixing of the meaning of racism in public imaginaries has been helped along in no small part by the plethora of ideological projects – such as 'colourblindness' or 'reverse racism' – that took shape in the post-war and post-civil rights period to insistently declare 'the end of racism', and thus to explain away persistent forms of racialized inequality as the result of cultural pathologies or individual failings.

In the US context, Touré F. Reed (2018) underlines how 'post-racialism is in step with postwar liberalism's tendency to treat racial inequities as if they exist in a world apart from the economic processes that generate them'. But the wider challenge, as Angela Davis argues, is examining how the 'persistence of historical meanings of racism and its remedies prevent us from recognizing the complex ways in which racism clandestinely structures prevailing institutions, practices and ideologies' (2008: 2). In this understanding, the postracial is more than a fiction, it is an active political force, operative in the contrast between the 'frozen' – 'there is no room for racism in this society' – and the shifting political, economic, social and cultural processes through which racism is reproduced and renewed, and through which 'problem' subjects are marked out.

David Theo Goldberg's concept of *postracialism* captures this generativity, for 'what is at work ... is the restructuring of the conditions of racist expression, and their terms of articulation' (2015: 113). That is, postracialism is more than confusion as to what now constitutes racism, or ideological denial of its enduring sociality. Rather, it is the totality of the ways in which racism is re-formed – through which populations and identities are marked out as suspicious, as problems to be contained, intervened in or disposed of – in societies where race is regarded as a historical deviation, overcome. Postraciality, Goldberg argues, 'increasingly erases or erodes the possibility of identifying racisms and their underpinnings, their structures and implications' (ibid: 88). It is a condition that both obscures the enduring historicity of racial arrangements and structures, while sanctioning and fashioning modes of racist expression that activate their racial underpinnings precisely because it is now difficult if not impossible to recall them to them:

> Postraciality ... rather than expressing the end of racism, conceals within its conceptual erasure of race the driving mode of contemporary racist articulation. Racisms dis-appear behind the formal deletion of racial classification, state regulation, and legal refusal of racial definition. They express themselves anew in the name of racial disappearance, disavowal, and denial. Racisms proliferate in the wake of the supposed death of race. (ibid: 152)

Debatability, in part, is animated in this space between the fixed and the motile, between the denial of racisms that do not map onto the assumed shape of the past, and the insistence on *speaking of racism* because what is taking shape requires the force of this naming. In proposing this idea, it should be clear that I do not mean that the experience of racism is open to debate, or that racially structured dimensions of social and political life are radically open to question. Rather, it is intended as a way of thinking about how the experience of racism and the operations of structural racism can be denied not only through silencing, but also through noise; not just through a lack of attention to racism, but also via an excess of particular kinds of attention. And as a theme that extends through the book, I want to suggest that this debatability, this incessant, recursive attention *as to what counts as racism and who gets to define it*, has political consequences for practices of anti-racism – practices that want to *name racism publicly*, the better to mobilize to confront it.

In contemporary theory, the tricky prefix 'post' is often too prevalent, and opening this analysis with a discussion of *postness* makes for an admittedly complex starting point. However, a more conventional approach, such as providing a linear treatment of definitions of race and racism, is simply inadequate to explore the contemporary political and communicative context. Understanding the productive political force of postracial confusion in contemporary societies requires that it is this recursive attention as to what counts as racism and what racism is taken to mean in public cultures, rather than an orienting set of theoretical definitions, that provides the analytical point of entry to this study. For these reasons, this chapter differs in its approach from those that follow.

It is structured around three intensively mediated incidents that sketch out a broad canvas of public dynamics produced through the intersection of 'postracial' confusion and digital profusion. They are snapshots, not case studies, and each one instantiates an important 'postracial' dynamic. By peeling away at the understandings of racism at play, they lay out an orienting sense of the confusion, contestation and polarization the idea of racism currently generates. These interpretative and political dynamics are produced through concentrated bursts of communicative energy, and examining their generation opens up ways of thinking about media dynamics and practices in the 'hybrid media system'. In short, they open up questions about racism, and about media, that map the analytical challenges subsequent chapters respond to, and help identify the theoretical resources they must marshal in order to get to grips with the generativity of networked communications on a 'postracial' terrain.

# The decidability of racism

Intensive and ephemeral concentrations of mediated activity and attention are a pronounced feature of contemporary media cultures, and debatability is generated when these discursive episodes pivot on confusion and polarization as to what constitutes racism.

On the 13th of January 2016 the French satirical newspaper *Charlie Hebdo* published a cartoon by Laurent Sourisseau, or 'Riss', a longtime contributor who had been injured in the lethal attack on the magazine on the 7th of January 2015. The edition for the 13th of January followed a highly publicized edition marking the first anniversary of the attacks. Riss's cartoon also generated significant publicity, for different if not altogether unrelated reasons. Under the heading 'Migrants', the cartoon posed a question: 'What would little Aylan have become if he'd grown up?' 'Little Aylan' is Aylan (or Alan) Kurdi, a three-year-old Syrian boy who drowned with his mother and brother while trying to cross from Turkey to the Greek island of Kos in early September 2015. A photo by the Turkish journalist Nilüfer Demir captured his lifeless body lying in the surf on a beach near Bodrum in Turkey. It was widely circulated in social media and on news sites, and representations of his body, captured in a pose redolent of nothing more than a toddler's slumber, rapidly circulated in symbolic forms beyond the original photo. Drawing directly on this iconic currency, a small drawing of his body bunched up in the lapping seawater is inserted in a circular inset in the top left of the cartoon, below which the main action unfolds. Two men, whose facial features are exaggerated through some hybrid of pig-like and ape-like characteristics, are chasing a woman who is running away and screaming as they advance. These figures are the answer to the headline question, and underscored by a written text: '*Tripoteur de fesses en Allemagne*' ['an ass groper in Germany'].

I first saw this image on the afternoon of its publication, when it was posted on the Facebook page of a French political activist with a large following, with the update 'Repeat after me: No, *Charlie Hebdo* is not racist'. The image of the cartoon was a re-post from the *Médiapart* journalist Faïza Zerouala, who posted it on Twitter – '*Charlie Hebdo mesdames et messieurs. Voilà*'. As the image spread rapidly through the social networks I access, it circulated across contexts and through languages, generating a concentrated period of interpretation and argument. Concomitantly, this social media 'furore' also became the raw material for rapidly blogged media coverage on established international news sites, with several social media 'curated' stories appearing on the 13th – 'Twitter responds to the latest *Hebdo* cartoon' – prior to full articles on the 14th, declaring, inter alia, a 'backlash' against the newspaper, and posing the question *is the cartoon racist?*

The meaning of Riss's cartoon prompted an 'enhanced news story', that is, a news story that circulates between social media platforms and content-intensive news sites, accumulating discursive value through circulation and participation (Fox, 2016: 24–5). The image of the cartoon I saw was a close-up photo taken on a mobile phone and shared via Twitter. Screen grabs of this photo, and others like it, circulated and mingled with licensed professional reproductions as the cartoon travelled beyond its allotted position in a newspaper's page layout, transformed into a 'digital object' that can be combined and recombined with other sets of digital objects through forms of remediation (Murthy, 2013: 26–7). The concentrated response to the cartoon was globally distributed, produced by clustered intensities of communicative action shaped by temporal dynamics of circulation across and within networked media spaces. Publics are always contingent, but this ephemeral communicative event took shape in a digital media environment characterized by the flow of content in and across social media platforms and news sites, accumulating reaction and commentary.

Its public, therefore, took shape in what Ingrid Volkmer describes as 'spheres of connected discursive consciousness' that emerge through these dense, convergent trans-border layers of communicative connectedness. This distributed discursive consciousness is conceptualized, in Volkmer's terms, as a *public horizon* rather than public sphere – a distinction captured in the fact that while the cartoon preoccupied me, and virtual interlocutors, for days, it barely charted on the consciousness of many people who actually have to live with me on a daily basis. Public horizons are both connective and individualizing, as they are produced through the 'techno-sociality' of digital media platforms, which, as Poell and Van Dijck remind us, 'are not *neutral* technologies that merely *enable* user activity [but instead] … *shape* how users share information, curate news, and express their points of view' (2014: 182, original emphasis). Public horizons are therefore ephemeral, not just because controversies such as this take shape in conditions where attention is the scarcest resource, but because the 'technological zones' of communication are also ephemeral – comment sections 'are now closed for comments', hotly contested Facebook threads vanish into the forgotten zone of 'older stories' (see Christensen and Christensen, 2013: 354).

If these are the communicative conditions under which this enhanced news story took shape, how did the question *is the cartoon racist?* emerge? A recurring characteristic of *Charlie Hebdo*'s cartoon satire is to fuse two topical stories or references into a pointed, overarching *second degré* comment. In this case, the blended elements were themselves recent news stories related to the intensification of the European borders crisis during 2015. Riss's cartoon was enhanced as a news story also because it referenced, and was inducted into, a cumulative sequence of mediated events. The photo image of Aylan Kurdi's body was shared first on Twitter, rapidly going 'viral' before being integrated into global news content. As Stanley Cohen writes in *States of Denial*, 'our knowledge is not dependent on chance. It is permanent and continuous; those single moments when a crying Rwandan orphan appears on screen are reminders of what we already know' (2001: 295). The appearance of this image on multiple screens was also the confirmation of a sublimated knowledge: of the extraordinary violence of the militarized borders of 'Fortress Europe', where borders organize hierarchies not just of mobility but also of viable human life, sifting those who 'belong' from what Zygmunt Bauman (2003) has termed the 'human waste' produced as an unwanted by-product of violent conflict and neoliberal globalization. Yet borders cannot ultimately prevent human movement, nor repress the needs and desires that propel it, and so 'by sea or by land, increased security at the EU's frontiers has not resulted in less immigration, merely in more deaths' (Trilling, 2015).

The velocity and scale of the circulation of the image of Aylan Kurdi generated a widespread representational reflex, the production of adapted versions of what was rapidly framed in media commentary as an *iconic* image. 'We live in an era', Limor Shifman notes, 'driven by a *hypermemetic* logic, in which almost every major public event sprouts a string of memes' (2014: loc 119, original emphasis). Tribute drawings and political cartoons; 'rehumanizing' images of Aylan alive and with his family; protest 'die-ins' against the inhumanity of the European border regime, with activists wearing his now indexical red t-shirt and blue shorts – the image was invested in as a 'never again' moment, willed, through its adaptation and circulation, to attain a power to shift 'public opinion' towards greater humanity, or hospitality, or justice, or at least to 'shift the media narrative' towards a focus on the *plight of refugees* rather than the *problem of migrants*. In that moment, according to Vis et al., 'the image of Aylan Kurdi created a social media event that looked capable of becoming a critical juncture in changing attitudes for the better' (2015: 71).

In Riss's cartoon, the 'unifying' moment of Aylan Kurdi's death is mashed up with another intensive media event connected to the 'refugee issue' in 2015, but one that was held to attest to the divisiveness of 'mass migration' – the allegations of widespread sexual assaults by 'refugees and migrants' on New Year's Eve in central Köln. If the photo of Aylan was charged with 'changing public opinion for the better', the confused but cumulative force of stories of widespread sexual assaults at the celebrations in Köln was framed as 'turning public opinion sharply against refugees in Europe'. It is clear that up to a thousand women filed legal complaints of theft, sexual assault and harassment after that night, and that in the region of 20 asylum-seekers and numerous men of 'North African background' were investigated as a consequence. However the truth of the women's experiences, and their voices and testimonies, were dissolved in a powerful – and frequently overtly patriarchal – desire to frame the fact of sexual assaults as a racialized truth about the problem of migration, Islam, and Muslim men (an elision compounded by attempts to combat the surge of racist framing by minimizing the extent and seriousness of the assaults).

That what actually happened that night in Köln would be subject to investigation and factual correction over many weeks did not prevent the rapid construction of *Köln* as a particular kind of event. As Ron Eyerman writes, occurrences become events through narration, and:

> … through a dialectic of actions and interpretations. Actions occur in time and space, events unfold and take shape. An event unfolds and takes shape in the interplay between protagonists, interpreters, and audience, as sense and meaning is attributed and various interpretations compete with each other. As this meaning struggle proceeds, various accounts stabilize, with perhaps one achieving some sort of hegemony, but counter interpretations or stories may continue to exist alongside. (2008: 22)

If Aylan's photo was a *we cannot say that we did not know* event, Köln was framed as a *now nobody can deny* event – a dramatic occurrence that is discursively framed as demonstrating or revealing an 'uncomfortable truth' about minority or racialized populations that must now, finally, in the light of this proof, be recognized (Demmers and Mehendale, 2010). From early January, stories in right-wing mainstream newspapers mingled with practised forms of disinformation propagated through a network of 'counter-jihad' news sites to push the insistent idea that the initially confused official response represented an attempt at a 'cover-up'. This initial framing expanded to suggest that 'rapefugees' and 'migrant rape gangs' were coordinating sexual assault plans internationally through instant messaging services. A narrative of a sexual and gendered 'clash of civilizations' has become increasingly important to radical right networks as Chapter 4 discusses; however, as Boulila and Carri's research on the events suggests, this narrative was reproduced far more broadly, for 'as the "terror of Cologne" came to stand for an exceptional attack on the German nation, anti-racist claims were said to deflect from the "real issues"'. Thus, 'what followed was the post-feminist emergence of a consensus that German sexism had long been overcome and that only extremists (read feminists) claim that Germany has a deep-rooted problem with misogyny' (2017: 289).

The transnational meaning struggle over Köln materialized in an online news environment characterized by speed and space, multiplicity and polycentrality (Fenton, 2010). As Mona Abdel-Fadil (2016) noted in an initial media analysis, the accelerated speed of coverage and the assemblage of sources and linked sites through rolling reports and content curation ensured that a plethora of what turned out, subsequently, to be fabricated stories circulated intensively, and the steady but relatively under-reported revision of assault figures did little to unsettle sensationalist news frames. Thus the serious but isolated sexual violence in Köln was subject to resilient ideological framing, racialized as the exclusive problem of the non-western migrant. In so doing, it indexed a particularly involved domain of postracial conflict that recurs throughout this book, as to how the contemporary racialization of 'Muslims' can be publicly contested in a context where the refrain 'Islam is not a race' is invested in, to varying degrees and valences, across the political spectrum in Europe.

Assembled and engaged in 'spheres of connected discursive consciousness', the media event of Riss's cartoon was driven by what could be termed a standing reserve of interpretative energy. This energy was accumulated not only through the intermeshing of these enhanced news stories from the border crisis, but also, of course, because of the iconic and conflicted status of the newspaper *Charlie Hebdo* in the aftermath of the lethal attacks on its offices in January 2015. A secondary dimension of the widespread expression of identification with *#JeSuisCharlie* was the rapid circulation of past cover images from the newspaper, which in turn generated a proliferation of political assessments of the paper, and symbolic investments in the values it was held to represent. To an important extent, this symbolic investment generated a media event that transcended any specific relation to the content and history of the newspaper. Nevertheless, a consistent dimension of the symbolic struggles over *who is and who is not Charlie* hinged on radically different assessments of their commitment to what was widely termed 'equal opportunities offensiveness', that is, to an abrasive satirical method that regularly drew on religious caricatures and racial stereotypes. Riss's cartoon not only coupled recent events fraught with racialized framing, but also evoked a standing reserve of interpretative dispute as to the racist/anti-racist character of some of *Charlie Hebdo*'s images.

A basic *News Journal* search retrieved 76 stories on online newspaper and news sites that were published about the cartoon between the 13th and 14th of January 2016, all of which referenced the question of racism in the story, while 13 articles referenced racism in their headline. It is either an accusation, where 'racism' is held in interpretative suspension through the use of quotation marks – 'backlash' over 'racist' cartoon – or a question: 'Is this cartoon of Alan Kurdi "racist"?' *The Guardian*, for example, featured the story 'Charlie Hebdo cartoon depicting drowned child Alan Kurdi sparks racism debate'. As with each of the other 13 headline stories, it drew heavily for its substantive content on social media 'reaction', and selected and organized – and also flattened and reduced – this material in terms of the established journalistic convention of balance, alternating positions for and against the proposition in the headline. What is of interest here is the main interpretative criteria applied to the cartoon, and the divergent understandings of racism they support. To tease this out, the main arguments I surveyed in the news sample and in online debates are summarized here in a dialogue form:

- The cartoon is racist because of its portrayal of Alan Kurdi. While the 'iconic' image of his body had entered into symbolic circulation, this did not provide a political justification for portraying him *as* a potential rapist. The cartoon, therefore, is both appropriative and insensitive to Alan and his family, while racializing 'migrants' through the reproduction of stereotypes being openly used to legitimate exclusionary politics in the political atmosphere in which it was published.

- This is a literalist misinterpretation of the cartoon's satire. By fusing two proximate events, the *second degré* humour takes aim at the fickleness of public opinion, which lurched from grief to hysteria. It clearly takes aim at the stereotyping structure present in sensationalist media frameworks that homogenizes and polices minority identities in polarized categories of 'angels and devils', or good and bad migrants.
- Intentionality is a distraction; if the cartoon is dominantly interpreted as an intervention that compounds anti-migrant and Islamophobic sentiment, then it is the public reception and broadly accepted meaning that matter. What is in question, therefore, is the inability or unwillingness of its publishers to act reflexively, to speculate on the consequentiality of these images rather than insist on the primacy of intentionality in a context of heightened public racism.
- Yes, but intentionality does not need to be based on an appeal to the general primacy of authorial intent. It can be deduced from specific histories of practice, and knowledge of *Charlie Hebdo*'s political history and mode of satire clarifies that this is not an expression of racism, but a satire of the popular irrationality of racism. They have a long history of anti-racist activism.
- Perhaps, but regardless, intentionality, even of the good anti-racist kind, does not guarantee control over the meaning of images. Images of 'non-European' people as beasts or monkeys cannot be extracted from historically generated repertoires of colonial and imperialist representations that worked to dehumanize and humiliate subordinated populations. In a context where white people still dress up in blackface and proudly Instagram the results, these caricatures inevitably still carry these accents and valences. Doesn't the fact that the Greek fascist party Golden Dawn approvingly shared the cartoon give pause for thought?
- How can an artist be held responsible for the uses to which their art is put? What is getting lost in this misdirected outrage is that *Charlie Hebdo* was reluctantly globalized when it was attacked, and decontextualized images now circulate and are open to misreading beyond the interpretative context of France, where the codes for this mode of satire are understood. This contextuality is important, for without some sense of this tradition it seems that Anglophone commentators lose all perspective.
- Yes, contextuality is important but there is not one unitary interpretative context. The juxtaposition of Anglophone incomprehension

and French semiotic fluency erases the – often racialized – voices in France that have an established history of criticizing how this satire supports repressive power relations in postcolonial France. Are these voices, therefore, less French? Didn't the French media critic Daniel Schneidermann point out that while he 'got' the cartoon, his younger colleagues, who have no biographical relation to this satirical tradition, 'totally saw a racist drawing'? And, that in a mediasphere increasingly organized by networked logics of sharing and mixing, an experienced author can find ways to 'signal that the message of your drawing (*"don't hassle me about Aylan, if he'd lived he would have become a rapist like the others"*) does not express your thought – the author's – but that of a narrator who might be, for example, a fat ugly racist Archie Bunker type?' (Ackermann, 2016).

- So what are you suggesting? That because something might end up somewhere on the internet as part of a meme, that artists and political commentators should censor themselves? This focus on one cartoon, especially given the recent history at play here, is disproportionate, but it also dilutes a focus on fundamental principles for some kind of symbolic or textual exercise. This kind of satire treats everybody *equally*, and as such it is radically anti-racist in some very important ways. It treats people as rational actors with the capacity to distinguish words from deeds in public life, and to accept being offended as a price worth paying for this.

- It's not just this one cartoon, it's the way it synthesizes so many recurring conflicts over what racism means and who gets to decide that. People of colour and anti-racist movements have consistently organized against demeaning and dehumanizing representations, not because of some superficial preference for 'symbolic exercises', but because the symbolic has material impact and political effect. If it didn't, why would institutions and nations invest so much labour in it? So why reduce all forms of communicative injury in unequal societies to the flat category of *offence*?

- The point is that this approach is radically egalitarian. It does not allow accidents of birth and the particularities of ascribed identity to relativize the public practice of democratic citizenship. It is only this kind of universal commitment to humanity that can negate the pseudo-biology of race and the false divisions of racism.

- Yes, a universal commitment to humanity is a critical horizon for life on this planet, but its promise has always been ambivalent, because it promises human emancipation while assuming a white

European subject as the measure of what it means to be free. We can't just ignore how people are racialized precisely because of accidents of birth and the particularities of ascribed identity, in a history that is still with us, and still inscribing these formations. To just assume that there is one set of public responses that count as rational, and that these happen to be the detached responses of people not relentlessly forced to negotiate racialized representations in a racially stratified society, well, that sets oneself up as gatekeeper of the universal.

The fraught and fractious rendering symbolic of *Charlie Hebdo* is further discussed in Chapter 5, where questions of free expression, hate speech, and the differing theories of communication and consequentiality assumed in these positions are examined. This complex thickening of one of its cartoons proposes some initial observations on the idea of debatability. In terms of media theory, what is clear is that the cartoon circulated in a media environment characterized by what Nick Couldry terms 'hugely increased incitements to discourse'; the ephemeral invitation to react, share, signal or comment (2012: 126). These compressed incitements to discourse on racism/anti-racism, as we shall see throughout this book, are an increasingly prevalent and ambivalent dimension of public culture, driven by the unexpected circulation of digital objects, or the capacity of ubiquitous digital technologies to make 'hidden racism' public, or the opportunities for publicity provided to racist groups by the 'always-on' prerogatives of content production in a hybrid media system.

In the cartoon dialogue, both imagined interlocutors deploy a complex set of understandings and associations in their interpretations of racism. This complexity is reinforced by the fact that they represent very different understandings of racism in the service of *anti-racism*, of opposing racism. This is not unusual, as varying traditions of anti-racism have always operated within a spectrum of different and often divergent definitions of racism, suggesting that anti-racism is never reducible to simply being against racism (see Bonnett, 2000; Lentin, 2004). However, as interpretations circulate and cluster in an irreducibly transnational space of mediated exchange, the cartoon as incitement to discourse amplifies the extent of 'postracial' confusion and polarization as to what counts as racism, where discussions of racism are characterized by competing social and personal understandings, political investments, interpretative frameworks and analytical foundations. These competing understandings are shaped contextually, but context in this event does not map onto neatly divided Anglophone and Francophone spheres. While some form of communicative event takes shape around digital objects such as this, the cartoon was contested not only as an interpretative text, but also as a medium for broader disagreement as to how racism should be understood, whose opinions or experiences register, and how it should be opposed.

# The definability of racism

In response to the circuitries of debatability, to this constant contest over what racism means and who gets to define it, a prevalent response is to reach for the clarity and certainty of a definition. Racism, after all, is an *ism*, and widely acknowledged as morally wrong – solid grounds for assuming that its meaning can be secured. In its list of top words for 2015, the American dictionary publisher Merriam-Webster reported that consultations of their definition of 'racism' increased by 50% in 2015 – a year where murderous police brutality, white supremacist murders in a South Carolina church, the *#BlackLivesMatter* movement and campus protests against institutional racism were the focus of significant media coverage. More anecdotally, anyone who has spent any time discussing racism in online or social media platforms may have encountered a moment when the disagreement and ambiguity peak, and a helpful interlocutor pastes a definition from Google Dictionary, or one like it, into the thread: 'prejudice, discrimination or antagonism directed against someone of a different race on the belief that one's own race is superior'.

The debatability of racism is certainly in part a product of its conceptual complexity, a complexity that has led some theorists to argue that we can only speak of *racisms* in the plural. One of the most challenging analytical dimensions of racism is that it is always dynamic, shifting in historical contexts and through social and political relations, a 'plastic or chameleon-like phenomenon which constantly finds new forms of political, social, cultural or linguistic expression' (MacMaster, 2001: 2). These forms of expression are also always intertwined and articulated with questions of class, gender, nationality, sexuality and religious identity. In addition, widespread use of the term 'racism', to describe structural and ideological modes of oppression and discrimination bound up in race-thinking and racially inflected beliefs and processes, is both modern in formation and very recent in usage (Hesse, 2004). Consequently, despite the harsh and violent realities of human exclusion and humiliation inscribed in the term, it is resistant to straightforward theoretical definition. Given, as Steve Garner argues, that 'racism is a phenomenon manifesting itself in such a diverse spectrum of ways across time and place', it is more productive in academic work to compare and contrast the foundations and elements of different definitions; how they combine the attention given to the historical power relationships through which certain groups are *racialized*, sets of ideas that legitimize these hierarchies and distinctions, and the forms of discrimination and practices that stem from them (2010: 10–11).

In order to grasp why racism is resistant to definition in public encounters, it is important to consider debatability as something more than primarily a question of conceptual complexity. The difficulty of producing adequate academic definitions, for example, is also a consequence of recognizing that 'the process of naming the problem is not simply a matter of semantics but reflects the intensely political process of conceptualization' (Bowling, 1998: 2). What holds for the convention-bound discipline of academic writing holds fast in less bounded environments – the meaning of racism in comment cultures is unlikely to be amenable to resolution through cut and paste definitions. This is because the act of defining is not just reflective, it is productive; it centres certain meanings, and marginalizes others. According to Sara Ahmed, 'if we recognize something as racism, we also offer a definition of that which we recognize. In this sense, recognition produces rather than simply finds its object' (2012: 44).

The incessant debatability of racism, therefore, is shaped not only by the contemporary complexity that has accreted to the term, but also because it is inherently *political*. The interpretative investment in the cartoon was less a semiotic competition than acknowledgement that the recognition of racism, and the racisms that are recognized, and by whom, entails political consequences. To recognize some form of racism may be in turn to admit to some form of reckoning with the systematic distribution of power, possibility, resources, legitimacy, belonging and even life itself over time and in contemporary socio-political relations. Consequently, definitions of what racism means in public culture have become sites of acute political contest, and intensive discursive labour aiming to derail or reverse racism's political implications. To return to the Google definition, anyone who has had it pasted their way may see how the recourse to the dictionary holds out the promise not of shared understanding, but of a full stop; inserted into dialogue it says to an interlocutor that what we are discussing cannot be racism, or that what you are experiencing cannot be racism, because it does not relate to the terms of this definition, it cannot be *recognized*.

Nevertheless, the desire to resolve debatability through definition is important because it is indicative of a powerful set of assumptions about public culture. Media Studies, as Peter Lunt and Sonia Livingstone (2013) argue, remains 'fascinated' with the concept of the public sphere, primarily through an extended critical engagement with the work of Jürgen Habermas on the conditions of political consciousness, ethical commitment and institutional procedure that could support communicative deliberation. For all the criticism directed at the undeclared class, gendered and racial exclusions implicit in the concept – a somewhat free-floating concept that does not always map onto Habermas's conceptualization – it has endured as a critical touchstone for considerations of the democratizing potential of internet-enabled participation (Papacharissi, 2011). For the purposes of this argument, it is also important to recognize that, in its most general sense, the idea of the public sphere provides a resilient framework of self-understanding for journalists, news organizations, media regulators and arguably many media audiences and users. In this vision, as James Curran summarizes, the media's primary role is to 'assist the collective self-realisation, co-ordination, democratic management, social integration and adaptation of society' (2002: 136).

Faith in the capacity of a definition to guide public understanding is informed by two intersecting ideas derived from this broadly liberal-democratic understanding of mediated public spheres. The first is that public life is characterized by the use of public reason, that ideas and arguments succeed by being tested in a 'marketplace of ideas', and that the public is united in turning attention to what Risto Kunelius terms 'inclusive argumentation'. This, he argues, is the

> ... imaginary idea type situation that informed a great deal of 20th-century public speech. It favors caution in naming others, emphasizes the epistemic (objective, fact-based) dimension of public argumentation and assumes there is at least a strategically motivated consensus or compromise that social actors can achieve ... this is the idea of publicity that provided legitimation for journalism (and the free press) in the period of both the political press and the commercial press. In the former, the public sphere was imagined to take place 'between' news outlets, in the latter (professionally and objectively) 'inside' news outlets

… freedom of speech in this mode is policed by references to the rationality of what is said. Rationality, in turn, is defined by what is taken to be true (factual arguments) or normatively acceptable, often using 'the nation' as the key ideological benchmark or container. (2013: 34–5)

The second is that this rationality is produced through debate between a plurality of voices, guaranteed at a systemic level by a – variously regulated and legitimated – diversity of media actors and institutions that address and constitute the public sphere. This plurality creates the conditions for *consensus*, a paradigm, as Des Freedman argues, that 'relates to a long-standing and highly influential notion of power that in advanced liberal democracies, power is widely distributed, pluralistically organized and contributes to a relatively stable social arrangement' (2014: 16). Students of these approaches may preempt the main critiques of how power is formulated in this perspective, and Freedman's three further paradigms of *chaos, control* and *contradiction* depart from them. It is critical to note, also, how the distribution of power in this paradigm has a postracial inflection. The assumption that consensus can be reached on a definition of racism, a definition that will in turn guide and discipline public contestation, is only imaginable if the public is imagined, however inchoately, as an aggregation of individuals whose lives are substantively unmarked by legacies and enduring conditions of structural, racial reproduction. To open these points out, the second snapshot explores these imaginaries of public understanding by considering the US context in which 50% more people in 2015 felt the need to consult their Merriam-Webster dictionaries for a definition of racism.

For many US commentators, the 2008 election of President Barack Obama represented definitive evidence of the transformation of racial realities in the United States. The substantial achievement of a black president in the context of US history was parlayed by many commentators into an encompassing narrative of a definitive break: with a *racial past* of slavery, legalized segregation and supremacist violence, and crucial proof that the enduring legacies and impacts of this racial system had been transcended. Reflecting on media coverage that combined 'assertions of racelessness with strikingly reductionist resorts to race to "explain" voting patterns', the historian David Roediger noted how 'such careening representations of the Obama campaign reflect an overwhelming desire to transcend race without transcending racial inequality, as well as the impossibility of doing so' (2008: 217). Roediger's formulation is important because it fixes on race as a political question, as a mode of ordering social relations where 'race defines the social category into which peoples are sorted, producing and justifying their very different opportunities with regard to wealth and poverty, confinement and freedom, citizenship and alienation ... Though genetic differences among groups defined as races are inconsequential, race is itself a critically important social fact' (ibid: xi–xii).

In 2015, as Americans reached for their dictionaries in record numbers, the social fact of race was killing black people and consigning them to premature death with such spectacular frequency that it forged the stark message of the main social movement to emerge in this period – *Black Lives Matter* (BLM). The phrase is stark not only because in its utterance it is impossible to evade the extraordinary fact that it must still be uttered, but also because of its contrast with the assumption that the Obama era marked the substantive inauguration of a 'postracial' society. As Joshua Paul writes, the symbolic meaning of President Obama's 2008 election was hailed as evidence that 'the democratic experiment had realized its meritocratic claims to be post-race. This narrative of social perfectibility positions president Obama as a bellwether for the fast-approaching post-racist society' (2014: 702). Keeanga-Yamahtta Taylor explicitly contrasts this framing with the formation of the BLM movement:

> There are ... periodic ruptures in the US narrative of its triumph over racism as a defining feature of its society ... The Black freedom struggle of the 1960s, while the United States was simultaneously waging a war in Vietnam (supposedly in the name of freedom), exposed the country as a whole as deeply racist and resistant to Black equality or liberation. More recently, the Los Angeles Rebellion in 1992 reignited a national discussion about the persistence of racial inequality. In 2005 the Bush administration's shameful response to Hurricane Katrina momentarily submerged the glowing self-appraisals of American society at a time when the country was, once again, locked in war and occupation ... Today the birth of a new movement against racism and policing is shattering the illusion of a colorblind postracial United States. Cries of 'Hands up, don't shoot', 'I can't breathe', and 'Black lives matter' have been heard around the country as tens of thousands of ordinary people mobilise to demand an end to rampant police brutality and murder against African Americans. (2016: loc 283)

The 'colorblind illusion' broadly refers to the assumption that the formal political equality won by the freedom movements of the 1950s and 1960s ushered in an era of official *racelessness*, a correction that recalibrated the essentially meritocratic character of US society. Yet in the absence of a substantive transformation of the stratified distribution of wealth and possibility that characterized a historically embedded racial system, gross material inequality endured, and according to some calculations, expanded on a range of fronts. As Taylor writes, 'poverty is but a single factor in making sense of the ever-widening wealth gap between African Americans and whites. Over the last twenty-five years, the disparity in household wealth has tripled; today white median wealth (as opposed to income) is 91,405, compared to 6,446 for African American households' (ibid: loc 315). In Dana-Ain Davis's terms, this legacy of segregated inequality has fused with the subsequent neoliberal contraction of the welfare state to produce what she terms 'muted racism', a product of official 'color-blindness' that, regardless of the historical legacies and contemporary structures that maintain racialized inequalities, 'forces claims of racism into silence' (2007: 349).

The Black Lives Matter movement is most intensely associated with the protests and resistance that followed the police killing of Michael Brown in Ferguson, Missouri on August 9th 2014 (see Lipsitz, 2015), but it is the acquittal of 'neighbourhood watch volunteer' George Zimmerman on July 15th 2013 for the murder of 17-year-old Trayvon Martin – on February 26th 2012 – that Deva Woodly (2016) identifies as a formative 'moment of painful politicization' for a renascent black liberation movement, a day where 'the virtual public sphere was awash with conversation, dissections of the trial and evidence, and polemical rants, but more prominent than all of these were outcries of pain'.

People had also taken to the virtual sphere following Trayvon's murder, as it took 45 days of organizing and protest before Zimmerman was arrested and subsequently charged (protestors adopted bags of Skittles candy – which Trayvon had bought in a local shop immediately prior to his murder – as a symbol, waving them at demonstrations, and mailing them to the local police department). Woodly's description of the visceral need for public sharing and mutual recognition recalls Zizi Papacharissi's discussion of 'affective publics', where latent ties and solidarities are activated by the networked structures of expression that digital media provide, often in the real time of an event. The impact of connective media on collective political mobilization has been subject to the equally reductive claims that 'social media' *cause* radical political action, or are a hyped-up distraction in understanding it. Writing against these approaches she argues that 'the connective affordances of social media help activate the in-between bond of publics, and they also enable expression and information sharing that liberate the individual and collective imaginations' (2014: 8).

Yet while the pluralizing and multiplying effects of connective media are often predominantly associated with progressive possibility – with the democratic redistribution of communicative power – the same structures and affordances facilitated the participatory dehumanization of Trayvon Martin. During the trial coverage, the meme genre of *Trayvoning* proliferated images of young white Americans posing for photos while playing dead, with a hood up and bag of Skittles in their hand. In a reflection on this practice, Lisa Guerrero and David J. Leonard (2012) observe that while the 'technologies of communication appear new, the technologies of oppression are anything but'. They place the meme-ification of Trayvon's murder in a lineage of practices that produced collective white supremacist pleasure in the destruction of black bodies, most notably the practice of taking photos with 'souvenirs' from bodies at lynchings. This lineage is simultaneously denied and deepened by the silence of the 'postracial':

> While the trend can be interpreted as a new technology of lynching, its character remains separate from lynchings of the past whose act, and the dissemination of lynching photographs highlighted White power and White supremacy. The ability to 'act' like a dead Trayvon Martin only to get up and head back into White suburbia is illustrative of this same feeling of power and privilege, but invisibly so. White people don't take part in 'Trayvoning' to 'declare' White supremacy; they take part in it because the declaration has been rendered unnecessary by various sociocultural, sociopolitical and socioeconomic forces. In fact, the absence of the explicit claim to it emphasizes the power and privilege even more.

Bags of Skittles entered into symbolic circulation to mark the innocence of a life violently taken, but once in circulation symbols are charged with memetic potential, in this instance appropriated as a mocking indicator of that life's historically sanctioned disposability. In their detailed study of media coverage of the trial, Erhardt Graeff et al. (2014) conclude that 'broadcast media is still important as an amplifier and a gatekeeper, but it is susceptible to media activists working through participatory media to co-create the news and influence the framing of major controversies'. Reviewing these circulatory dynamics at the scale of the media system, Safiya Umoja Noble, in her essay 'Teaching Trayvon', turns to Guy Debord's notion of the *spectacle* to examine how the political desire to get justice for Trayvon through publicity, and to link his murder to a 'national conversation about racial justice', was subordinated to 'the creation of Trayvon and George as commodities', as mediated stories for consumption (2014: 14). The idea of 'the spectacle' is in a tradition, stretching from Frankfurt School analyses of the Culture Industry to 'definitive' conceptualizations of contemporary mediatization, that seeks to theorize the ever-deeper penetration of mediated representations to subjectivity and social relations (see Jensen, 2013). In Debord's aphoristic *The Society of the Spectacle* (1967), the spectacle is the insistent flow of media content and commodity drive that extends capitalism's structuring force into how people communicate, formulate desires, and shape their understandings of political and social possibility. The spectacle is not just distracting, but also alienating, as 'the spectacle is not a collection of images but a social relation among people mediated by images' (thesis 4).

Noble traces how the coverage of Zimmerman's trial inevitably produced Trayvon as a commodity, a story primed for dramatic rendition, opinion generation and sensationalist revelation regardless of the trial's outcome ('The spectacle aims at nothing other than itself', thesis 14). However, this spectacle was also racialized. The adversarial narrative of a trial, intensively mediated in its day-to-day 'revelations', accentuated the ways in which race, in the postracial moment, was rendered both hyper-visible and invisibilized – hyper-visible, in that Trayvon Martin was marked out as an object of legitimate suspicion by nothing more than his blackness, presumed out of place in the undeclared but potent *whiteness* of the private property of a gated community. For Zimmerman this was enough to conjure up and act upon a stereotypical mélange of risk, threat and criminality, and during Zimmerman's trial, it was sufficient for Trayvon to effectively be put on trial, his behaviour and character scrutinized for exonerating confirmation of threatening black masculinity. As Noble argues, media narratives were suffused with an established textual repertoire of 'black male criminality' that shaped the commodity of 'Trayvon'. These narratives were not uncontested, as significant mobilization went into 'counter-narratives' designed to reclaim Trayvon's humanity. Moreover, the spectacle had something for everybody, as competing news outlets emphasized different angles and frames according to the presumed positionality of their target audience.

Rather, 'what we know is that despite the efforts at counter-narrative and empathetic outpourings, the dominant narrative of black criminality prevailed in one of the most important sites of power – the courtroom' (op.cit.: 17).

In order to seek justice for the racially ordered taking of his life, Trayvon Martin entered into symbolic circulation as 'Trayvon', in part framed and scripted in terms of constructions of threatening and suspicious blackness historically generated with the 'racial formation' of the US (Omi and Winant, 1995). He was symbolically reproduced within a capitalist media system where texts of black male deviancy are exchanged for profit, an assembly of associations that in turn produced 'Trayvon' intertextually, as a commodity to be projected onto and consumed. And this hyper-visibility, the suspicious fact of blackness, enforces the concomitant invisibility of race understood in Roediger's terms as a 'social category into which peoples are sorted, producing and justifying their very different opportunities with regard to … life and premature death' (op.cit.: 17). Media forms obscured the systemic dimension, as the adversarial story of a trial was mediated through short news segments and updates, and narrated as a tragic encounter between two individuals. Postracialism is present in the interplay of hyper-visibility and invisibilization that erases the historical and systemic conditions that positioned Trayvon as a suspicious body fatally out of place in a private gated community. Racism, again, appears everywhere and nowhere.

Noble's use of Debord's famously elusive idea of the spectacle is primarily designed to mark distance from pluralist imaginaries of the public sphere. By highlighting the communicative work invested by an affective public in attempting to undermine the commodification of 'Trayvon Martin', her theory of media power is less Debord's treatise on mass delusion than Freedman's fourth paradigm, that of *contradiction*. The media system, Freedman argues, is neither an undifferentiated power bloc (*control*) nor a field of power radically diffused and fractured by the digital media revolution (*chaos*) (2014: 18–24). Rather, it is comprised of actors and institutions that have material, social and ideological relations with vested interests and elite power, that regularly reproduce hegemonic forms of 'common sense', but that are nevertheless 'not immune from the movements and ideas that circulate in society at any one time and the seek to challenge these power structures' (ibid: 25). Analyzing the contradictions of media power, Freedman argues, requires an approach that

… emphasizes structure and agency, contradiction and action, consensus and conflict; an analytical framework that recognizes the existence of unequal power frameworks but acknowledges that they are not forever frozen; and a perspective that takes seriously the activities of producers and audiences while recognizing the existence of uneven consciousness. (ibid: 28)

Noble's approach layers an analysis of media power with the attention given to the undeclared power of racial articulation. In focusing on the challenge of teaching 'Trayvon', she emphasizes the ways in which activists and academics can work with media logics by strategic reframing and contestation, and also work against them by creating spaces for relocating 'racial incidents in socio-historical context' (op. cit.: 25). Yet this necessary embrace of contradiction underlines the intersection of inequalities in communicative power with the power of (post)-racial stratification, the processes through which, as Robin D.G. Kelley (2013) observed, a murdered teenager was put on trial for the crimes 'he would have committed had he lived past 17'. By foregrounding this mesh of power relations, the idea of debatability marks a critical distance from the pluralist understanding of 'debate'. Put bluntly, definitions of racism or other forms of oppression are unlikely to be shared in what Stuart Hall (1980) called 'societies structured in dominance', and thus the proposition that conceptual consensus is possible is latent with postracial presumption. Similarly, 'national conversations' on racism can never simulate the inclusive argumentation among individuals idealistically attached to deliberative notions of debate, because such discussions occur in public cultures where powerful, historically produced discourses and repertoires of racialized representation circulate and shape hierarchies of value in the 'marketplace of ideas'.

The integration of connective media and participatory networks to the hybrid media system certainly diversifies public discourse; however, the liberal imaginary of public debate rests on an inadequate examination of how power is challenged, reproduced and re-formed within its structures and dynamics. The 'affective public' of #BLM illustrates how the recognition of racism in 'postracial' societies depends on political mobilization and struggle; and in media cultures of endless and abundant content creation, interventions in 'debates' by those with less power and resources will always be strategic, and exact an affective cost. The idea of debatability foregrounds this, and underlines the need to examine how discourse unfolds in and through interlocking and sometimes contradictory forms of power.

# The deniability of racism

The prominent hashtag response to #BlackLivesMatter, #AllLivesMatter, is an evocative artefact of the postracial formation. That is, its ostensibly agreeable, universal *raceless* message is only expressed in this form as a specific negation of the lethal social fact of race. It attempts to force BLM's claims of police and structural racism into silence by positioning their reference to black lives as a divisive reaction, as 'bringing race into it'. This form of denial is important because it signifies how 'postracial' racism may be silencing but it is not silent. The discursive game-playing of reversals and negations represented by this hashtag response has been a defining feature of the politics of racism since at least the 1970s. As its logics are now rehearsed every day in radio interviews, comment threads and Twitter storms, this discursivity must be regarded as an important dimension of debatability.

In the build-up to the 2015 UK general election, the BBC screened a documentary 'Meet the Ukippers', about the anti-immigration and anti-EU United Kingdom Independent Party (UKIP). It featured an interview with a Kent city councillor, Rozanne Duncan, who openly and somewhat cheerfully discussed her deep and visceral dislike of 'Negros' and 'people with Negroid features' – features she helpfully described in detail – and to ensure that the viewer understood the depth of her aversion, even recounted a story about overtly discriminating against 'Negro children' in housing allocation decisions in council affairs in the past. If the previous sections have emphasized racism's political motility and mutable modes of expression, Duncan's openly phenotypical anti-black racism appears to reach back into the repudiated past and stage a defiant revival. This is particularly jarring in the context of the UK, where anti-racist movements powerfully combatted the racism brought to bear on 'postcolonial' migrants to Britain from the Caribbean and Indian sub-continent; where legislation banning various forms of racial and ethnic discrimination has been enacted over decades; where the development of ethnically mixed working-class communities in many British cities complicates and often actively unsettles nationalist assumptions; and where a stylized but nonetheless resonant notion of multiculturalism has become part of official attempts to re-position Britishness as an inclusive identity. In this context, as Ben Pitcher argues, 'to openly proclaim racist beliefs is effectively a declaration of one's moral degeneracy' (2009: 13). Yet even after the programme was broadcast, and Duncan was fired from the party, she continued to insist through the media that she was *not racist*.

'I'm not racist, but ... ' is a globally resonant cliché, thickened with layers of ironic deployment and mimetic enjoyment. This over-exposure does not prevent it from enduring as a vital political grammar, as *denial* has historically been formative in the expression of racism. In the extensive international literature on racism, a recurring theme is the layered resilience of racism denial; assumptions, practices and tactics that relativize or dismiss forms of racism and minimize their impact on the lived experience for those racialized in 'societies structured in dominance'. Denial takes different forms and is produced by different actors and agencies, but forms of denial serve to 'close down any space in which to question racism and the structures that produce and sustain it' (Macedo and Gounari, 2005: 3). Consequently, many key works on contemporary racism find themselves positioned as having to write about, and write against, the denial and disavowal of racism as dominant modes through which contemporary racisms are consolidated and rearticulated.

Such contemporary theoretical ideas as 'colour-blind racism', 'racism without racists' (Bonilla-Silva, 2006) and 'muted racism' (Davis, 2007), for example, seek to explain the shifting yet obdurate nature of racial stratification, inequality and discrimination in contexts with significant official and popular commitment to ideas of equality, diversity, multiculturalism and anti-racism. These system-level analyses are complemented by a literature on social and communicative interaction, where notions of 'racial paranoia' (Jackson, 2008), 'the racism of denial' (Giroux, 2003), 'ambient racism' (Sharma and Brooker, 2016) and 'racial equivalence' (Song, 2014) examine how denial works as a formative aspect of what Philomena Essed (1991) termed 'everyday racism', a silencing of the experience of racism that must be negotiated in social interaction and institutional context (see Harries, 2014, for a discussion of young people's response to these micro-processes). Sara Ahmed (2010), in her work on 'willfulness', has explored the reversals that proliferate in the gap between the 'official prohibition' of racism and the lived experience of racialized exclusions and dynamics:

> It can be willful even to name racism, as if the talk about divisions is what is divisive. Given that racism recedes from social consciousness, it appears as if the ones who 'bring it up' are bringing it into existence ... racism is very difficult to talk about as racism can operate to censor the very evidence of its existence. Those who talk about racism are thus heard as creating rather than

describing a problem ... when you use the language of racism you are heard as 'going on about it', as 'not letting go'. It is as if talking about racism is what keeps it going.

Read in these terms, Duncan's resolute refusal to recognize the character of her speech is coherent with the variegated ways in which racism is denied even as it is being performed. Further, her dehumanizing focus on 'negroid features' positions her racism as a spectacular outburst that serves to confirm the positioning of UKIP at the extremes of the electoral party system, and the contention of other parties that UKIP are uniquely responsible for racism in British politics. Such outbursts also fit an established form of mediated scandal – the interview with Duncan was released to the media prior to the BBC's broadcast of the documentary – that is routinely read as distracting from the silenced operations of structural racism, precisely because their event-like irruption drives a ritual of public repudiation of racism-as-anachronism (Davis, 2008; Hartigan Jr, 2010). However, comments like Duncan's have significance beyond this, in that while they act to silence, they are far from silent acts – they are fluent.

Duncan sought at length in the programme extract for an explanation for her aversion and willingness to discriminate. She was, in short, fascinated with her own racism. And her fascination produced a kind of fluency as her explanations ranged across a repertoire of forms of denial, derived from decades of political investment in silencing the experience of racism from being heard and taken seriously. In his examination of the politics of racism in the UK, Ben Pitcher describes a 'language war over racial reference', whereby 'any direct approach to the question of race must be channeled through a public discourse that explicitly signals the illegitimacy of racist beliefs and practices' (2009: 14). This language war is a result not only of the success of anti-racist movements in opposing public manifestations of racism, but also of the concerted emphasis on adaptive discourse and communicative strategy that characterizes the 'new racism' diagnosed in western Europe since the 1970s. The public inadmissibility of race after the Holocaust, and the strong post-war aversion to parties and movements that laid claim to a Nazi and fascist lineage, forced movements of the 'new right' to turn to a discourse of irreconcilable *cultural difference* rather than *racial hierarchy* to publicly justify the politicization of migration.

This complex heritage is explored in a variety of ways in subsequent chapters, but a sense of it emerges from the compressed fluency of Duncan's explanations. Firstly, and recalling Hesse's argument that 'what remains (of racism) … is consigned to pathology' (2004: 10), she speculates as to whether she needs regression therapy to identify a repressed fear, 'something in my psyche' that would explain her behaviour, because 'I don't know why, I wish I did'. From this reproduction of the broadly liberal conviction that racism is now nothing more than an individual maladjustment, she segues into one of the key strategies of the so-called 'new racism', *differentialism*. She stopped 'young negroes' getting social housing in the 1980s because back then there were no black people and foreigners living in Thanet, and it would have been unfair to them. Unfair, because as the post-Powellite new racism in the UK or *Nouvelle Droit* in France then argued, cultures have their own place, and are better off kept separate as contact leads inevitably to conflict. It isn't the 'colonials'' or migrants' fault, they're better off in their own place, as they 'too have natural homes'. It's not about race, it's about culture; but if there is racism it is *reversed*, as it is the act of migration that threatens national unity, and the refusal/inability of the racialized to integrate to a unified, national way of life. To refuse these 'uncomfortable truths' is to bow, inevitably, to 'political correctness'. And while ultimately she accepts that 'there is no justification' for her attitudes, she also appeals to context, recounting how she reminds her daughter that she was born in a different time and place, and that while she is marked by it, she is reflexive enough to recognize the need to change. Performing for the camera, she replicates the 'subjective, autobiographical and confessional modes of expression (that) have proliferated … across print journalism, literature, factual TV and digital media' (Dovey, 2000: 1).

While we might expect this fluency from an experienced party activist of the political right, it is also a feature of what Miri Song regards as a wider 'culture of racial equivalence'. Song situates her discussion of public understandings of racism in the contemporary UK in an argument about the critical need for concepts that are adequate to the shifting dynamics of racism in a multicultural society. Echoing John L. Jackson's notion of 'racial paranoia' in the US, Song argues that contemporary society is characterized by high levels of awareness of 'racial identity', and of the dangers of committing 'public racial indiscretions', yet also by understandings of racism that are 'often highly imprecise, broad, and used to describe a wide range of racialized phenomena' (2014: 1). This imprecision is more than the product of the multivalent disagreement and confusion elicited by Riss's cartoon. A significant consequence of this, she argues, is the 'growing tendency in Britain to regard almost any form of racial statement, made by anyone (of any hue), as automatically, and indiscriminately, "racist"' (ibid: 4). This collapses a 'bewildering' range of racialized interactions into a catch-all category of racism, without attention being given to formative social relations and the distribution of power in a historical and political context. Further, this equivalence is secured through a proliferation of mediated accusations of 'reverse racism' – that is, of a discursive tactic designed to extract the consideration of racism from a shifting yet historically structured 'system of power and domination' and reduce it simply to a prejudice that anybody can hold.

Song's examination of a 'culture of racial equivalence' demonstrates how the fluency compressed in Duncan's denial has become widely distributed. Discursive tactics that emerged and have transnationally proliferated since the 1970s for strategic political advantage in countering anti-racist politics are now routine scripts. They are part of a discursive sedimentation that is amplified by the communicative forms of both mainstream media debates and, as Song's central evidential focus on Twitter responses to 'scandalous' incidents of purported public racism demonstrates, social media interactions. In emphasizing the immediacy and potential networked reach of connective media platforms, and the issue of anonymity, she argues that the problem with 'soundbyte technologies' is that

> ... such charges of racism (and reverse racism) tend to be monolithic, and delivered in formats which are not conducive to the elaboration of detailed and careful argumentation and explanations; as such, these brief articles, blogs, and Tweets do not properly assess the nature and specific of each racial interaction or event.

This is undoubtedly true, but by privileging the assumptions of rational critical debate as the normative horizon for social media interaction, the argument neglects to account for the variety of ways in which communication is motivated, and *mediated*. As Geert Lovink argues, the textual flow of 'comment cultures' has 'created systems that are no longer solely concentrated on interpretation of the text itself. We do not care so much what the text precisely "says" but what the wider ecology is. Instead of a close reading, we practice intuitive scanning' (2011: 57). In a hybrid media system 'racial incidents' have a generative value, driving interaction and sharing, yet outside of such spectacles, there is also, as

Sharma and Brooker (2016) show in their study of the hashtag *#notracist*, a constant use of the hashtag in steady but low-volume tweeting that 'is not about any specific event or issue as such ... but (gathered) around a wide array of sub-topics which bubble away on Twitter without ever trending or becoming visible'.

Public debate as to what constitutes racism is constituted through discourse. A pronounced dimension of 'postracial' societies is that debate is filtered through discursive repertoires and scripts of denial that are now sedimented into public culture, and that are given expression through a complex range of communicative dynamics and motivations. They are amplified as sense-making frameworks both within the tensions of a political conjuncture and by the mediating configurations of communicative forms and platform specificities. In the surfeit of searchable and flattened-out evidence and sources, they can always be 'proven' through instantly linkable examples of 'reverse racism', or political correctness, or multicultural censorship, and injected into any unfolding discussion of racism. Debatability suggests that we need to examine how denial is effected not just through silence but also through noise.

# 2

## The politics of representation in postracial media culture

# Debatability and the politics of representation

'It would not be too far-fetched to suggest', Roger Silverstone writes in *Media and Morality: On the Rise of the Mediapolis*, that the 'primary cultural role' of the media is 'the endless, endless, endless playing with difference and sameness'. Media work cannot help but involve what he terms 'boundary work', from the macro-boundary work of addressing and shaping publics, to the micro-boundary work that shapes the every-day flow of representations and constructions of the social world. This is a world assembled from 'the continuous inscriptions of difference in any and every media text or discourse: from the crude stereotypes of other-ness to the subtle and not-so-subtle discriminations of dramatic charac-terization, narrative construction, political punditry, internet chat rooms and talk radio' (2007: 13). Silverstone's characterization at once cap-tures why the analysis of representation is a foundational focus of Media and Cultural Studies, and the breadth of genres, texts and practices that the idea of *representation* has come to encompass and implicate. The idea of 'boundary work' does more than underline the fact, both patently obvious and frequently obscured, that representations are constructed, crafted, curated and circulated. It emphasizes that they proceed from and through forms of economic, institutional and symbolic power, the power to draw, delineate and attempt to define.

Representations of race – and its intersections with gender, class and sexuality – have provided a critical focus for this constructivist project of 'the politics of representation', and decades of studies have empha-sized the role of media representations and narratives in propagating and resisting racialized mythologies, premises and 'commonsense' assumptions. Writing in 1981, in this then nascent area of research, Stuart Hall argued that 'amongst other kinds of ideological labour, the media construct for us a definition of what race is, what meaning the imagery of race carries, and what the problem of race is understood to be. They help us to classify out the world in terms of the categories of race' (1981: 35). Studies of this 'ideological labour' now comprise a vast body of literature, spanning fiction and non-fiction media genres and the racialization of groups, populations and identities in their histori-cal and contextual specificity. Yet even as Hall underlines the signifi-cance of 'the media' in the boundary work of race, he warns against the kind of deterministic, mediacentric and sometimes quasi-conspiratorial understandings of power that the homogenizing shorthand of 'the media' invites. 'It would be simple and convenient', Hall continues, 'if all the media were simply the ventriloquists of a unified and racist "ruling class" conception of the world. But neither a unifiedly conspiratorial media nor indeed a unified racist "ruling class" exists in anything like that simple way' (ibid).

Further, the meanings of representations are shaped by their circulation and integration into flows of images, narratives and other forms of symbolic content. The representations discussed in the previous chapter – the *Charlie Hebdo* cartoon, the construction of 'Trayvon Martin', the BBC programme taster – became 'debatable' when they entered into wider and unpredictable circulation as objects of media commentary, memetic engagement and 'real-time' critique or satire. The sheer flow of symbolic content in contemporary transnational, hyper-visual digital environments intensifies and extends the terrain of representation even as it renders public horizons of reception and engagement more complex. The unevenly distributed yet markedly changed practices of everyday media representation in and through connective media alter this terrain's relations and terms. The 'politics of representation' today, therefore, is more than an academic field of textual research. It is a distributed practice increasingly integrated into everyday media engagements with the flow of symbolic content, and honed to contest or accentuate, however ephemerally, the register of representations of race.

The aim of this chapter is shaped by exploring this observation in relation to the established field of study. The significance of mediated representation, and the sheer scale of the research that has been produced, places a generic demand on studies of media and racism, such as this one, to provide some kind of inevitably partial yet purposeful survey of the field. In some survey or introductory texts discrete studies are often decontextualized and knitted into a patchwork diagnosis of both 'racism' and 'the media', providing a model of how not to address this demand. Beyond such mechanistic applications, it is difficult for survey or summary approaches to draw out the relationality of racisms when ranging, however reflectively, across a sample of media genres, political contexts and modalities of racialization. The first section, therefore, foregoes this more conventional approach of providing a thematic and theoretical overview. It instead suggests that what is currently at stake in the 'politics of representation' can be assembled from a discussion of recent critical perspectives that question the limits and purpose of representational analysis. These criticisms provide points of orientation for thinking through fundamental questions of representation, politics and racism, and thus this alternative survey approach is used to build a critical scaffolding for thinking about representation and postracial debatability.

It does this by focusing on a recurring form of controversy in postcolonial nation-states, the critique of racist representations in contexts where race is held to be a 'frozen' dimension of the past. It draws on the idea of 'racial debris' (Amin, 2010) to approach how images derived from colonial modernity continue to be reproduced, circulated, invested in and contested in the current 'postracial' moment. The first step involves a discussion of the work of Stuart Hall and Frantz Fanon on the vital question of how and why representations figure in the 'work' of race, and what this tells us about the idea of 'race' itself. The final section then takes these conceptual approaches to the politics of representation to the contemporary politics of 'blackface' in the Netherlands and Flanders. It explores a situation where anti-racist activists and racialized communities have politically opposed forms of media and cultural representation as images indexed to particular historical archives, provoking a politics of representation that takes shape in and through the circulation of images and texts across time and space. But in so doing, these images also act as a prism for a conjunctural critique of contemporary racism under socio-political conditions characterized by a now-familiar contradiction – the denial of race coupled with a relentless focus on the problem of 'ethnic and religious difference'.

## What is living and what is dead in the politics of representation?

Over the decades of the broadcast era, an enormous body of work has been produced on what is often called the 'politics of representation', a formula which emphasizes that, under conditions of massively unequal access to symbolic resources, the process of representation cannot be separated from the power to represent, and the cultural power of representations from prevailing socio-political relations and structures. Assessing how the social order and social relations are reproduced and made meaningful through the symbolic production and circulation of images and stories is regarded as critical to understanding the operation of ideology and hegemony. Examining how boundaries are inscribed is important to unsettling and challenging the naturalization

and legitimization of exclusion from, or coercive inclusion in, the imagined community. Dominant media and cultural studies methodologies
draw on a rich body of constructionist theory and semiotic concepts to
approach representation as a fluid and active process of meaning production, where the irreducibly polysemic dimensions of representation
must be examined in relation to the power relations through which representations are produced, and which are encoded in their construction
of the social world. Such approaches, Shani Orgad argues, focus on
the ways in which media representations 'are involved, often in subtle,
latent and highly sophisticated ways, in the reproduction and/or contestation of power relations and inequalities, for example of class, gender,
race, sexuality, ethnicity, age and nationality' (2012: 25).

Despite, or perhaps because of this centrality, recent critical evaluations have suggesting that the academic 'politics of representation' is a
somewhat exhausted enterprise. Exhausted does not mean empty; as we
shall see, in contexts where anti-migrant sensationalism, Islamophobic
discourse and anti-black mythologies circulate resiliently, 'the field
of representation remains a place of struggle', as bell hooks argued a
quarter of a century ago in *Black Looks* (1992: 3). What is less clear,
this body of critique contends, is what this struggle can hope to achieve
under contemporary media and political conditions, and what insights
and possibilities it contributes to beyond an analysis of the text. In the
following discussion, some main lines of critique are examined in order
to build points of orientation for situating the politics of representation
under the conditions outlined in the previous chapter.

One such trajectory is an assessment of the suppleness of central
concepts employed in the analysis of representation, such as the question of *mediated visibility*. In contexts where indigenous peoples have
been dispossessed and erased from stories of the nation, and racialized
populations framed as ambiguous supplements to the nation's taken-
for-granted whiteness, 'inclusion and exclusion' from the imagined
communities and social worlds of media representations features as an
organizing concern of the field. Historical accounts of film and television, for example, document regimes of unquestioned invisibility or
tightly circumscribed inclusion; as John D.H. Downing argues in an
essay on broadcast history, 'American television in its first two genera-
tions inherited and diffused – on an hourly or daily basis – a mythology of
whiteness that framed and sustained a racist national self-understanding'
(n.d.). And, of all the issues that have informed academic analysis, the
question of visibility/inclusion in non-fiction programming is the one

that most keenly animates public contest. Here there is an important contrast between theoretical and mobilizing understandings. Cultural theory generally underlines the instability of meaning, and broadly postmodern approaches insist on the death of referentiality in image-saturated environments. However, the idea that media texts that make a discursive claim to represent the social world should *reflect* aspects of what is recognized by those who inhabit that social world retains a powerful ethical and political charge. Reflectionist assumptions suffuse media professional understandings as to the media's capacity to truthfully capture what is happening in society, and these assumptions are dialectically engaged by the various monitoring and advocacy projects that work 'premised on the idea that the media should somehow mirror the society on which they report' (Orgad, 2012: 19).

In media cultures characterized by the incessant proliferation of images and a diversification of producers, audiences and markets, the question of visibility is often regarded as quaint. Yet it is a form of postracial fiction to consider it 'fixed' in a linear progression towards greater representational complexity. Over the last few years, for example, the exclusion of actors of colour from dramatically meaningful film roles has been subject to significant public commentary. A 2016 report by the British Film Institute demonstrated that almost 60% of British films made in the preceding ten years had 'no named black characters', and only 13% had a 'black actor in a leading role' (Addley, 2016). In the same year, a widely-publicized Tumblr page 'Every Single Word' featured edits of well-known Hollywood movies where all dialogue spoken by white characters was removed (allowing one to watch the entire *Harry Potter* series in 5 minutes and 40 seconds, and the reduction of what seems like forever before the ship finally sinks in *Titanic* to 54 seconds). In 2018, a collective of 16 actors and comedians in France published *Noire n'est pas mon métier* ['Black is not my profession'], which, as well as discussing the racism and sexism they experienced in the film industry, documented the near absence of any roles that did not conform to resilient stereotypes – 'do you speak African?' – and called for the 'right to banality' as actors (Maïga et al., 2018).

Nevertheless, the question of visibility is often understood simplistically or instrumentally, lending itself to essentialist and reified ideas of racial or group identity that elide the intersectional dimensions of oppression and the complexity of lived identities. And, as Herman Gray (2013) has argued, the objective of greater visibility and 'representation as an end in itself ... perfectly expresses the logic of market choice, consumer sovereignty, self-reliance, and cultural diversity', and thus cannot integrate a consideration of how the proliferation of images undercuts the foundations of a politics of recognition predicated on exclusion and overt marginalization under past conditions of 'media scarcity'. Of course, as these cinema controversies suggest, the question of visibility/inclusion shades almost immediately into interpretative evaluations of the discursive construction of representations; the 'right to banality' is explicitly framed as a demand to play 'all the women in film and theatre' and not just stereotypical roles of 'African mamas and prostitutes' (du Boucheron, 2018). The question of *stereotypes* thus provides a further imperative of media analysis, for, as Simon Cottle summarizes,

> It is in and through representations ... that members of the media audience are variously invited to construct a sense of who 'we' are in relation to who 'we' are not, whether as 'us' and 'them', 'insider' and 'outsider', 'coloniser' and 'colonised', 'citizen' and 'foreigner', 'normal' and 'deviant', 'friend' and 'foe', 'the west' and 'the rest'. (2000: 2)

Like the question of visibility, the relevance of *stereotyping* is also subject to postracial assumption; in a context where media consumers/users are schooled in the constant play of intertextuality and ironic referentiality, stereotypes, the story goes, are a dwindling product of a less sophisticated, more 'overtly racist' past. Yet it is precisely this postracial sensibility through which stereotypes are recomposed. The idea of 'ironic racism', or 'hipster racism', for example, describes the recuperation of racist or gendered stereotypes as nothing more than ironic signifiers, curiosities and remnants of a past that *we* have repudiated, and which can now be enjoyed on the licence of knowing referentiality and performative self-awareness. Nevertheless, the resilience of particular repertoires of representation, the practices which have produced them, the forms of symbolic reduction and containment they propose, and the contemporary investments and mutations they acquire, require understanding 'the content of stereotypes historically – to bring the repressed historical dimension of stereotyping back into the light of its analysis in the present' (Pickering, 2001: 8). Without this attention to historicity and the shifting investments of contemporary articulation, the analysis of stereotypes is quickly reduced to a hunt for binary relations, inadvertently naturalizing race and soliciting idealist proposals as to how to 'correct' or 'smash' them. As Shohat and Stam argue in *Unthinking Eurocentrism*, 'The focus on "good" and "bad" characters in image analysis confronts racist discourse on that discourse's favoured ground. It easily elides into moralism, and thus into fruitless debates about the relative virtues of fictive characters ... and the correctness of their fictional actions' (1994: 200–1).

Further lines of criticism depart from a widely-held methodological reservation. In a review of 'research on racism, ethnicity and the media', Downing and Husband point to the dominance of *textual research* in relation to representation, suggesting that it is a consequence of a general disciplinary focus on 'deciphering' communication as a symbolic process, the relative ease of accessing media content for research, and the primacy placed on analyzing meaning as a determining dimension of cultural and political significance (2005: 26). While this proposes a somewhat pragmatic case for this dominance, it is also important to underline how this situation emerged. That is, the focus on *reading* the products of media culture, interpreting how texts signify and make meaning in a wider field of intertextual interaction, was informed by the shift in cultural and critical theory in the 1970s/80s to take 'ordinary' cultural processes seriously: to think about how 'dominant meanings' are encoded textually but never stable in their signification; to grapple with how mediated images and narratives are interpreted and put to work in identity negotiation, political ideology and social understanding; to depart from primarily behavioural, transmissive or functional models of media's significance, and normative theories of implicit cultural value, to examine complex and often contested circuits of cultural production. Representation, it was argued, is a process, and the 'struggle', the aim of deconstructing racialized representations, bell hooks argued, is not about sifting 'good and bad imagery', but about intervening in these circuits by 'transforming the image, creating alternatives, asking ourselves questions about what types of images subvert, pose critical alternatives, and transform our worldviews' (1992: 4).

The issue with the prevalence of textual analysis is that it has come to dominate *over* those other dimensions necessary to support such an intervention. Trumping the other 'components of a Critical Cultural Studies approach' that requires attention to also be paid to production and political economy and the reception and use of cultural texts (Kellner, 2015: 10–16), it has detached from the necessarily relational dimensions of media research. Nick Couldry, for example, models media research as a 'pyramid with four apexes' of media *texts*, *political economy* of media production, the *technical properties* of media, and the *social uses* of media technology and content – the pyramid can be turned to prioritize any one apex, but they remain mutually implicated (2012: 6–7). Otherwise diverse lines of critique stem from a reckoning with this dominance as *limitation*, including its neglect of the materiality of representation. 'Non-representational' theories of digital media and assemblage emphasize that it is not enough to analyze media-as-text as digital objects are processual, 'a particular articulation, the end result of specific interactions with specific programs at that specific moment' (Jarrett and Naji, 2016: 6). In his research on race and the cultural industries, Anamik Saha argues that this limitation in respect of digital technology is the continuation of a pronounced research deficit, and that understanding representation as a process requires a rebalancing away from how the cultural industries '*represent* race to how cultural industries *make* race' (2018: 11, original emphasis). The limitation of textual analysis is that while it 'can highlight the discourses and ideologies that underpin racialized representations of difference, they cannot tell us how and why these representations come to be made in the first place' – a limitation that also stymies the transformative goal articulated by hooks, as the marginalization of production studies stunts a consideration of how and in what ways practices and strategies may shift representational politics (ibid: 21).

The question of limitation underpins further lines of critique. One of the most consistent is the contention that the politics of representation is a *distraction*, or, as Adolph Reed Jr (2013) puts it, a 'cultural politics is worse than no politics at all'. In a juxtaposition of *The Help* – a 2011 film set in 1960s Mississippi about a young white journalist's attempt to write a book from the point of view of black house maids – and Quentin Tarantino's (2012) *Django Unchained* – a 'revisionist' slave revenge spaghetti western – Reed's focus is on why the latter received a reading as 'subversive', while the former was dismissed as patronising for erasing the multiplicity of ways in which black people were organizing their own emancipation during the Civil Rights period. They are, he argues, in effect 'different versions of the same movie', as both dissolve the prevailing social relations and structuring political economy of historical formations into individualized narratives of overcoming. He criticizes readings of *Django* by 'black and leftoid commentators' who framed the film as validating a 'history of autonomous black agency and "resistance" as a politico-existential desideratum', as assigning significance to representations of heroic or resistant 'black heroes' effects a discursive casting of 'political and economic problems in psychological terms'. It also artificially separates the signifying text from its status as a commodity produced within what Reed defiantly refers to as a 'mass culture ... thoroughly embedded in capitalist material and ideological imperatives', and thus integral to the reproduction of the very conditions of injustice the politics of representation seeks to engage.

Defiantly, as Reed's argument draws explicitly on one side of 'mass culture versus popular culture' debates that have taken a variety of shapes over decades, from the Frankfurt School critique of 'the culture industry', to theories of cultural imperialism, to often exaggerated though nonetheless substantive disagreements between political economy and cultural studies (see Fenton, 2008). It is not my intention to rehearse these debates here, and Reed's resistance to investment in the transformative power of images/narratives also suffuses a number of other critical positions, from scepticism regarding the individualizing drive of narratives of empowerment to a more profound critique of the *mediacentrism* which the politics of representation can cultivate, where the 'world is considered to be a product of representation, with the media then being the central means of that representation' (Hesmondhalgh and Toynbee, 2008: 12; see also Couldry, 2012).

Rather, the focus here is on Reed's contention that a politics of representation *is worse than no politics at all*. Firstly, it should be noted that what he sees as the neglect of sustained anti-capitalism in some representational politics is not an oversight, but quite conscious. Racialized people can object to racist imagery from a variety of political positions, and community or media watch groups may be motivated to confront prejudicial representations, without implying that 'this reform will have greater impact on society than other reforms' (Alcoff, 2006: 28). Beyond this, Reed's delineation of the 'politics of representation' is organized around two assumptions: that the dominant purpose of textual analysis is to recover resistant or transformative dimensions, and that textual analysis inevitably obscures the political economy of production. While this certainly describes particular trends in academic production, including a much commented tendency to distil political hope from 'resistant' readings of popular cultural texts, it is hard to see how this delineation incorporates research that takes seriously the need to interpret the texts of the media industry in terms of the context of their emergence and production. In her study of representations of Arabs and Muslims in US television drama after 9/11, Evelyn Alsutany, like Reed, critiques the focus on 'positive' or empowering images, not because this kind of cultural politics distracts from more fundamental political struggle, but because it fails to understand how cultural politics intersects with this wider political struggle.

In the post 9/11 conjuncture, US television drama conspicuously featured 'good Muslim' characters to an extent that comprised 'a new representational strategy whereby sympathetic representations are standardized as a stock feature of media narratives' (Alsutany, 2012: 10–11). To consider these representations in isolation from a wider, interactive 'hegemonic field' of 'government and media discourses', however, would be to miss how this emergent strategy fictively inscribed the wider discursive distinction between 'extremist and moderate' Muslims, honed during a period of military imperialism, domestic surveillance and coercion, and exaggerated, compulsory patriotism. These 'simplified complex representations', while appearing to directly challenge the negative stereotypes associated with racism, 'simultaneously produce the logics and affects necessary to legitimize racist policies and practices' (ibid: 14). That is, by projecting an attachment to multiculturalism and a postracial consensus capable of withstanding the temptation to 'demonise' an enemy, they circumscribe 'acceptable forms of Muslim American identity' and obscure how the securitarian response to the attacks involved intensively racializing forms of collective surveillance, profiling, and immigration 'reform' (see Kapoor, 2018). Alsutany's argument that 'it is no longer the case that the Other is explicitly demonized to justify war or injustice' (op. cit: 16) is critical to understanding how, as the next chapter examines, racialization often proceeds not by rejecting multiculturalism or diversity *tout court*, but by sifting and ordering acceptable and unacceptable forms of diversity. Her method of examining the emergence of a particular representational strategy in and through the political conjuncture opens up more possibilities for understanding political formations in heavily mediated societies than insisting on capitalist media as a superstructural distraction, *tout court*, from the underlying political real.

A very different line of critique builds on this circulation of racial meaning in public culture to argue not that a focus on representation distracts from politics, but that certain tendencies reduce representations solely *to* politics. In a reading of Bob Marley's image in consumer culture, Ben Pitcher (2014) argues for thinking about how racial meaning is shaped and shifted through articulation, performance and adaptation, and thus often 'exceeds the parameters' of racism and anti-racism, necessitating ways of thinking about race in cultural circulation which is not reduced to this categorical approach. Pitcher's argument is a departure from prevalent critiques of representation in consumer culture which emphasize how the mediated imaginaries of consumer societies are inconceivable without an 'aesthetic cosmopolitanism' (Urry, 2003) that is semiologically voracious: commodifying, co-opting, hybridizing and riffing on cultural styles and referents, on *difference*. Scholarship on the commodification of race, as Anamik Saha summarizes, examines how racial markers are used to differentiate cultural products 'that have no discernible difference between them in terms of use value; in which case symbols of race and ethnicity, especially when tapping into the fears and desires bound up in imperial nostalgia or postcolonial melancholy, are able to give commodities a competitive advantage' (2018: 67).

Some assessments of the commodification of difference hew towards the paradigm of distraction by arguing how a 'soft cosmopolitanism' predicated on mobility and the appreciation of difference provides cultural capital for liberal individualism (Calhoun, 2002) and a form of stylized multiculturalism that is the 'ideal form of ideology of global capitalism' (Žižek, 1997). Pitcher's argument is different, conceiving of consumer culture as a space in which meaning is produced and reproduced in artefacts and practices often dismissed as trivial but which are part of the 'ensemble of relations' which constitute race as a site of meaning. As a consequence, the tendency to read solely ideologically is reductive, as 'to try to confront racism without acknowledging the full complexity of racial meaning is to undermine anti-racism and place an arbitrary and rudimentary limit on how we conceptualise it' (2014: 23). This complexity, therefore, requires a vigilance against critical readings that sift representations according to whether they confirm or contest forms of racism, eliding the 'meanings of race in excess of racism' (ibid: 17). Pitcher's emphasis on processes of meaning generation suggests a final point of orientation; *intertextual circulation* and the accretion of commentary as productive dimensions of the process of representation. In an assessment of media sociology scholarship on race and representation in the US in recent decades, Ronald N. Jacobs (2014) emphasizes the need to recognize how

> … racialized representations derive meanings from intertextual circulation of factual and fictional media. Consequently, it is important for media sociologists to study the full range of mediated representations. Second, media representations of race are connected to the larger field of political and social representations. Third, while media representations have clear ideological tendencies, they are also multivalent and polysemic texts, offering a variety of interpretative paths. Because of this fact, it is important to

study racial representations as part of a larger struggle over mean-ing, in public as well as private communicative spaces. We can-not only study texts themselves; we must also explore how media texts become objects of commentary and critique in a variety of multiple yet overlapping publics.

Jacobs is focused here on the need to consider representation beyond the hermeneutic relationship between the media text and the reader/audience, yet his emphasis on how racialized representations derive meaning, and what this demands of analysis, provides an insightful starting point for thinking about the digital media environment. Herman Gray, in echoing Pitcher's dissatisfaction with a 'binary formulation of dominance and resistance' in critical analysis of issues of representa-tion and meaning, similarly underlines that the generativity of circula-tion is critical to analyzing digital media. Circulation mobilizes public sentiment and resonance, and requires 'thinking about the work of race in media (and media on questions of race) along the lines of media cir-culation, intensification and proliferation of affective investments and not just the legibility and authenticity of representation' (2013: 792–3). Conceiving of circulation in these terms is not a preamble to a celebra-tion of connective media's modes of participation or the 'resistant prac-tices' of users (an assessment of how digital media platforms both enable and constrict anti-racist politics is undertaken in the final chapter). For one thing, this is not simply a question of social media users 'talking back' to media representations, as the increased production and circulation of commentary is a political economic imperative of the 'high choice' media environment. A consequence of this accelerated, attention-seeking dynamic is media hyper-responsiveness, if not reflexivity, regarding potentially racist representations.

Further, in a context where online news sites have significantly expanded the competition for attention, accelerated news cycles demand concerted content production, and news sites must compete in a context of 'distributed discovery' through social media platforms and aggregator sites, it is no longer simply that 'a more participatory media environment ... provides digital media users with new opportunities to engage with the news by commenting on stories, sharing them, discussing them with others' (Nielsen et al., 2016: 14). What was often termed 'user-generated content' has shifted from being a celebrated – if in practice highly cir-cumscribed – complement to news witnessing and story elaboration (Peters and Witschge, 2014) to providing a source and topic of news. Take the video 'This is America' by Childish Gambino/Donald Glover, which was released on May 5th 2018 and accumulated ten million YouTube views in 24 hours (Beaumont-Thomas, 2018). The layered and allusive video invites a reading in terms of the history of anti-black violence in the US, and a reading is what it received; by May 8th, *Time*, *Business Insider*, *The Guardian*, *The Washington Post* and *The New York Times*, to name but a few, had published online responses collating and building on social media disseminated 'decodings' of the 'hidden meanings you may have missed' as 'the internet was quick to pick up on tons of hidden messages that were scattered throughout the video' (Yzola, 2018).

The oft-neglected hermeneutic overspill of circulation and commentary that Jacobs integrated into the intertextual process of representation is now structured into the economy and operations of contemporary 'news-as-comment' culture. Concomitantly, this structural intensification of circulation and comment overlaps with, and undoubtedly shapes, the extent to which symbols and representations have become mediating conduits for the politics of race. The politics of representation has acquired a renewed visibility as a distributed digital practice, commercial media imperative and modality of racialized politics, and the critiques of representation analysis discussed provide points of orientation for responding to it. The following sections attempt to carry these points forward by focusing on a recurring form of the politics of representation shaped by the dynamics of debatability – the politicization of image repertoires derived and adapted from the colonial past as ways of forcing a reckoning with the coloniality of the 'postracial' present. The next section moves towards a discussion of that generativity by revisiting the relationship between representation and race.

# Human chains, chains of equivalence

In a lecture first delivered in 1994, Stuart Hall called for an account of 'why race is so tenacious in human history, so impossible to dislodge' (2017: 43). In 'Race – the Sliding Signifier', Hall juxtaposes the fact that all attempts to 'fix the idea of race foundationally' in biology, genetics, physiology or various formulas of pseudo-science have failed, and yet the widely-cited conviction that 'race is a construct' has not dislodged forms of racialized 'commonsense' in society. Hall is pointing to the durability and motility of racialized meaning and logics beyond the radical break announced, following the Second World War, with race as a putatively scientific concept. As Mark Mazower notes in his history of twentieth-century Europe, 'In an age of empire and social Darwinism, notions of racial hierarchy were ubiquitous, and few Europeans on Left or Right did not believe in ideas of racial superiority in one form or another, or accept their relevance to colonial policy' (1998: 101). While the late nineteenth and early twentieth centuries constituted a period of significant political and institutional investment in racial eugenics, targeting both the 'unfitness' of the industrial working class and the threat of racial mixing across colonies and metropoles (Sussman, 2014; see also Rowbotham 2011: 87–94), in practice 'the concept of race had an exceptionally amorphous and indeterminate meaning' (Mazower, op. cit.: 102). It is this indeterminacy that Hall picks up on, yet it is important to recognize that, following the implacable genocide of European Jews in the *Shoah* and Roma in the *Porajmos*, the need to refute biological knowledge that justified hierarchical categories of human difference was a compelling political, scientific and civil prerogative.

The problem that Hall outlines is that despite this discrediting of phenotypical and genetic discourses of racial difference, it is symptomatic of racial discourse 'that the physical or biological trace, having been shown out of the front door, tends to sidle around the edge of the veranda and climb back in through the pantry window' (2017: 36). It is this relation between persistence and indeterminacy that leads Hall to underline the insufficiency of proclaiming that race doesn't exist, not because of a conceptual or political investment in it, but because the lack of a scientific base does not account for race as a 'sociohistorical fact'. Race is a fiction, but not an easily dispelled story, because it works as discourse:

> I do nevertheless want to advance the scandalous argument that, socially, historically, and politically, race is a discourse; that it operates like a language, like a sliding signifier; that its signifiers reference not genetically established facts but the systems of meaning that have come to be fixed in the classifications of culture; and that those meanings have real effects not because of some truth that inheres in their scientific classification but because of the will to power and the regime of truth that are instituted in the shifting relations of discourse that such meanings establish with our concepts and ideas in the signifying field. (ibid: 45–6)

Hall introduces this key move by pre-empting objections to it: How could something with the historical weight of race be explained at the level of signification, of cultural meaning? His argument stresses the importance of representations to the 'concrete historical work' of racism, but this turn to a semiotic vocabulary does not entail that race only exists as a system of self-referential differences. Rather, visible differences are made meaningful *through* discursive practices. There is no point denying, Hall notes, that there are differences in appearance between humans; however, it is when these differences are encoded and organized within discourse 'as a system of marked differentiations, that the resulting categories can be said to acquire meaning, become a factor in human culture, regulate conduct, and have real effects on everyday social practices' (2017: 50). This key move requires an account of how race works 'like a sliding signifier', and it also propels the argument into a colossal field of study and controversy as to the specifically modern production of race under colonialism, capitalist modernity, and the formation of European nation-states. Lingering momentarily at the edge of this field, appreciating Hall's argument requires recalling the sheer historical pervasiveness of racial frameworks and logics. In *Traces of History: Elementary Structures of Race* (2016) Patrick Wolfe follows other historians in insisting on the modern status of race (see also Bethencourt, 2013; Fredrickson, 2002; Hannaford, 1996). While race is striated with older forms of religious, phenotypical and civilizational prejudice, these relations are not 'imbued with the discursive formation that today we call "race" ... a distinctive configuration of ideological elements that we do not find configured in this way before the late eighteenth century' (2016: 7).

This configuration establishes linkages between physical characteristics and 'cognitive, cultural and moral ones' and classifies these differences in hierarchical terms, marking out levels of inferiority from the European norm. Ideologically, the production of race is marked by a form of reconciliation between two dimensions of Enlightenment discourse, 'the great taxonomies of natural science with the political rhetoric of the rights of man' (ibid: 8). Race produced populations as not capable, or yet ready, to be integrated into the universal as 'bearers of the rights of man'; 'Race enabled universality to presuppose distinction' (ibid: 15). As Goldberg (2002) has demonstrated, these practices of distinction involved both 'naturalist' convictions of immutable and inferior difference, which were consolidated in the rise of 'racial science', and 'historicist' ideas of 'native' civilizational improvement under the supervision of European governance. Wolfe's account stresses that the attention given to these ideological developments is insufficient without a consideration of race in practice, or *racialization*, the 'assortment of local attempts to impose classificatory grids on a variety of colonised populations, to particular though coordinated ends' (op. cit.: 10). Race was integral to the legitimation and organization of regimes of European colonialism, but as a mesh of knowledge and practices circulating and adapting across territories, and shifting according to the subject populations and varyingly exploitative and exterminationist ends of 'bodily exploitation' and 'territorial dispossession'. And, as European colonial domination was conducted through racializing rationales and practices, 'reciprocally, colonialism subsequently came to furnish a racialised mythology that could be displaced back onto stigmatised minorities within Europe itself' (ibid: 11).

MacMaster (2001) underlines this displacement in a discussion of the factors which drove the 'simultaneous appearance of a modern, exclusionary racism in its anti-black and anti-Semitic forms right across Europe after 1870'. The dislocations of rapid industrialization and urbanization, and the seemingly uncontrolled growth of the working class, fuelled a romantic and reactionary rejection of modernism and a nostalgia for 'organic' community and the aristocratic order. Racism provided a 'powerful ideological means of expressing a much more rigidly defined nationalism', one where the 'imagined community' is defined by blood and lineage, and where the tensions created by the expansionist militarism of the nascent international order required the fitness of an internally coherent 'race nation'. What Étienne Balibar terms the 'reciprocity of determination' between racism and nationalism is manifested not only in the aim of conferring 'the political and cultural unity of a nation on the heterogeneity of a pluri-ethnic state' (Balibar and Wallerstein, 1991: 52–3) but also in the concomitant elevation of political and racial antisemitism. Across Europe, though with different national emphases and political articulations, Jewish populations were increasingly subject to racial science, but also cast as a 'stateless other', unassimilable to the national 'family', and inherently suspicious because of their presumed rootlessness and relations to corrosive forms of internationalism. MacMaster links the extension of male suffrage and the growth of mass politics to the marked mobilization of antisemitism, while the growth of associative life, transport and communication networks, the press and 'mass culture' 'vastly increased the channels through which colonial and racist ideas could be diffused' (op.cit.: 26).

It is within the historical force of these factors that Hall sets out his argument about the 'sliding signifier' and the resilient adaptability of race. The key to this notion lies in noting that, counterintuitively, race is a signifier, not the signified. In Saussure's theory of the sign, the signifier is the form a sign takes, while the signified is the concept communicated. In naturalized understandings of race, it is race that is signified by a signifier such as skin colour. Yet Hall inverts this relation, because 'what looks literally as if it fixes race in all its materiality – the obvious visibility of black bodies – is actually functioning as a set of signifiers that direct us to read the bodily inscription of racial difference and thus render it intelligible' (op.cit.: 63). And these signifiers are 'sliding', that is, they are constantly linked to other signifiers, such as gender, producing meaning relationally through representation. Thus 'there is always a certain sliding of meaning, always something left unsaid about race'. Hall draws on Ernesto Laclau's idea of a 'chain of equivalences' to argue that race is stabilized only by sliding between different domains of 'truth'. The level of obvious visible differences slides towards the 'domain of science', the genetic truth which can only be accessed by sliding back to reading the body, and can also 'be metonymically displaced further up the signifying chain' to behaviour and background to secure assumed differences in cultural achievement or intellectual capacity. The work of discourse, therefore, is neither purely symbolic nor scandalously superficial, as

> ... the chain of equivalences that race *makes possible* between genetic, physical, social and cultural difference does actually exist. Not only does this chain of equivalences remain extensively present in the world, in the meanings we use to make sense of social life and social practices everywhere, but also, even though it is 'only a discourse', it has for that very reason a reality because it has racial effects – material effects in how power and resources are distributed, symbolic effects in how groups are ranked relationally to one another, psychic effects that form the interior space of existence of every subject constructed by it and caught up in the play of signifiers. (ibid: 69)

To understand the chain of equivalence at work in 'the practices and operations of *relations of power* between groups' under colonialism, consider a famous passage from *Black Skins, White Masks* (1952 [2008]), where Frantz Fanon excavates a moment of profound disjuncture that occurred shortly after his arrival in Lyon from Martinique in 1946. He encounters a child on a train, and the child turns to her mother:

'Look, a negro!' It was an external stimulus that flicked me in passing. I smiled slightly.

'Look, a negro!' It was true. I laughed.

'Look, a negro!' The circle was gradually getting smaller. I laughed openly.

'Mum, look at the negro. I'm frightened!'. Frightened! Frightened! Now they were beginning to be frightened of me. I wanted to laugh till I burst, but that had become impossible.

Impossible, as Fanon finds himself not merely looked upon but 'fixed' by a gaze, a way of seeing that suffuses the child's field of vision. Far more than simply an uncomfortable and insulting encounter, Fanon realizes he is 'the object the other is looking at', an object pre-figured by the weight of race. 'The force of language, through the mouth of a child', Lewis Gordon observes, 'froze Fanon in his tracks. He found himself dried up and laid out in a world of ice-cold exteriority' (2005: 15). The encounter is not just with a child, but with the historically produced, racialized schema of the 'white gaze' that seeks also to compel him to recognize himself in violently circumscribed ways, 'to be black in the eyes of the white man'. This stark ascription is Fanon's often misunderstood 'fact of blackness'; the fact is not any essential or natural state of racial difference, rather it is the implacable force of racialized objectification. It is the *social fact* of being subjected to and positioned by the historically accrued ideas and practices of race, through which he is 'over-determined from the outside'. In this ephemeral exchange, Fanon realizes that his body is encoded by the 'epidermal racial schema' produced, distributed and enforced by the world-making of colonial modernity – the 'fact' that Fanon is subject to is the 'crushing objecthood' thrust upon him by racial formation. As his biographer, David Macey, writes, 'For the Martinican Fanon, the experience of coming under the white gaze reproduces the primal experience of his island's history: slavery and a colonization so brutal as to be a form of trauma or even annihilation' (2012: 166).

Fixed by the putative 'truth' of race, Fanon must cast 'an objective gaze at myself, discovering my blackness, my ethnic characteristics – and I was battered down by tom-toms, cannibalism, intellectual deficiency, fetishism, racial defects, slave-ships, and above all, above all, "*Y'a bon banania*"' (2008: 85). The inscription of racialized blackness, the codification of skin under conditions of administered subordination,

Hall's scandalous exposition and Fanon's anatomy of a moment trace the discursive shaping of race in very different historical contexts from the present moment. And yet 'chains of equivalence' lattice the examples encountered in the book thus far: the assumptions of 'black male criminality' that were fatally inscribed on Trayvon Martin's body; the insurmountable cultural differences that justified discrimination against young black British people in Rozanne Duncan's imagination; the orientalist fantasy of hyper-sexuality rendered through physiological caricature in Riss's ambivalent cartoon; the surveillance of 'radical Islam' which in practice implicates anyone of 'Middle Eastern appearance'. Racism, as Hall emphasizes in a different essay, 'Race and reaction' (2017[1978]), is always historically specific, though 'it may draw on the cultural and ideological traces which are deposited in a society by previous historical phases, it always assumes specific forms which arise out of *present* – not past – conditions and organisation of society' (ibid: 146, original emphasis). The next section examines a politics of representation shaped around such historical deposits, their contested circulation, and what they articulate about the present conditions of a society.

# Blackface: discourse and debris

In October 2011, a video was uploaded to YouTube showing the artist and activist Quinsy Gario being violently arrested by Dutch police in Dordrecht. Along with another artist, Kno'ledge Cesare, he had been attending the *Sinterklaas intocht*, the start of the national Saint Nicolas festival, which is broadcast live from a different city every year. Stopped from unfurling a banner with the slogan 'Zwarte Piet is Racisme' – Black Pete is racism – the police proceeded to use considerable force in removing the artists from the festival for the crime of wearing t-shirts with the same slogan. The ritual will be televised; in the build-up to Sinterklaas celebration on December 5th, St Nicholas arrives in the Netherlands from Spain on a steamboat laden with presents for the good children. The wise old saint enters on a white horse, and he is assisted by a troupe of clownish *Zwarte Piets* who are played by white Dutch women and men with their faces 'blacked up' while wearing 'Moorish' costumes, wigs of black curly hair, thick red lipstick and golden earrings. In the widely recounted version of the story, the Petes are merely blackened by chimney soot. However, the video of Gario's treatment intensified hitherto sporadic protest against 'Black Pete' not just as a racist representation, but, as the slogan suggests, *as racism*. At the same time, the zealous police action indicated the depth of cultural investment in the figure, and anger that the innocent fun of children could be politicized in this way. Not only is Black Pete not racist, but how can there be racism in the Netherlands, when race does not exist?

The annual festival is major business, and images of Sinterklaas and Zwarte Piet abound in advertising, television programmes and public images. The period between the characters' entry and the present-giving festivities of December 5th is characterized by media presence and private rituals, marking out the period as especially oriented towards families, children and the enjoyment of shared national tradition. For these reasons, Gloria Wekker argues, Zwarte Piet constitutes what Stuart Hall termed a 'ritualized degradation', that is, a 'representation that is so natural that it requires no explanation or justification' (Wekker, 2016: 140). Above all, above all, Zwarte Piet; sporadic protests against the caricature had been organized by people who had migrated from former Dutch colonies such as Suriname since at least the 1970s (Esajas, 2014). However Gario and Cesare's protest marked a significant intensification of protests, not only because of the immediate response to their virally witnessed treatment, but because the ritual image provided a generation descended from these 'postcolonial' migrants with a potent and versatile focus for anti-racist activism, including the basic need to insist on the salience of racism to understanding society in the Netherlands (Coenders and Chauvin, 2017: 1245).

This insistence confronts, as Markus Balkenhol and colleagues (2016) argue, a denial of racism which goes hand in hand with a 'nativism' informed by a 'preoccupation with Dutchness' and the problem of the 'cultural and religious alterity ... associated with postcolonial and labour migrants and their descendants' for this thwarted national essence. Thus Zwarte Piet became not only a contested representation and prism for anti-racist critique, but also a mediating object for the defensive, racialized reproduction of national identity and culture. This dynamic of denialism and insistence thrusts Zwarte Piet into ferocious circuits of debatability, a struggle over the meaning of racism conducted through contesting how 'shared, often unexamined fantasies with regard to race continue to shape the ways in which "we" and "they" are constructed and perceived, while dominant common sense has it that race is thoroughly absent in the Netherlands' (Wekker, 2016: 31). This is played out through a politics of representation that activates many of the dimensions and questions accumulated in the chapter thus far, and analyzing it requires unravelling main lines from the mesh of ways in which Zwarte Piet is made to mean.

The period of renewed protest from 2011 witnessed increasingly high-profile actions and counter-actions which began to generate international media coverage. In 2012 the Saint Nicholas Society began petitioning for the festival, including Zwarte Piet, to be protected as 'national cultural heritage'. In response to this attempt to fix Zwarte Piet's meaning within the framework of heritage, activists insisted on the question of history, requesting a United Nations human rights body, the Working Group of Experts of People of African Descent, to draw attention to its roots as a degrading representational *practice*. In a subsequent letter to the Dutch government in 2013, the Working Group situated Zwarte Piet in Fanon's 'galaxy of erosive stereotypes', contending that 'the character and image of Black Pete perpetuate a stereotyped image of African people and people of African descent as second-class citizens ... [they experience it as] a living trace of past slavery and oppression, tracing back to the country's past involvement in the trade of African slaves in the previous centuries'. This internationalization of the issue intensified the affective nationalism of the response, particularly after a television interview with the group's chairperson, the Jamaican historian Verene Shepherd, who stated that 'the working group cannot understand why it is that people in the Netherlands cannot see that this is a throwback to slavery and that in the 21st century this practice should stop'. A Facebook page, *Pete-ition*, set up to rally support for a wilfully misunderstood tradition, garnered nearly two million likes within a few days (Groot and de Kroon, 2013).

The general contention, therefore, that Zwarte Piet signified within a modern tradition of dehumanizing stereotypes, that, like *Y'a bon*, took archival shape under colonialism's relations of domination, triggered a public hermeneutic contest as to the figure's fixable meaning. Insistence on the putative non-racial signification – it's just soot – became so repetitive and scripted that the European Network Against Racism (2014) was able to publish a list of suggested responses to common justifications for Zwarte Piet (e.g. 'Why aren't his clothes black as well then? And going down a chimney does not give you big painted red lips or afro hair'). Establishing the origins of the Sinterklaas tradition, and plausible links with similar figures elsewhere in Europe, became, Wekker argues, a 'national pastime' where 'the reasoning seems to be that if it can be proven that there are figures comparable to Zwarte Piet in other parts of Europe, or if he can be shown to have Norse or

Germanic origins, then there is no possibility that he can be associated with racism' (op.cit.: 154). As a corollary, by establishing a genealogy for Zwarte Piet's blackness that preceded modern coloniality, the tradition could be distanced from the forms of 'blackface' closely associated with the US and the UK – the associative framing that loomed large in international criticism.

In order to understand these implications, it is necessary to draw attention to two intersecting traditions of colonial representation, the first of which is the practice of representing people of African descent as primates. Because they are held to resemble humans but are still regarded as animals, '"ape", "gorilla" "monkey" and related terms became favorite epithets to degrade those whose otherness and inferiority were believed to be manifested by and *inscribed* upon their bodies, people who, while they appeared human, were seen as less than human' (Greene, 1998: 5). In representational terms, simians, Donna Haraway notes, 'occupy the border zones between (the) potent mythic poles' of nature and culture (1989: 1). The fusion of assumptions about Darwinian evolution with eugenicist racial science in the late nineteenth and early twentieth centuries fixed 'negroes', immigrants and the industrial working class as sub-populations defined by their immutable hereditary characteristics (Sussman, 2014: 88–106). The established simianization of blackness and racial otherness in (settler) colonial popular cultures rapidly integrated this new imaginary of racial hierarchy, and the production of such images proliferated during turbulent periods when the border zone between human and those racialized as less-than-human was socially and politically contested.

Consequently, regimes of racialization have drawn on the unsettling proximity of the primate to reinscribe the racial difference of the insurgent or troublesome 'primitive', in representations frequently laced with gendered and hyper-sexualized motifs: post-emancipation Black Americans as 'urban coons', inferiorized by the absurd contrast of their grotesquely magnified lips and facial features with the ill-fitting pretension of their dandified outfits; the cartoonish simianization of post-famine Irish people in Victorian and Edwardian popular culture, their bestial stupidity and innate propensity for violence underlining, as the historian Thomas Babington Macauley wrote, that 'they did not belong to our branch of the great human family' (de Nie, 2004: 10); the 'more ourang-outangs than men' framing of Aboriginal Australians, slated to die out 'naturally' as a species through slaughter and neglect, even as early twentieth-century scientists wondered if they represented the 'missing link' in the Darwinian puzzle (Foley, 1997). Donning 'black-face', like simianization, is a practice that inscribes racial difference; however, its genealogies produce slightly different inferences. The popular cultural spread of blackface minstrelsy in Victorian and Edwardian Britain, Michael Pickering (2008) suggests, represented a form of 'symbolic expulsion' bound up in processes of national self-definition:

> In this way, what was constructed as 'racially' inferior became *interior* to national identity even as this was hidden behind its exterior front of civility and progress. The civilizing process of modernity required its de-civilized counterpart, and it found this in its own racial fantasies. Built as they were around its peculiar and complex conflation of mimicry and mockery ... blackface fantasies set up a sense of contrast between the modern self, upright in the prow of its rationality, and a disorderly black low-Other who confirmed white racial superiority and advancement while appearing to have been made safe by being made ridiculous. (Original emphasis)

Research on the modern sources of Zwarte Piet's iconography emphasizes the myriad ways in which images of the figure emerge from an archive of representations of blackness in Dutch visual culture, with significant variation in its appearance before it became more standardized in the second half of the twentieth century, with the proliferation of commercial and festive images on a national basis (Brienen, 2018). Prior to this, however, certain dimensions become increasingly fixed through representational practices at different moments. While the very inclusion of a 'Moorish' courtly servant is 'embedded in the systems of exchange and commodification as well as the circulation of images during the nineteenth century' (Smith, 2014: 228), it also signifies an earlier period of the 'Dutch golden age' of commerce, overseas expansion and involvement in the slave trade. As Brienen documents, the contemporary visual form is heavily influenced by nineteenth-century children's books' illustrations, which display over time an 'altered visual tradition ... responding to the hardening of racial categories and hierarchies that occurred during the nineteenth century' as well as to the possible influence of blackface minstrelsy and the nascent popularity of 'golliwog' dolls in books and as consumer products (2018: 182–7).

While these genealogies are important for understanding the transnational chains of signification which have shaped a localised repertoire, Wekker's observation as to the limits of empirical assertion also pertain to critiques of Zwarte Piet. As Jasmine Cobb has argued, 'there is never a culturally neutral ground for racial depiction – no place where our representational contexts have taken a reprieve from old ways of knowing race that create enough distance for the postracial to occur' (2011: 418). In other words, the racism at stake in Zwarte Piet does not depend on establishing a determining connection to 'old ways of knowing race', but rather on recognizing the chains of equivalence at play in how blackface practices signify under changed socio-historical conditions. The idea of 'racial debris' provides a compelling way of approaching these practices. In his essay 'The remainders of race', Ash Amin offers this metaphor as a way of understanding the circulation of such racial references, images and logics held to be 'past' but which are rearticulated under particular social and political conditions. His argument is particularly pertinent to self-consciously 'postracial' contexts, where racism 'quickly resurfaces even when thought to be thoroughly dismantled' (2010: 2).

Simianization and blackface practices constitute forms of such debris, and often it is the postracial assumption of their non-referentiality which informs their reproduction. In 2014 when Barack Obama travelled to Brussels for a NATO summit, the Flemish-language Belgian newspaper *De Morgen* published a satirical 'special article' presented as having been sent to the newspaper by Vladimir Putin. The article included an image where the faces of Barack and Michelle Obama are digitally altered with distinctly ape-like features. Putin, the joke set-up suggests, is capable of anything, including the kind of 'open racism' that is no longer tolerated in such post-racial western polities as Belgium. Stung by the appalled response on social media, *De Morgen* apologized, noting that 'we wrongly assumed that racism is no longer acceptable and that in this way it could be the subject of a joke' (Mackey, 2014). However, Amin's notion presses beyond such familiar postracial fictions to suggest paying attention to 'the potentiality of accumulated racial debris, variegated and dormant from different eras'. This requires, he argues, digging into the 'archaeology of a racial present' to explain the relationships between endurance and change in the dynamics of racism, and how 'mixes of past and present racial practices become especially vengeful towards the racialized other' (2010: 3). That is, when does racial debris become weaponized as racial shrapnel?

In some readings of the Zwarte Piet controversies, the reactive insistence on the innocence of tradition cannot be understood without thinking about forms of not just affective investment, but racialized pleasure. For Philomena Essed, Black Pete and the broader proliferation of social media-enabled 'blackface scandals' can be understood as what she terms 'entitlement racism', a turn to a discourse of freedom of speech as a 'licence to offend' and recuperate racist practices as a pure or sophisticated instance of free expression to which one is entitled (Essed and Muhr, 2018). For Egbert Alejandro Martina (2013), the intensity of investment in the ritual despite the argument that it constitutes a form of dehumanization suggests it endures also as a form of enjoyment, where 'racial domination as a pleasure in the Sinterklaas tradition is produced through a ritualised denial of race and an intimate choreography between Sinterklaas and Zwarte Piet, in which the figure of Zwarte Piet acts as a sign of subjugation, punishment and pleasure'. The reproduction of Zwarte Piet, therefore, is suffused with the vengefulness towards the racialized other that Amin detects, but these forms of investment must be explained, as per Hall, conjuncturally. With a preemptive nod to the kind of criticism of the politics of representation offered by Adolph Reed, Gloria Wekker points out that to focus on the Zwarte Piet conflict is not to prioritize 'cultural politics' above the violence of socio-economic inequality, but to work from how it has become 'the symbolic spearhead of a now year-round debate on fundamental racial inequalities in Dutch society' (2016: 143).

The protests against Zwarte Piet were multi-layered: disrupting the reproduction of a dehumanizing practice, through this disruption insisting on the representation's connections to a disavowed colonial past, and through avowing this past demanding a reckoning with the contemporary coloniality of racial arrangements in the nation-state. That is, Black Pete is both racist, and, as the slogan insisted, racism. While assessments of the movement's impact in forging an expansive agenda vary (for discussion see Esajas, 2016), in connecting the power to exclude through representation to the power to exclude in terms of belonging and citizenship, it created a space of 'intersectional social justice activism' connecting struggles against anti-black racism and an 'increasingly gendered Islamophobia discourse and practice' (de Jong, 2019: 273). In so doing, it disrupted the public fictions of what Wekker terms 'white innocence': 'an important and apparently satisfying way in which the Dutch think of themselves as being a small, but just, ethical nation; color-blind, thus free of racism; as being inherently on the moral and ethical high ground, thus a guiding light to other folks and nations' (op.cit.: 2). That there is no racism in the Netherlands, as with all European postracial fictions, is woven both from specific threads and the loom of the post-war 'break with race' discussed previously. As de Leeuw and van Wichelen summarize:

Dutch victimhood of Nazism during the Second World War fuelled the idea that a *real* racism equals antisemitism. It was impossible for the Dutch to conceive of themselves as being antisemites and by extension racists. The terms 'anti-fascism' and 'anti-racism' – strong in the 1970s and 1980s – indicate a general social rejection of racism. Hence it was not because the Dutch had worked through their own racist past (colonialism/slavery/antisemitism), but because of moral outrage towards French colonialism in Algeria, Apartheid in South Africa, racism in the United States, or the perception of the Vietnam war as a new imperialism. The lack of self-reflection with respect to Dutch history ... created the strange paradox that the Dutch perceived themselves as exemplary anti-racists defined in relation to racism and racist regimes outside the Netherlands rather than their own racism within Dutch society. (2016: 348)

The protests' insistence that the Netherlands cannot be innocent of the 'reciprocal determination' between race and nation intensified the dynamics of debatability, and in destabilizing Black Pete as an 'innocent' image, produced a series of ancillary questions and complexities for both media practices and the wider 'political and social field of representation'. As Chauvin et al. note in their (2018) study of children's television programmes, the public resonance of the Zwarte Piet protests provided mainstream media producers aiming to cater to an 'inclusive' public with a dilemma to navigate, for 'in an increasingly disputed narrative field, it takes more and more work to never have been racist'. Representational tactics also picked away at the seams of innocence; if racism is something that always happens over there, then let's take *Zwarte Piet* 'over there' to see what they think. To frequently bemused reactions, the journalist Thijs Roes made a video report where he showed pictures to passers-by on the street in Montgomery, Alabama, where in 1955 Rosa Parks refused to give up her bus seat. Sunny Bergman's film 'Our Colonial Hangover' (2014) parlayed London's 'conviviality' (Gilroy, 2004) into a sustained admonishment, where as a blacked-up *Zwarte Piet* in Hyde Park she is met with astonishment and aggression, while just happening to bump into Russell Brand, who informs her that 'we're scared of your tradition'.

At the same time, these tactics are ambivalent. Roes' video plays on the irony of Black Pete being judged negatively in a supposedly racist heartland, while further universalizing the North American experience of racism as the gold standard against which variations are judged (see Salem and Thompson, 2016). Bergman's role-play raises the question, as Chandra Frank (2014) notes, as to the forms of privilege at play in a white film maker dressing up in blackface and deciding that 'perpetuating the very racist structures that underlie Black Pete are not as important as "proving" that Black Pete is racist'. This criticism echoes a recurring limitation experienced in various public processes aimed at producing alternative Black Pete images acceptable to 'both sides' (see Wekker, 2016: 143–50). In analyzing the irruption of a 'Zwarte Piet' debate in Flanders in Belgium, Olivia Umurerwa Rutazibwa argues that the public dynamics of discussion reproduced the coloniality inscribed in the image of the exotic, childish helper, with primarily white male experts tackling the objective question of 'what constitutes as racism and what not', while the 'affected visible minority communities' were primarily invited to 'anecdotally expand on the emotional pain that Zwarte Piet might cause them and their community' (2016: 196). And as Chauvin et al. (2018) examine, the commercial prerogative of navigating social conflict served to strengthen modes of recognition that furthered denial through the floating inclusivity of 'diversity':

> Media producers claimed to have found a middle ground between the (misplaced) racial sensitivities of a minority and the majority's attachment to tradition. Multicultural compromise was thus deployed to undercut criticisms of racial discrimination, replacing the latter with a liberal call to respect emotional diversity. Unsurprisingly, the focus on respecting 'black feelings' – while presenting them as mistaken – was mirrored by calls for mutual tolerance between the proponents and opponents of Black Pete. By portraying multicultural society as free of conflict, these calls resulted in framing persistent anti-racist critique as disrespectful of 'white feelings' and this ultimately as anti-liberal and anti-multicultural.

What, then, of the politics of representation under conditions of postracial debatability? This case study examines how the image of Zwarte Piet is the subject of contested interpretations that link it in time and space to archives of colonial images and racialized stereotypes, and also to folkloric depictions and carnivalesque figures, shaping a tension between varying attempts to establish genealogies of the image and the inescapable ways in which it signifies in and through resilient practices of 'blackface'. As the image circulates under conditions of intensive contestation, it accrues adaptations, idealizations and subversions, and what Gray (2013) terms an 'intensification and proliferation of affective investments'. This media circulation and affective politics implicates the image in the wider field of social and political representation, indexing it not just to an elision of the nation's colonial past, but also to attempts to make visible the enduring colonial relations in the contemporary social formation of the nation-state. That this can never simply be separated out as a 'cultural politics' is demonstrated by the force of the reaction to the protests. Wounded innocence is not just evasive, it is vengeful, and Zwarte Piet was inevitably reloaded as racist shrapnel, made to stand, in nativist politics, as evidence of a culture under threat and a national tolerance betrayed by the ungrateful – and sliding – cultural, religious, racialized other (Balkenhol et al., 2016). The prevalence of racisms vested in the myth of the overly tolerant nation and the overly-tolerated other is further explored in the next chapter, which examines the question of representation more specifically in relation to journalistic framing.

# Endnote

1   The poet and first president of an independent Senegal, Léopold Senghor, who served in the French army during the war, took aim at the paternalistic caricature of the loyal child-like subject in a 1940 poem dedicated to African soldiers killed fighting for France, promising to 'destroy the Banania laughter on all the walls of France'. Its charge as an 'erosive stereotype' was heightened in the aftermath of the liberation of France, when the role of soldiers from North and West Africa in the Free French Army was deliberately elided, and in 1944 Senagalese Tirailleurs were massacred by French troops in a camp in Thiaroye for protesting against the appalling conditions of their demobilization.

# 3

Reasonable aversions: journalism and the Muslim/ Migrant 'problem'

# Let's just have the debate

In December 2016 the German chancellor Angela Merkel addressed a convention of her ruling Christian Democratic Union party, in which she stated that the burka is culturally unacceptable in Germany, as Germans 'show our face in interpersonal communication', and should be banned when legally possible. In response, a popular online news site in Ireland hosted an online debate, asking 'should we also ban face veils here in Ireland?'[1] The first comment set the tone: 'Ireland has never colonised an Islamic country ... They (Muslims) are guests here. No way should we tolerate their provocative fundamentalist practices.' One should never read the comments; however, the immediate chain of equivalence in this response is telling, slipping from the 'issue' of the burka, to all Muslims, to Muslims as migrants. This chain of equivalence is not only pronounced in contemporary politics, but also invited by the form of the poll and the purported debate. It is this transnational construction of the Muslim/Migrant problem, and the significance of being endlessly cast as the object of debate, which this chapter explores.

Merkel's sudden interest in the burka was transparent, widely reported as a 'counterweight to her refugee policy' (Aleem, 2016). During 2015, Germany had allowed hundreds of thousands of people fleeing the Syrian civil war to seek asylum, a period vaunted for its display of '*wilkommenskultur*', welcome culture. However, as apparent levels of public support for the policy fell during 2016, and it became associated with the highly mediated events in Cologne (see Chapter 1), Merkel feared being outflanked to her right by the AfD (Alternative for Germany) party, which had continually accused her of allowing potential terrorists, fundamentalists and hordes of Muslim men into the country, unchecked.

The 'demonstrative religiosity' of the burka, Nilüfer Göle argues, and its symbolism as a repudiation of the values of secularism and sexual freedom, is highly unusual in European Islam. It has emerged as a radical form of normativity in urban multiculture negotiating the 'coherence and incoherence between ancestral sacredness, personal experience and global modernity' (2017: 239–40). That it is a demonstrably rare practice which is subject to debate and critique by Muslim feminists is elided by its status as a gendered 'master symbol of Islamic difference' (ibid: 135) that acts as a trigger not just for the staging of wider and more inchoate aversion, but also for the rehearsal of those values that define *us*, the nation. As the openness of the political calculus in Germany and other national 'burka debates' over several years indicates, the significance of 'burka debates' lies primarily in their political form.

While they are validated in democratic terms, as a process of public opinion formation, the function of such debates, as Ghassan Hage (1998) argues, is ritual. The political invitation to 'have an open debate' about immigration and 'migrants' provides an opportunity for 'white governmental buzz'. It is an invitation – call the phone-in show or post below the line – to occupy the fantasy position of the 'national manager'. It promises an affective sense of privileged governmental belonging, adjudicating over who should and shouldn't stay, what they can and cannot do, restoring some felt sense of control over the destiny of the nation. In so doing, the lives of people who migrate are defined as a problem that requires majority deliberation on the admissible solutions (1998: 240–3). (Scroll down, a little more, to one of the next comments in the Irish 'debate' thread: 'When in Rome, do as the Romans. Yes of course ban it, it is not part of our culture, if muslims (sic) want to live amongst us they should adhere to our laws and customs as we would have to do in their land'.) The online poll transplants the 'issue' into a context, like Ireland, where the lack of a meaningful social referent for the burka is far less important than the generic invitation to worry over the nation and adjudicate who belongs, and to what extent, and what terms and conditions apply. Yet this transposition also succeeds because it is easy to achieve *fluency* in burka debates; they are extensively transnationally mediated, marked by the circulation of popular 'knowledge about Muslims and Islam' as translated from context to context, and vested in the assumption that the presence of Muslims, in any context, leads, if not now then eventually, to similar problems and controversies.

This fixation in political discourse has been formatted by the geopolitical chaos of the post 9/11 'war on terror', in which 'Muslims' have been produced as a source of political fear and a screen of socio-cultural anxiety, but its constitution is complex. For while Muslims are homogenized and essentialized as a politically productive problem population, contemporary anti-Muslim racism is shaped through a confluence of socio-political factors and a collage of ideological elements. While it is transnationally derived and shaped, it is also an extension and transfiguration of particular, longer-standing racialized social relations within divergent national contexts. (In an analysis of the 'email bombardment' sent to the Van Abbemuseum in Eindhoven when it staged a critical exhibition about Zwarte Piet in 2008, Gloria Wekker notes the extraordinary prevalence of 'anti-Muslim sentiments' in the emails. Despite the protests confronting anti-blackness, Muslims, as the most 'unwelcome, unassimilable, the disposable of the disposable', were ultimately held responsible for this dis-cohesion [2016: 154–5]).

As this suggests, the figure of the Muslim is integrated to powerful chains of equivalence co-joining Muslim, non-white and *migrant* difference. To simplify somewhat, if the 'migrant' is easily cast as a social enemy, a drain on resources, employment, housing and welfare, this figure slips and slides in relation to the 'Muslim' as a cultural enemy, incapable or unwilling to integrate or 'respect our values'. Whether the language is one of culture and civilization, or values and compatibility – or a mixture of both – the result is that people who are Muslim and 'Muslim-looking people' have become the subject of relentless media surveillance and speculation, a constant object of public debate, those who are 'spoken about *as if they are absent*, as the subjects of gossip' (Amiraux and Fetiu, 2017: 72, original emphasis).

Central to this chapter is the argument that the distributed banalization of this 'gossip', its apparently endless reproducibility, cannot be understood without a particular inflection of postracialism; that the relentless focus on a 'problem population' is solely a response to the problems caused by benevolent histories of migrant welcome and accommodation. *We tried, you failed*; the problem of the burka, as with many other controversies, is framed as a problem not only of self-segregation but also of excessive generosity and tolerance towards minorities which, having unfortunately failed, must now be corrected 'without apologies'. This discourse is explored in this chapter as a justificatory framework of *reasonable aversion*. The chapter proceeds by discussing the racialization of 'the migrant', firstly by examining the paradigms of security and risk which have come to organize migration governance, and then by discussing research on reporting migration and asylum-seeking, which tracks the structuring tension between securitarianism and humanitarianism in journalistic frames. The second half of the chapter integrates the racialization of 'the Muslim' to this analysis, also positioning it in relation to geopolitics and the rise of integrationist politics in Europe, and then examining the discourse of 'values' at work in reporting about Muslims – values that 'we' are all alleged to share, but which 'they' must prove themselves willing and capable of living by in an otherwise diverse nation.

# Racializing the migrant

## The constitutive outside

Hall's analysis of how race works in and across symbolic signification and material effects underlines a point made by Alana Lentin that race must be examined as a '*doing* rather than a *being*' (2017). This doing is never complete or uncontested, and shifts in time and space. The idea of 'racialization' has developed to capture the processual and dynamic productivity of how groups or populations become or are renewed as 'sites of racial inscriptions' (Meer, 2013: 390). Accordingly, a focus on how identities become racialized offers 'enhanced understandings of the discriminatory practices performed in the name of race by not taking race for granted and critically examining how race is symbolically invented and materially made' (Paul, 2014: 711). As with many such terms, the breadth of application of the idea of racialization has provoked critiques as to its imprecision (Barot and Bird, 2010); however, as Nasar Meer argues, its value may be as a 'meta-concept' that both cautions against singular approaches to racism while inviting an explanation for how chains of equivalence between physical appearance, 'culture', class, gender and religion are produced, and how they work in particular contexts to produce racialized groups and identities (Meer, 2013).

This 'meta-conceptual' approach is useful when it comes to examining how the category of the 'migrant' is racialized. National and intergovernmental organizations underline the crossing of territorial boundaries in definitions of migration, and 'migrants' as persons who live temporarily or permanently in a country other than that of their birth, and who have worked or acquired social ties in the country of relocation. Yet the 'migrant', in the context of the postcolonial nation-state, has long stood as a 'catch-all category, combining ethnic and class criteria, into which foreigners are dumped indiscriminately, though not *all* foreigners and not *only* foreigners' (Balibar and Wallerstein, 1991: 221). That the putative difference between 'ex-pats' and 'immigrants' is a regular media talking point suggests a basic intuition of racialization in action. The point is further illustrated by the plethora of terms that exist in European polities for delineating people 'of migrant background' in contra-distinction to the ethno-national, implicitly more legitimately belonging population. In Swedish, for example, the term '*invandrare*', immigrant, is used to describe those who are not of western European origin or appearance, including those born in the country, and is thus used to mark out non-whiteness rather than being applied to everyone who has migrated (Valluvan, 2017a). In part, such divisions are integral to the active production of the nation, which has always required a conception of who does not belong to configure the 'imagined community'. However the force and texture of these exclusions must be explained over time, not marked down as a 'rejection of the Other' that floats free of context, politics and practices (Delphy, 2015). As Sivamohan Valluvan (2017b) argues:

> ... if one basic proposition about what constitutes nationalism is to be advanced, one proposition from which all else follows, it is the relationship between political discourse, ideology and nation that is the most helpful. Namely, western nationalism can be read as the formation by which a self-appointed normative community attributes its putative socioeconomic, cultural and security concerns to the excessive presence and allowance made to those understood as not belonging. Those who comprise the relevant field of non-belonging include the variously constituted insider minorities but also various foreign peoples and/or international forces, some of which intertwine with and reinforce the pathologies attributed to those internal, generally non-white groups.

This process of attribution is a constitutive feature, not a static dimension of nationalism, and its articulation is never singular, fully coherent or uncontested. Take once again the language of symbolic division of the nationally resident population. The *Zwarte Piet* protests were regularly cast, in nativist discourse, as a provocation by *allochtonens,* a putatively administrative term for anyone born abroad or with a parent from abroad, but one that can be invested with particular anxieties and animus when 'employed to refer to those who are considered most troublesome and are most strongly raced as Other: Dutch citizens with Turkish, Antillean and, particularly, Moroccan backgrounds' (De Koning, 2016). Thus the rejection of Zwarte Piet was politically recast as spectacular evidence of the problem of particular category of backgrounds who have, symbolically, divided *themselves* from the nation. It is not just the meaning of the images that is at stake but also the ascribed identities and status of those criticizing them, a combination of actor and action that performatively reinforces their estrangement from a normatively imagined national subject. The question is, therefore, why and under what conditions do particular forms of racializing anxiety and aversion become stuck to the (sliding) figure of the migrant?

## Politics and the governance of anxiety

No one framework can fully do justice to this question, but, in the limited foray possible here, I propose to draw heuristically on the notion of 'domopolitics', a mode of population governance emergent in liberal democracies under neoliberal capitalism (Walters, 2004). Walter's argument begins with mapping transformations in the contemporary state. The 'openness' of markets required by globalization makes a particular image of the (welfare) state, as a territorially defined and nationally coherent economic system and social order, untenable. Instead, the 'business' of governance becomes a contingent exercise in tapping 'good' flows of resources such as investment and useful (human) resources, while also staunching 'bad' flows of mobile risks and disruptions such as terrorism, asylum-seeking and unwanted forms of immigration. This unsettling of the isomorphic vision of the nation is compensated for through domopolitics as a 'politics of home', a 'reconfiguring of the relations between citizenship, state and territory. At its heart is a fateful conjunction of home, land, and security. It rationalizes a series of security measures in the name of a particular conception of home ... the home as our place, where we belong naturally, and where, by definition, others do not' (2004: 241).

While particular articulations of this obviously vary, the summary value of this idea is how it facilitates an analysis of the interlocking material and discursive dimensions of migrant racialization. Domopolitics represents an intensification and expansion of the securitization of migration regimes in the post-Cold War era. Asylum-seeking rights, in this period, have been eroded, nationally and transnationally, through spatialized systems of bordering and deterrence, and punitive reception, determination and deportation processes. Asylum-seeking has been inducted into a 'security continuum' that encompasses terrorism and immigration, and that reconfigures the border not only as a territorial frontier but also as an assemblage of practices of surveillance, policing (e.g. 'random' ID checks in urban spaces) and outsourced 'buffer zones' (e.g. asylum camps in 'non-European' transit points). This securitization works in tandem with the stratification of access to social and economic rights, types of residence, and citizenship. Stratification in turn requires a concomitant production of migrant 'illegality' through blocked or constricted modes of entry, and often rapidly shifting visa regimes and prohibitively complex conditions on entry and stay.[2] The 'illegal immigrant', as Eithne Luibhéid stresses, 'is not an inherently undesirable "type" of person but rather a position of social and political vulnerability that is constructed through multiple relations of power' (2013: loc 272). Desirable migrants, in this complex, must not only be advantageous to the economy, but also have assumed competencies for autonomy and non-reliance on the state, and be regarded, as is discussed subsequently, as capable of *integration*.

What is striking in so much debate about the problem of migration is that the highly militarized and expansive border apparatus remains hiding in plain sight, while migration, in discursive terms, is everywhere always presented as being 'unmanaged' and spiralling out of control. While the explicit 'populist' politicization of immigration is integral to this hyper-visibility, a theory of domopolitics locates a more sustained reason for this in a logic of governmentality; that being seen to identify and manage 'risk' and 'insecurity' internal to the population has become a dimension of governance, a process that requires also cultivating anxiety about the risk to be managed. In a framework similar to Walters', Didier Bigo (2002) argues that the explicit securitization of immigration under neoliberal globalization informs a 'governmentality of unease', a process which has ideological elements but which must primarily be understood as a 'political technology' comprised of intersecting dimensions, including the enormous growth in technologies of surveillance and the security industry; the 'fears of politicians at losing their symbolic control over the territorial boundaries'; an affective register among citizens whose experience of everyday life is suffused with uncertainty and precarity (2002: 65).

Securitization not only generates unease but also simplifies it. It links the figure of the migrant to forms of insecurity, typically through 'repertoires of justification' concerning crime, terrorism, unemployment and urban degeneration (see Kryżanowski and Wodak, 2009). Structural problems and the 'social distribution of the bad' are written onto a figure that, while varying in profile across contexts, is the product of a 'political game' which delineates 'the figure of the migrant by inverting an image of the good citizen', thus also marking a 'citizenship by difference with these outsiders inside the state' (Bigo, 2002: 70–8). The productivity of this political game is evident in the degree to which the fallout from the post-2008 global economic crisis was shifted to focus more on a 'migrant crisis' than on neoliberalism and austerity, where 'politicians and pundits increasingly began to link economic woes to the presence of migrants, despite little in the way of evidence supporting this link' (Gilmartin et al., 2018: 82). This apparent productivity under conditions of heightened insecurity should not be taken to mean that resurgent nationalism or nativism are an 'epiphenomenal' effect of capitalist crisis. The emphasis in the 'governmentality of unease' framework on scales of action, and the intersection of a spectrum of actors and practices in producing the 'political spectacle', caution against this. However it does allow for an unflinching focus on anti-immigrant racism as what Jacques Rancière (2010) has termed a 'cold racism':

> Our states are less and less able to thwart the destructive effects of the free circulation of capital on the communities under their care – all the less so because they have no desire to do so. They then fall back on what is in their power, the circulation of people. They seize upon the control of this other circulation as their specific object and the national security that these immigrants threaten as their objective – to say more precisely, the production and management of insecurity. This work is increasingly becoming their purpose and their means of legitimation.

Cold racism is articulated politically as a form of anti-racism, as dealing with the 'problems caused by immigration' in order to prevent the expression of racism as a 'popular passion', or as responding to the people's 'ordinary fears' (which have a right to be expressed without 'accusations of racism'). While the securitization of migration clearly has an affective register within electorates, this conceit serves to disguise how it is in fact a 'passion from above' that prosecutes state racism as nothing more than responsible management of conditions that would otherwise give rise to – frozen – racist expression (the 'hot passion' of the masses, increasingly coded as 'the white working class'). Cold racism involves both the legal and institutional construction of stratification and exclusion and an intensely symbolic politics. It can be seen overtly at work in the highly mediated 'spectacles of migrant illegality' which have become important set pieces in simultaneously stoking and assuaging anxiety (De Genova, 2013).

One form of spectacle involves a performance of securing the 'external' border. In 2018, shortly after the post-fascist leader of the Italian Lega Nord, Matteo Salvini, became Interior Minister, he prevented the landing of a Doctors Without Borders' refugee rescue ship *The Aquarius*, declaring that 'from today Italy will start to say no to human trafficking, no to the business of illegal immigration'. A second genre of border events involves disciplining the internal 'borderland'. In 2018 the Danish government passed a 'ghetto deal' law that identified 25 urban areas with high proportions of 'ethnic minority background' residents as 'parallel societies'. These will be subject to spectacular forms of justice – for example explicitly punitive double sentencing for crimes – and where those of 'non-western' background must, according to the Danish Justice Minister Soren Pape Poulsen, 'profess to the values required to have a good life in Denmark' (Ngo, 2018).

The domopolitical defence of home is performative, hailing the crisis it seeks to then handle through spectacular intervention. Ambalavaner Sivanandan captures how the border is secured through chains of equivalence, as

> the war on asylum and the 'war on terror' – one, the unarmed invasion, the other, the armed enemy within, has produced the idea of a nation under siege, and, on the ground, a racism that cannot tell a settler from an immigrant, an asylum seeker from a Muslim, a Muslim from a terrorist. All of us non-whites, at first sight, are terrorists or illegals. We wear our passports on our faces. (2008: 48)

The racialization of the 'migrant' proceeds through this anxious dialectic of external threat and internal problem.

## Between security and humanity: reporting migration and asylum

Border spectacles are dependent on what Eric Louw describes as the 'routines and practices of media-ized politics'; the deep penetration of public relations, media logics and stage-managed events into the 'communicative steering' of public political processes (2010: 195–7). It does not follow from this, however, that media coverage of migration and asylum issues corresponds to any neatly prescribed role within this logic of governmentality. Certainly, there is copious research, in discrete national and comparative international studies, that demonstrates the persistence of stereotypical and often actively 'demonising' representation. The Glasgow Media Group, for example, in a study of British newspaper coverage samples in 2006 and 2011, identified the prevalence of key themes which regularly linked asylum-seekers to security risks (crime, terrorism) and social threats (primarily welfare and employment; Philo et al., 2013). In a similar thematic review, but this time of a significant European-wide corpus of studies of the representation of migrants in news discourse, Bennett et al. (2013) identified three recurring tendencies: 'fuzzy group designations' (including collapsing the categories of asylum-seeker, refugee and 'migrant' into each other while using these as all-encompassing terms for highly heterogenous groups); a tendency to oscillate between binary constructions of threat or victim, with a particular 'persistence of stereotypical portrayals of immigrants juxtaposed to crime and violence';

and a consistent tendency to primarily source and centrally quote 'authority figures' involved in the management of migration (2013: 249–52).

However, reporting is frequently contradictory, reflexive and sometimes involved in migrant and refugee advocacy[3] and this is illustrated by recent studies of how journalism negotiates the domopolitical logic of migration governance. A key analytical focus here is on news frames, that is, 'the process of *defining what is at issue* in public debates' produced through journalistic patterns of interpretation and patterns of presentation (Brüggeman, 2014: 62, original emphasis). In Entman's widely-sourced formulation, to 'frame' is to 'select some aspect of a perceived reality and make them more salient in a communicating text, in such a way as to promote a particular problem definition, causal interpretation, moral evaluation, and/or treatment recommendation for the item described' (1993: 52). 'Issue-specific' frames in news are produced through the interaction of these dimensions as 'frame elements' which foreground and emphasize particular aspects over others (Matthes and Kohring, 2008). Research also suggests, unsurprisingly, that news media framing of migration stories has considerable potential influence over 'story-telling practices in other media', political communication and policy discussion, and public conceptions and understandings (Moore et al., 2018).

The first aspect of note is the extent to which navigating a tension between, broadly speaking, securitarian and humanitarian frames recurs in news coverage. While unexpected events and border spectacles sharpen the tension between these frames, longitudinal studies reveal how they become reproduced through the marking out of particular types of deserving and undeserving subjects. Kerry Moore's study of the emergence of the signifier 'asylum-shopping' over the 1990s/2000s, approaches it in the context of a 'hegemonic asylum discourse' in Britain where 'narratives dominant in mainstream media and political discourse seemed to assume a default position of suspicion, reproducing a "culture of disbelief" about asylum claims' (2013: 349). In this context, a plethora of terms emerged positing hard and fast distinctions between genuine/deserving refugees and bogus/fake asylum-seekers or migrants. 'Asylum-shopping' first began to appear in British newspapers in the early 1990s, but became a regular feature of predominantly broadsheet reporting during the 2000s, particularly in periods when particular policies or incidents were subject to public discussion, such as the European Union's restrictive 'harmonisation' of asylum procedures.

'Asylum shopping' recategorizes the practice of asylum-seeking as a consumer activity. While the term was routinely presented in scare quotes in articles, the fact that the signifier seems to nevertheless describe a self-evident practice serves to position state actions as a 'logical response' to a given problem that requires deterrence. Though Moore does not describe it in these terms, the category of 'asylum-shopping' is shaped by domopolitical logics. Implicitly linked to a 'discursive pre-history of national anxiety about immigration, race relations and potential social unrest', it does not articulate any seemingly explicit racialized valence. Instead, it identifies the British nation with a privileged socio-economic status that is vulnerable to exploitation, thus requiring decisive state action to address any threats to those who are at home by unwanted forms of intrusion. Consequently:

> Instead of a structure providing protection, the asylum system becomes metonym for the nation, re-articulated as that which requires protection from exploitation. Indeed as part of a myth so in accordance with the prevailing neoliberal social imaginary it is perhaps no wonder that, despite the extraordinary novelty of the expression, calls to combat 'asylum shopping' should have been naturalised and incorporated so uncritically within the UK press discourse surrounding asylum and refugee issues. (ibid: 361)

Comparative studies conducted in relation to the sharp intensification of asylum-seeking in 2014–2015 also reflect the dominance of intersecting humanitarian and securitizing frameworks. As Daniel Trilling (2018) argues, the 'refugee crisis' precipitated by the increased scale of movement, particularly as a consequence of the Syrian civil war, along two principal routes – from North Africa to Italy across the Mediterranean, and through Turkey to south-east Europe – is better understood as a 'border crisis', that is, a crisis in the system designed to deter, warehouse and filter people before, at and after the border-as-frontier. The international nature of the 'crisis' as a political phenomenon and news story lent itself to comparative media research, and here two studies are considered, the first conducted by researchers in Cardiff University media researchers for the UNHCR and focusing on the dominant news frames through which the 2014–2015 'migration crisis' was articulated in national newspaper coverage in Germany, Italy, Spain, Sweden and the UK (Moore et al., 2018). Their approach drew faithfully on the 'frame elements' discussed previously, while underlining that framing processes are contingent on the specific socio-political context, and that 'multiple, mixed and even seemingly contradictory frames may feature within a single news narrative' (2018: 69–70).

The most pronounced frames across the contexts studied were a focus on immigration numbers, search and rescue/aid operations, political and policy responses, and humanitarian considerations. Some of their findings identified striking national findings; the right-wing and tabloid press in the UK, for example, is marked out by a 'consistent, hard campaigning edge' present not just in editorial or opinion material but also in the angles consistently taken in stories. However, more significant than any form of negative framing is the question of causal interpretation of 'crisis'. From the majority of articles sampled across newspaper genres and across countries, causal explanations of war/conflict/disease and poverty/economic factors were not followed by 'treatment recommendations' trained on the causes of these factors, but on a 'shifting set of anxieties between benevolent humanitarian concerns to save refugees and a securitising fortress mentality to better police the borders of the EU, and/or nation' (ibid: 90). In other words, the refugee/border crisis is primarily mediated as a crisis for and experienced by Europe. As such, it is a narrative produced through *both* humanitarian and securitarian frames.[4]

A study by London School of Economics (LSE) media scholars of broadsheet newspapers in eight countries – the Czech Republic, France, Germany, Greece, Hungary, Ireland, Serbia and the UK – examined coverage along an 'axis from militarization to humanitarianism' in a geopolitical scope that captured something of the spatial logics of the border crisis, and in a temporal framework that sampled reporting around key events in 2015: Hungary's construction of a border barrier with Serbia, the publication of images of Alan Kurdi, and the Paris attacks in November. As with the Cardiff study, striking patterns of distinction emerge, such as the significantly higher prevalence overall of securitization and militarization frames in 'western' European coverage, though this became widely pronounced after the Paris attacks. The study emphasizes the dynamics of reporting on a fast-moving and multi-polar event and the consequences of this for the 'frame element' of consequentiality. Necessarily speculative, 'negative consequences' were narrated in concrete geopolitical, economic and cultural terms, whereas positive consequences were presented as the intangible civic fruits of humanitarianism – empathy and solidarity (Georgiou and Zaborowski, 2017: 8–10). Their conclusion also underlines the instability and fragmentation of news frames, while linking this to professional practices and media–political interaction:

Many of the media organisations and journalists were unprepared to cover such events and there is little evidence of European media initiating systematic training for their staff on how to deal with the events and the sensitive issues involved. Such training opportunities have been scattered and exceptional. Furthermore, media coverage of "the crisis" was inevitably interacting with political decision-making and popular opinions. Thus, the mainstream political narratives, which sometimes promoted hostility and sometimes solidarity towards newcomers, were inevitably reflected in the press coverage. However, questioning political decision-making and engaging critically with the narratives of the "crisis", which is a responsibility associated with independent journalism, was very uneven across Europe. (ibid: 13)

The scale, spatiality and intensive mediation of the 2015 border crisis have prompted a significant body of research on journalism and the news framing of migration and asylum-seeking, capturing its complexity and contradictions. That frames of securitarianism and humanitarianism emerge as unifying research dimensions, and that these frames work both against and with each other in the construction of a 'European crisis' is nevertheless reflective of the pervasiveness of the politics that ideas such as 'domopolitics' attempt to historicize and situate. While these studies do not substantively examine the question of 'migrant' racialization, the key events of 2015 they address reveal how a border crisis focused on the border-as-territorial-frontier soon extended to a crisis of those, to adapt Sivanandan, who wear the border on their faces.

The politics of 'migration' is enmeshed in chains of equivalence, sliding between external threat and internal failure, unknown risk and familiar problem, social cost and cultural burden. 'There is no stable space of "Europe"', Nicholas De Genova argues, 'towards which the figure of "migration" can be understood to move, as from an imagined periphery toward a presumably fixed centre' (2016: 76). Instead, the sliding of the migration question between new arrivals and the native-born children and grandchildren and great-grandchildren of migrants 'entails a persistent conflation of migration, "race" *and* "Muslim" identity as relatively floating signifiers for the ... mediation of the contemporary, protracted postcolonial agony' (ibid). The 'Muslim' has come to represent in turn the most acute form of contemporary alterity in this play of sliding signifiers. As the archetype of that which is not 'European' but that is already visibly and volubly within the gate, it is a projection that sutures border politics and contemporary cultural and political anxieties into a figure of *reasonable aversion.*

# Racializing the Muslim

## We need to talk about Islam

The racialization of Muslims has generated a complex theoretical discussion, both because of the ways in which it draws on religious, cultural, ethnic, national and gendered dimensions, and because of the divergent ways in which these dimensions combine in different contexts, where pronounced anti-Muslim racism emerges from particular histories of migration, discrimination and the complicated 'becoming Muslim' of 'migrant background' populations (see Yilmaz, 2016). The centrality of religion has served, until recently, to inure theories of race and racism from discussions of 'Islamophobia' (Meer, 2013). The gradual force of the recognition that, as Abdoolkarim Vakil summarizes, 'religion is "raced" and Muslims are racialised' (2010: 276) has prompted engagements with the race critical literature, which in turn have generated new ways of approaching it, particularly in theorizing the early modern co-constitution of race and religion (see Bethencourt, 2013; Meer, 2013), and the analogous relations between anti-Muslim racism and antisemitism (Klug, 2014; Renton and Gidley, 2017).

This complexity has been ratcheted up by the dynamics of debatability, as the very terms used to conduct the discussion are themselves subject to significant public scrutiny and political contestation. The idea of 'Islamophobia', for example, is the subject of discussions as to its origins and etymology (Allen: 2012: 5–7), and as to whether the conceptual conjunction of Islam + phobia captures or obscures the intersecting structural, political and cultural ways in which Muslims are racialized as a practically homogenous population (Garner and Selod, 2015). However, the term, particularly in the UK following the publication of the influential *Islamophobia: A Challenge for Us All* report in 1997, is incorporated into a highly antagonistic and polyvalent conflict over its meaning. Some of this criticism is a question of anti-racist strategy; does the concept reify the supposed primacy of religion over the clustered practices that target Muslims, or does it provide a communicable concept with public use value in a context where 'racism' is too confusing? Does it produce a monolithic image of Islam, and provide Islamic 'extremists' with an accidental means of deflecting criticism from hate speech, or does it capture the ways in which it is precisely the prevalence of the image of Islam which anchors and legitimates processes of racialization?

Much of the criticism, of course, is motivated by varying political projects. For a hard right ideologue like Douglas Murray, author of the recognizably generic *The Strange Death of Europe: Immigration, Identity, Islam* (2017), the idea of Islamophobia as an irrational prejudice masks the host of rational reasons for worry. For the ostensibly liberal 'new atheist' Sam Harris, the term is designed to silence criticism of religion by disingenuously aligning hostility to adherence to belief with the legacies of racism. In France, resistance to the concept is pronounced among left-liberal intellectuals who dismiss it as political rhetoric masquerading as an analytical term, one that creates space for, at best, communitarianism within the secular public space of the Republic, and at worst, leftist sympathy for 'Islamism'. This ideological kaleidoscope is significant, but its primary significance is not the difficulties posed for defining 'Islamophobia' – the twentieth anniversary follow-up report *Islamophobia: Still A Challenge for Us All* (Alexander, 2017) bluntly cuts through these layers of objection to offer the definition 'Islamophobia is anti-Muslim racism'. Rather, this kaleidoscopic effect serves as an invitation to step back and note the sheer array of ideological trajectories and political projects centred on the problem of Islam, and of Muslims.

This, in and of itself, clearly does not render 'criticism of Islam' racist. Nor does it require evasion of how reactionary practices are justified as Islamic, or downplaying the agency and ideology of armed Islamist groups by reducing them to inevitable reactions to western imperialism. It matters after all that attacks in European cities are conducted in the name of Islam, Markha Valenta argues, 'but not because of what it can tell us about "religion" or "religion and violence" or "Islam and political violence". Instead it matters because "Islam" has become a name, a sign, a gesture through which to rally, act, to make history' (2017). Instead, stepping back from the detail of both patient conceptual work and debatability's frenetic fluency allows us to note something fundamental. Considerable discursive labour is invested in carving out public space for criticism of Islam in a conjuncture where, through war, securitization, social discrimination, political scapegoating and widely reported everyday humiliation, 'the totality of these images and practices creates an inescapable feeling among many that today "Muslim" is short for "the wretched of the earth"' (Hage, 2017: 6). The logics of migrant racialization contribute to this, but there is more to how Islam and Muslimness have been positioned as 'an overriding symbol of difference against which national identities are dressed and political agendas are set in the Western world' (Göle, 2017: xvii). The political agendas in question are forged by the racializing force of the 'war on terror', and the 'new integration' politics which overlaps with but is not fully explained or contained by this era of conflict.

In the opening lines of *Radical Skin, Moderate Masks,* Yassir Morsi writes of asking himself, after the second plane was piloted into the World Trade Centre, a 'rather worrying question': 'No evidence as to who was responsible for the attacks had been provided, yet somehow, I knew of a responsible Other and I whispered to myself, "what have *we* done?"' (2017: 3). Morsi's retrospection is written to be read in the light of what we now know; that the globally destabilizing 'war on terror' which followed the 9/11 attacks did not just target armed Islamist groups, but also civilian populations in Afghanistan and Iraq, and did not remain constrained to these invasions, but was extended to cast suspicion on and intervene in the lives of Muslims resident in western nation-states. The hunt for Osama Bin Laden, and the geopolitical strategies informing these imperial adventures, were wrapped up in a number of forms of legitimation. These shifted as the war spilt over from a conventional attack on sovereign nations to extending indefinitely in time and space and across multiple forms of armed conflict (Chamayou, 2015). The extent of the death toll in the 'war on terror', Arun Kundnani argues, 'could not be sustained without the racialised dehumanisation of its Muslim victims. A social body dependent on imperialist violence to sustain its way of life must discover an ideology that can disavow that dependency if it is to maintain legitimacy. Various kinds of racism have performed that role in the modern era; Islamophobia is currently the preferred form' (2014: Loc 197).

'[S]omehow, I knew of a responsible Other' – Morsi's hesitant answer to himself stresses what is often overlooked in narratives of a world changed forever on 9/11; the Islamophobia which was institutionalized and legitimated by this critical juncture drew on and compounded powerful discourses about Islam which were long in circulation. The 'Clash of Civilizations' framework, for instance, popularized by Samuel Huntingdon in the immediate post-Cold War period, drew on powerful imaginaries of Islam and the West shaped over centuries of religious antagonism, romantic projection, and the colonial forms of knowledge production about 'the Muslim world' often summarized as orientalism.[5] As a return of the 'split colonial geographies' (Gregory, 2004) of civilization and barbarism, the narrative of the War on Terror at once rendered inhabitants of Afghanistan and Iraq not only as disposable forms of life, but also as cultural subjects requiring the benevolent intervention of 'nation-building', articulated as an ideal form of liberal democracy. The shifting rationales of the War on Terror thus oscillated in emphasis between essentialist visions of the dangers to the West of the 'Muslim world', and a 'clash *within* civilizations' discourse underlining the need to empower 'moderate Islam', develop civil society and foster gender equality (Kumar, 2012: 128–35 original emphais). In a formulation not unlike Amin's notion of 'debris', Yasmin Ibrahim (2007) describes the 'referential archive' of associations with, knowledge about and images of Islam that circulated in media and political discourse in this period as 'dis-orientalism', a dizzying intertextuality given coherence by demanding that Muslim communities in western nation-states respond to this debris in their narratives of Islam.

'What have *we* done?' Morsi's recollection is also an intimation of the forms of racializing surveillance and collectivization which were instigated after 9/11, and which, having been sutured into domopolitical governance, have since taken a variety of forms. The post 9/11 geopolitics of 'preemptive strikes' on potential enemies was reflected in the development of elaborate and coercive systems of domestic terror prevention, often predicated on the suspension of civil liberties (Fekete, 2009; Kumar, 2012). These focused initially on international mobility, but also rapidly incorporated those suspicious, national 'migrant-Muslim' populations which may knowingly harbour or culturally incubate future attackers. These chains of equivalence were structured into forms of racial profiling – for example in airports and the policing of public spaces – that 'fluctuate between the Arab, the Muslim, and "Islam" between the racial phenotypes, the ethnic stereotypes, and the religious generalisations' (Hage, 2017: 8).

The counter-terrorism discourse accelerated in the aftermath of urban attacks by Islamist groups or their opportunistic fellow travellers locates the risk of violence in a combination of Islam and psychology. While totalizing accounts locating terror in the irrational rage of Islam's non-modernity have largely given way to a focus on the impact of 'extremist political Islam', the net result of the emergence of a discourse of 'radicalization' is that the prevention of terrorism is bound up in monitoring Muslim religious and political life for signs of 'dangerous beliefs and identities', an approach that locates causality in 'individual psychological or theological journeys, largely removed from social and political circumstances' (Kundnani, 2014, op. cit.). This has resulted in the construction of a 'racialized surveillant assemblage' justified by a 'pre-crime logic of security' that produces not just phenotypically pro-filed populations, but also 'datafied bodies' assembled from behavioural analysis, biometric information, mobility data trails and surveillance of religiosity (Sharma and Nijjar, 2018).

This domopolitical fixation on the as-yet-unknown threat, by locat-ing risks as internal to Muslim populations, is profoundly performative. As Valenta puts it, 'To be interpellated by the state as "Muslim" makes one subject to the treatment meted out to "Muslims", locking into place these citizen's public-political subjectivity regardless of the subject's own identification' (2017: 133). And, despite ritual recognition of the ethnic, cultural, ideological and social diversity of Muslim populations, the politics of radicalization produces a performative 'Muslim culture' not only as a product of surveillance, but also as a site where 'moder-ate' Muslims must continually be seen to dissociate themselves from 'dangerous beliefs and identities' in a coercive politics of recognition. The 'moderate' is a subject that fits an imagined spectrum of acceptable cultural diversity. Shorn of any dissenting form of politics, resistance or spirituality, the typology demands, Morsi argues, that 'we overpolice ourselves' and 'begin to fight the war on terror along the lines of it being a cultural "we" and not a world we inherit' (2017: 91).

As with media coverage of migration, there is no shortage of research on how journalism has contributed to the construction of Muslims as the threat already within the gate. This is particularly pronounced in reporting of political violence. A longitudinal study of national news-paper coverage in the US between 2006 and 2015 concluded that attacks by Muslim extremists garnered 357% more press coverage than attacks by non-Muslims, despite white supremacist groups carrying out almost twice as many attacks in this period (Kearns et al., 2018). In examining how media coverage contributes to a 'myth of radicalization', Hoskins and O'Loughlin have noted the affinity between media narrativization and the governance of anxiety, as 'for security policymakers and jour-nalists alike, radicalization can anchor a news agenda, offering a cast of radicalizers and the vulnerable radicalized, and legitimating a policy response to such danger' (2009: 107). Consequently, potential dangers are afforded a 'continuous discursive presence' that not only encourages anxiety but can also serve to tether any political activity by Muslims, such as Palestinian solidarity protests, to the possibility of future rad-icalized violence (2009: 107–8). In a study of UK press coverage of British Muslims between 2000 and 2008 commissioned by Channel 4 for a *Dispatches* documentary, Moore and colleagues (2008) found that 36%

of stories in their sample were about terrorism, with references to 'radical' Muslims 17 times more likely than references to 'moderate', while the most common adjectives used were 'radical, fanatical, fundamentalist, extremist, militant'. When the distribution of stories over time is considered, '2008 was the first year in which the volume of stories about religious difference and cultural differences (32% of stories by 2008) overtook terrorism related stories (27% by 2008)', with increased reference to social problems or 'opposition to dominant British values' (2008: 3).

This shift in reporting frames captures a fundamental dimension of Muslim racialization, which is the intersection of post 9/11 securitization with the dominant forms of 'integration' politics which have taken shape in Europe over the last two decades. Integration has emerged as the policy and rhetorical rubric charged with projecting the current and future cohesion of globalized nation-states. While the idea of integration, loosely conceived, seems to promise a process of social and institutional inclusion into the polity of the nation-state, ultimately as a citizen, integration regimes are domopolitical in orientation:

> Integration functions as another regulatory technique for the state to manage access by the non-national – not to the status of citizen – but to the act of entry, the security of residence, family reunification and protection against expulsion ... Integration determines the legality of human mobility, and constitutes another frontier to be considered as a 'legal immigrant'. (Guild et al., 2009: 42)

The integration regime, therefore, ranks and orders not only desirable and undesirable immigration statuses according to economic utility, but also perceived *integratability* – the potential of the subject to be socio-economically autonomous and coherent with a preordained cultural order. Integration, therefore, is comprised of technologies of cultural precondition: pre-migration tests, integration tests, integration indicators, citizenship tests – that attempt to shape the desired subjectivity of the compatible migrant subject.

However, even as integration regimes in effect dis-integrate by extending the stratification of status, residence and legitimacy, and creating hierarchies of belonging, integration politics has become fundamental to the political need to sustain a plausible vision of home – the bounded and cohesive national society. In *Daily Lives of Muslims*, Nilüfer Göle notes the irony that 'Muslim culture' has come to stand for the dis-integrating force of migration even as 'Islam gains visibility in Europe at this particular stage as a post-migration phenomenon. It seems paradoxical that those who have already integrated into host countries feel most confident asserting their Islamic identity, thereby making manifest their religious difference' (2017: xviii). It is this visibility that has been relentlessly politicized, and framed not only as cultural or religious difference, but also as a self-segregating rejection of the national community that gains temporary coherence through this contrast. This is most evident in the rash of manufactured symbolic controversies in western Europe that function as spectacles of cultural prohibition; hijabs, burkas, minarets and halal food have all been held up as evidence of the dis-integrating tendencies of Muslim 'migrant communities', and proof of the need to insist on demonstrative fidelity and loyalty to Our Way of Life.

As the chapter opening suggested, visions of the national community and way of life threatened by Muslim incompatibility vary. The next chapter discusses far-right politics, and its integralist, ethno-pluralist and differentialist understandings of the national people. However, integration politics has been dominantly articulated over the last two decades through what Adam Tebble (2006) terms 'identity liberalism', advocating a national culture of shared values, compulsory forms of immigrant assimilation and the duty of the state to protect liberal national culture, up to and including the exclusion of non-liberal subjects in the interests of democracy. Identity liberalism's claim to distinctiveness is not based on a singular national ethnos threatened by incompatible cultures, but instead on a defense of the liberal principles that define the way of life of the national community, and which must be protected against illiberal and regressive cultures. The national community is not homogenous and embraces its diversity, but integrationist politics adjudicates between 'good and bad diversity' (Lentin and Titley, 2011) – the moderate and the radical, the faithful and the fanatics, the willing and the willful, the civic and the communitarian, the idealist and the ideologue, the free speaker and the offended. This articulation is profoundly gendered and sexualized, positing gender equality and sexual freedom as established dimensions of a hegemonic national culture, pointedly contrasted with the resilient patriarchy and homophobia of non-white, non-western others.

It is this over-determined contrast between a national culture defined by universal freedoms and liberal norms, and subjects struggling to shed their regressive particularisms, that structures what I have been calling a politics of reasonable aversion. What could be more reasonable than insisting that living here involves trading bad values for the good values that just happen to define our way of life? While the ideological content of integration politics is defined by appeal to progressive values, in its form and force it 'ought instead to be understood to epitomise a dynamic of subordinate inclusion ... 'inclusion through exclusion''' (De Genova, 2017: 107). This dynamic is given political expression differently across national contexts, from an avowedly right-wing discourse of *leitkultur* – leading culture – in Germany to the dominant exclusionary interpretation of secular republicanism in contemporary France (see Mondon and Winter, 2017). In the discussion that follows, the focus is on the particular mode of subordinate inclusion enacted through a politics of 'British values'.

The final section examines this inclusion through exclusion at work in media discourse. Discourse analysis in Media Studies has been used in particular to interrogate news and current affairs journalism, including the generic dimensions and structural conventions of texts, the interdiscursive and intertextual dimensions at work in a text, and to 'examine how media representations inflect the discursive constitution of different social phenomena' (Phelan, 2017). As Sean Phelan argues, there has been a tendency to focus on textual analysis *as* discourse analysis rather than providing an account of texts in context and as embedded in and produced within specific political conjunctures (ibid). Discourses, Ruth Wodak argues, spread not just through texts but also within different fields of action, and texts 'as they relate to structured knowledge (discourses), are realized in specific *genres*, and must be viewed in terms of their *situatedness*' (2015: 49–51, original emphasis). The approach here, therefore, is to provide a close reading of a recent documentary about British Muslims in terms of the integrationist discourse of 'British values', detailing its discursive saturation with the assumptions and myths that structure reasonable aversion. Located in historical relief through a rolling comparison, situating it in journalistic, generic and sociopolitical terms, helps to explain what this discursive structure achieves in postracial terms: endless public surveillance, gossip and frequently fantastical speculation about the Muslim problem, freed from the frozen baggage of 'race'.

# Genres of reasonable aversion

Shortly before the 1979 British general election that brought Margaret Thatcher to power, Stuart Hall and the journalist and actor Maggie Steed presented a BBC 2 programme on racism in the media. Produced as part of a community access programme called *The Open Door*, the programme was made by the Campaign Against Racism in the Media (CARM), an initiative involving anti-racist groups of media workers and community groups and activists aiming to oppose and counter racist reporting in the context of regular fascist street activity, the anti-immigrant authoritarianism of the ascendant Conservative Party, and sensational reporting of 'black crime' and uncontrolled immigration (Cohen and Gardner, 1982). Entitled *It Ain't Half Racist, Mum* (IAHRM)[6] – a reference to the 1970s sitcom, *It Ain't Half Hot, Mum* about British soldiers in India and Burma towards the end of the Second World War – the programme mainly examined news and current affairs, offering an intervention that Hall described as '*about* the media and racism, *on* the media, *against* the media' (quoted in Malik, 2002: 48, original emphasis).

The programme features the presenters reframing news and documentary footage, talking the viewers through journalistic conventions, sequence editing and framing practices, emphasizing at every point the editorial choices made in source selection and narrative logic, priming the viewers to notice how seemingly impartial approaches are saturated in 'the dominant consensus constructed by popular representations of race' (ibid: 50). It documents an egregious field of practices; the total absence of the 'Blacks' and 'immigrants' who are the focus of demographic and cultural problematization, treating racist gossip as to what they do to us as public claims worthy of investigation, basing programme topics and choosing narrative points of entry in relation to the contentions of far-right ideologues. What the programme excavates is a recurring set of narrative assumptions: problems are caused by their presence, not by the hostility and discrimination they face. These journalistic presuppositions are congruent, as Hall laid out in his 1978 essay 'Racism and reaction', with racism as a 'dynamic political force in Britain', 'the mechanism by which problems which are internal to British society, not ones which are visited on it from the outside, come to be projected on to, or exported into, an excessive preoccupation with the problem of "race"' (Hall, 2017: 142). In a multi-ethnic context where ideas of 'immigrant return' and assimilation were no longer tenable, but also a broader political conjuncture of industrial conflict, economic recession and high youth unemployment, a palpable sense of national crisis demanded ideological containment and public scripting. In strings of stories of black youth violence and mugging of Asians living it large in council houses:

> Blacks become the bearers, the signifiers, of the crisis of British society in the 1970s ... This is not a crisis of race. But race punctuates and periodises the crisis. Race is the lens through which people come to perceive that a crisis is developing. It is

the framework through which the crisis is experienced. It is the means by which the crisis is to be resolved – 'send it away' ... It is, above all, the language of racism which has the effect of connecting the 'crisis of the state' *above* with the state of the streets, and little old ladies hustled off pavements in the depths down *below*. (ibid: 152–3, original emphasis)

In April 2016 Channel 4 broadcast a documentary presented by the broadcaster and former chair of the Commission for Racial Equality Trevor Phillips entitled *What British Muslims Really Think* (WBMRT).[7] The documentary explores significant shifts in British society since Hall's diagnosis of racialized crisis politics, and unsurprisingly its journalistic and generic approach is markedly different from the programmes IAHRM subjected to forensic examination. The familiarity of Phillips – whose parents emigrated from Guyana, then British Guiana, to London in the 1950s – to British television audiences marks the stark political and cultural distance since, as Hall and Steed note acerbically of one excerpt from a BBC programme about a troubled Blackburn housing estate, 'Blacks may outnumber whites 3 to 1 but the BBC seems to have trouble finding them, since none from the estate are interviewed'. The BBC's subject matter was 'Britain's non-white population'; now Channel 4 is concerned with an altogether different construction: British Muslims, part of the national community, and described by their faith, not crude racial negation. Far from being voiceless and invisible, they are extensively polled and featured in interviews, and in vignettes of their activities in workplaces and community contexts. And, as Phillips emphasizes in the introduction, the documentary is about 'what British Muslims really think' – an in-depth attempt to get to grips with the thoughts of a population subject to relentless gossip, and as the intro continues, hostility, much of it emanating from 'sheer blind prejudice, but not all of it'.

'[N]ot all of it'; the qualification is jarring, a momentary recall of the remorseless, presumptive logic assessed by Hall that racism, such as it is, is a result of their presence. Philips elaborates, identifying the compelling contemporary question as being 'how increasingly diverse societies like ours can cope with racial and religious differences. There's no shortage of difficult issues to tackle, but I think there's little doubt that it's the extremist adherents of one particular faith, Islam, who have created a major fault line in this country'. While assessments of the significance of the crisis may vary, the issue of some connection between radical interpretations of Islam and political violence, no matter how vexed, is real. Phillips, however, has not finished qualifying the question. Situating his inquiry in the period since the '7/7' London bombings, the dominant media and policy narrative has been that extremist views are held only by a tiny minority of British Muslims. However, on the basis of an in-depth opinion poll that forms the basis for the programme, and which explores whether British Muslims 'reject extremism, and share the values of British society', Phillips concludes the introduction by suggesting that such a picture is naïve, as 'our findings will shock many ... they propose a profound question about how we confront the looming threat to our very way of life'. What threat can this be, and what way of life is this? With the help of a handful of guiding quotes from Hall and Steed in IAHRM, this final section reads WBMRT in terms of patterns in reporting about Muslims, and the contemporary domopolitics of British values.

*Once you mention numbers, it doesn't matter how you wrap it up, there is only one lesson to be drawn, the numbers are growing, there are too many of them.*

WBMRT is based on a survey conducted by the polling company ICM, providing 'as accurate a picture of the views of British Muslims as science can deliver'. It was precisely this science that drew intensive criticism in newspaper reviews of the documentary. The frequently repeated claim that the poll is a 'fully representative sample of Muslim opinion', and thus generalizable from 1,081 interviews, was based on the decision to conduct all the interviews in areas where Muslims formed more than 20% of the local population, a decision that limited the sample to 'some of Britain's most deprived areas' and skews the results by polling in areas that 'are poor and more religiously conservative ... making them indicative of these areas and not of British Muslims nationally' (Versi, 2016). The category of 'British Muslims', of course, is slippery from the start, looping a communal frame around a hugely heterogenous population comprised of a diversity of national and ethnic backgrounds, not to mention socioeconomic conditions and political, cultural and religious differences (Modood, 2005). An opinion poll, as Michael Warner cautions, is an 'elaborate apparatus designed to characterize a public as a social fact independent of any discursive address or circulation' (2002: 54). The methodology performs a double erasure, not only generalizing 'Muslim attitudes' from a very limited and particular sample, but also assuming that 'Britain's Muslim community' pre-exists the perlocutionary effect of the poll as a technology, that it exists and can be made knowable. And, made knowable in a particular relation: what Muslims are really thinking compared with what is described, at different points, as 'the rest of the community at large', 'wider population', 'rest of Britain', 'the majority' and 'orthodox British society'.

Methodologically, there is an important difference in how this polarity was studied, as a phone poll was used to produce a control sample of the 'rest of Britain' rather than the face-to-face interviews conducted with Muslims. In stressing the importance of the interviews, the documentary shows a halal market in south London, and its Muslim owners joking with customers of different backgrounds. This everyday conviviality is not 'our way of life', however, as such scenes of social interaction are not where people reveal their 'innermost thoughts'. The interviews were thus designed to allow the respondents to be truthful and avoid the 'social desirability' answers they may feel they have to give in such situations. This juxtaposition of inner truth and social performance is revealing, not just because of its superficial understanding of everyday sociability, or because of how thoroughly it misunderstands the profound influence of context, interaction, expectation and reflexivity on our social subjectivities, or how it exempts interviews from these social dynamics, or because of how it echoes the 'historically enduring Orientalist contrivance of the inscrutable Muslim "other"' (Sharma and Nijjar, 2018: 73). It is because, in the programme's imaginary, to harbour private thoughts and values, and to not let these influence how you express yourself in the social spaces of complex multiculture, is not a sign of integration or civic virtue, but of the depth of worryingly unknown difference. In the governmentality of anxiety, Muslim sociability becomes a cause for worry as it means that risk resides elsewhere, hidden from view until it can be rendered subject to surveillance.

*This is the programme where the black majority, who are said to be the problem, are invisible, and the whites, who are having the problem, hold the camera.*

This structuring distinction of British Muslims and the rest of Britain is starkly dichotomous, yet it endures in part because of its textual instability. The script makes several references to the diversity of British Muslims, while consistently, in its presentation of poll results, moving from the percentage of sample respondents to generalized results as to 'what British Muslims think', and then immediately addressing the social and political significance of the finding. At the same time, the documentary includes many interviews with well-known and other British Muslims, and hosts discussion groups interacting animatedly with Phillips. The tension between this relentlessly binary framing and the range of inclusion is not as surprising as it may seem. While some research insists on the representational marginalization of British Muslims as a dimension of their portrayal as an 'alien within' (Saeed, 2007), there is also significant research into press and media sourcing which demonstrates not just increased inclusion over time, but also an increased plurality of positions.

Richardson's study of press coverage in the late 1990s noted that less than one-fifth of primary sources in stories about Muslim issues were Muslim, but also 'when Muslim activities are not criticised – or when reported actions are not labelled as *Muslim* actions – Muslim sources are, almost without exception, absent from journalistic texts' (2006: 115, original emphasis). In a study focusing on 2004, Meer and colleagues (2010) detect a comparable limitation of sourcing to issues of 'integration and citizenship'. At the same time, while following 9/11 and 7/7 – 'the explanatory purchase of Muslim cultural dysfunctionality has generated a profitable discursive economy in accounting for what has been described as "Islamic terrorism"' – they argue that the reporting of news issues affecting Muslims is now characterized by a greater plurality of voices articulating divergent interpretations and positions. This is attributed to a public 'assertiveness' among Muslim groups and people prepared to speak 'as Muslims', pushing past both multicultural logics of community representation and challenging the 'fundamentalism-moderate couplet'. In a more recent study of journalist–source interaction in Glasgow, Michael B. Munnik complements this with a focus on routines of media production to 'trace a shift from a "gatekeeper" model of representing the community, resembling the monolithic depiction which the media are allegedly guilty of reproducing, to that of a plurality of sources which reveals and insists on the diversity of Muslim communities and voices' (2017: 272). This shift is analyzed as resulting from changes in journalistic routines, recognizing the need for 'fresh voices', and a greater willingness among 'younger, media-savvy Muslims' to present themselves to journalists (for a broad European comparison, see Göle, 2017: 49–60).

The range of contributions to WBMRT is congruent with these broader shifts in practices of representation and sourcing. At the same time, it replicates particular forms of mediated inclusion shaped by the presumptions of integration politics. The contributors to WBMRT, despite their plurality, are compelled to speak to the assumed truths of the poll, what these results say about a presumptive silent majority of British Muslims, and what they mean for a vision of integration that proceeds from the premise that British Muslims constitute a given population uniquely required to prove their compatibility. As a report by the Institute of Race Relations (IRR) based on research with Muslim groups in the UK, Netherlands, Germany and France noted, increased inclusion is also a product of increased surveillance. The participants in the IRR research spoke of being made subject to an ongoing 'integration debate' shaped by the political and journalistic presumption that Muslims should respond to violent events in other countries *as Muslims*, and to the 'scare scenarios' circulated through political rhetoric and 'intellectual public contributions'. This creates a double-bind whereby responding legitimates the issue as a matter of public concern, while not responding legitimates the idea of a 'community apart' (Fekete, 2008: 22–38). In a comparable study, Bangstad's interviews with Norwegian senior media editors revealed that many imagine themselves involved in a struggle for public reason, conceiving of 'Norwegian Muslims as potential and future threats against freedom of expression, by virtue of their alleged "religiousity" and purported "conformity"' (2013: 367). This practice of the 'nationalisation of liberal values' informed sourcing and commissioning practices that favoured 'Muslim voices' prepared to perform 'auto-critique' that cohered with a vision of 'modernizing Islam', and excluded those who, regardless of the nuance or substance of what they may have to say, refuse to perform this circumscribed role. WBMRT reinscribes its dichotomy through similar circumscriptions; the contributions of 'liberal Muslims' are removed from patterns of discursive and political plurality and antagonism amongst diverse Muslim actors and predominantly used to mark just how 'out of line with the rest of society' the poll results are.

*Formal balance is one thing, and the impression that strong images make is another.*

Poll respondents are not interviewed in the programme, but they are dramatically represented. As the poll methodology is being explained in a voice-over, the visual cuts to a young woman wearing a headscarf and walking through run-down streets, before knocking on a particularly dingy door. The door is answered by a young man who says nothing in response to a polite explanation of the survey, but whose facial expression suggests hostility to the intrusion and invitation to participate (in the interests of dramatic reconstruction, he evidently assents). As different poll questions are introduced the dramatization accompanies them; they sit in a darkened room, the researcher poses the question, and the camera cuts to the increasingly uncomfortable and incalcitrant young man, who only answers verbally once, his emphatic No! almost cutting in on the question 'Does any publication have the right to publish pictures that make fun of the Prophet?'. Surly and uninhibited by a hankering for 'social desirability', his increasing discomfort and hostility visually render the key finding that structures the main thread of the documentary narrative: 'There is a clear cultural gap between a significant section of Britain's Muslims, and the wider population. Equality of women, social tolerance, freedom of expression, are now all taken-for-granted as features of British way of life.'

So taken-for-granted that they seemingly merit no discussion at all, but the power of the discourse of values is precisely its platitudinous valence; no one can deny that some Muslims do not share these values, nor substantively object to this thin delineation of broadly progressive positions. Its routine articulation does not require elaboration, as the British way of life is presumed to be coherent, settled and given, comprised of values that happen to be British but that simply guarantee the common good. The question of integration is not an issue of majority cultural particularity, but simply the cohesion of the good society. Bad values may lead to extremism and violence, but they are also bad in and of themselves, and there 'are some things on which a society will not compromise'. That the British way of life is represented through a gendered dramatic reconstruction is not incidental, as the ascendency of British values marks a society excised of gendered violence, misogyny and homophobia other than the attitudes of those who doctrinally, culturally, set themselves outside of this settled consensus.

This is a pronounced dimension of comparable integrationist discourses of 'national values' in western Europe. Balkenhol and colleagues (2016) have described a Dutch 'nativist triangle' of race, sexuality and religion that positions the tolerant traditions of Dutch culture as requiring 'protection from the nefarious consequences of postcolonial and labour migration'. In assessing the context of the burka ban in France, Éric Fassin (2012) discusses the 'defence of sexual democracy' as an imagined secular emancipation fully achieved and threatened by regressive, communal particularity. Sara Farris, in a wider European perspective, describes this process of political articulation as 'femonationalism', a space of political convergence between the (far) right and some forms of liberal feminism that invoke the threat to national values posed by the uniquely patriarchal relations of Muslim communities. The consequence of this politics is to pit anti-sexism against anti-racism in two ways. It serves to elide the voices and perspectives of movements and struggles, particularly anti-racist feminists, already engaging and confronting reactionary social politics in various social contexts. It also exteriorizes and relativizes; as Boulila and Carri argue in their study of journalistic event framing of the disputed events in Cologne, it was coded in mainstream debate as specifically an assault on 'the "German value" of gender equality, after decades of political indifference towards sexual violence', and of 'hysteria' about racism resulting in a refusal to acknowledge the problems caused over years by liberal immigration policies and illiberal immigrant cultures (2017: 286).

*Myths keep working their way back into the programme. TV reinforces those myths simply by using them as a colourful lead into the next race story, just good strong television.*

The causes of this 'clear cultural gap' are complex, the script concedes, but this complexity admits only cultural and religious explanation over and above any social or political dimensions. The migrant and diasporic 'ancestral backgrounds' of many British Muslims are briefly promoted as a reason, but beyond this speculation what can be verified is that 'our survey suggests that significant amounts of British Muslims don't want to change, and don't want to move to adopt the behaviours of the majority'. In fact, it is not just that they 'have no desire to integrate to orthodox British society', but also what the 'survey shows is the emergence of what you might describe as a nation within the nation, where many hold many different values and behaviours from the majority'. The question remains as to why, in a society characterized by different and often antagonistic values and behaviours, it is the putative values of 'many British Muslims' which pose a problem for the coherence of the nation. In part it is the connection the poll analysis proposes between 'illiberal values' and radicalization. This link is forged on the basis of a question as to 'sympathy towards terrorist acts' – where 'sympathy' remains deliberately unqualified, and could mean anything from 'understand but not justify' to 'openly celebrate' – and where, Phillips notes, 4% of those polled 'expressed some form of sympathy towards terrorist acts ... which equates to just over 100,000'. Yet while this putative sympathy remains wholly unexplored, the problem of values is recalled to the threat of terror yet it is not anchored to it. For, as Phillips makes clear in turning to the question of what must be done, the problem is the 'illiberal attitudes' themselves, and the task is for everybody to 'reassert the liberal values that have served our society so well for so long'. This statement certainly invites skeptical historical analysis, but again, the demand for respect for British values is as much if not more about form than content. It is a historically pronounced demand for national allegiance from a suspect population, but one that takes a particular contextual form.

*It isn't only what the media say, it's what they don't say and take for granted.*

The language of a 'nation within a nation' recalls a conceit of modern antisemitism, that 'the Jew', whether spatially contained in the ghetto or worryingly assimilated to metropolitan society, ultimately owes spiritual, ethnic and political allegiance *elsewhere*. Its logic, however, is shaped by a recent political history that is substantively absent from the documentary, but is hinted at when Phillips argues in conclusion that this 'bad diversity' has been incubated by the problem of excessive tolerance. It is, he argues, the traditional British 'live and let live philosophy' which has failed to set the limits of pluralism and recognize the extremism and self-segregation it has 'unwittingly created fertile ground for'. This is a pivotal moment, as it is here that the documentary narrative actively represses the socio-political history which has produced the discourse it is constructed through.

The emphasis on 'British values' as a guarantee of social cohesion and deradicalization emerges from intensive decades of governmental intervention in Muslim and minority ethnic communities in explicitly culturalist terms. The idea of a dominant 'live and let live philosophy' is only possible by ignoring this history of active, highly publicized and often socially coercive 'community cohesion' initiatives aimed at mitigating socio-economic problems through a focus on the problem of 'parallel societies' and, tellingly, 'self-segregation' (Kundnani, 2007). The assumption that cultural difference is a primary driver of social conflict, and that the answer to 'too much diversity' is a domopolitical focus on not just complying with but also demonstrating a belief in 'British values', was intensified by its cross-pollination with the counter-terrorism Prevent agenda. This presents 'British Muslim communities as marginal to the mainstream of British life and as a threat to the British way of life', and as a dimension of its operations, assesses the willingness of community groups to 'promote British values' (Alam and Husband, 2013: 249). This complex recent history[8] is fully absent from the programme even as it replicates its dominant political logic of 'community' surveillance and inclusion through exclusion, and a nebulous but performative articulation of shared values that 'define what it means to be British'.

\*\*\*\*\*\*

In the twentieth anniversary Runnymede report on Islamophobia, Claire Alexander argues that the 'de-raceing' of Islamophobia in Britain is achieved through 'four interlinking conceptual sleights of hand': a reduction of racism to a narrow, frozen definition; the denial that people who identify as Muslim or are 'Muslim-looking' experience racism as 'Muslims'; the related presentation of religion as volitional and 'therefore separate from the embodied being of its adherents ('culture' rather than 'race'); and, despite this volitional understanding, the deterministic emphasis on '"Islamic culture" or "Muslim culture" as a foundational explanation for the slew of assumed pathologies' (2017: 14). In building on similar points, this chapter has sought to emphasize that understanding how 'Muslims' are racialized must take account of how contemporary geopolitics, integration governance and border anxieties consistently rely on migrant-as-Muslim and Muslim-as-migrant intersections. The social threat of always 'uncontrolled' migration is intensified by the figure of the Muslim as a 'global public enemy, which is seen to threaten the coherence of the social body worldwide' (Fadil, 2016: 2264).

If the figure of the migrant exemplifies and renews the politics of sovereignty in a globalized world, the figure of the Muslim sharpens the question of the nation – the security of the community at home, but also its coherence. This coherence is articulated both as (ethno)national culture and as a community of defining liberal values, and through fusions of these visions that, in practice, are more complementary than contradictory. The postracial articulation of this politics, varying in intensity and texture across European polities, depends on an affective and ideological sense of reasonable aversion; it is not just that they may be incapable of integrating, but also that their provocatively visible difference and behaviour amount to a refusal to do so. They set themselves outside of the nation, and our only mistake has been to accommodate that and turn a blind eye to how bad diversity threatens a community largely defined by good things.

As the discussion of migration news frames and discourse in reporting 'about Muslims' suggests, the journalistic response to this picture is complex. There is certainly significant evidence, as for example Chris Allen laid out in a report on research conducted on UK media between 2001 and 2012, that media coverage is implicated in creating a 'form of order about who we are and who we are not (that) feeds into an ideological understanding of Islamophobia' (2012: 13). However, these tendencies rub up against increasingly reflexive practices concerning source plurality and the diversity of Muslim 'communities', not to mention journalistic practices openly hostile to reductive and stereotyping comment and reporting, and troubled by the role reporting may play in stoking and legitimating hostility. Concomitantly, the discussion of WBMRT demonstrates the fluency with which journalistic frames and media discourse can reproduce 'Muslims' as a population required to answer questions and explain their lives through controversies and talking points latent with securitarian and culturalist anxiety and aversion. For all the legitimating insistence on uncomfortable truths, these approaches not only demand that Muslims respond to any and all anxieties projected onto 'media-generated Muslims' (Rane et al., 2014: 29), they also serve to obscure the complex, convivial social realities they proclaim to reveal.

# Endnotes

1   www.thejournal.ie/readme/should-we-ban-the-burqa-in-ireland-3130204-Dec2016/
2   A 2018 study by *The Guardian*, for example, documented 5,700 changes to British immigration rules since 2010, with the rules governing the visa system running to 275,000 words. See Bozic et al., 2018.
3   The most high-profile example of this was *Al Jazeera*'s editorial decision to substitute the word 'refugee' for 'economic migrant' in all reports and to publicly explain this as an intervention, challenging journalists to think about how their reporting frames may contribute to the reactionary politicization of asylum-seeking in the context of the borders crisis. As Christopher Kyriakides (2017) noted, while this captures how 'migrant' is used to delegitimate the mobility and personhood through a moralized negative relation to the 'refugee', the issue remains that 'Although the migrant–refugee policy couplet seemingly mobilizes oppositional, contrary categories, they are better understood as complementary, interconnected and interdependent. The discursive distancing of "negative economic migrant" from "positive non-economic refugee" in news content does not dislodge their mutually reinforcing power to define "legitimate migrant" status' (2017: 934). Qualitative studies of journalistic practice are, at the time of writing, beginning to be published. Ojala and Pöyhtäri (2018) have studied how journalists in Finland conceived of their professional roles in relation to three 'reference groups' – officials, asylum-seekers and mobilized 'anti-immigration publics'. In relation to each conceptions of their roles varied – between forms of collaboration and 'watchdog' in relation to official sources, and 'advocacy versus objective dissemination' in relation to asylum-seekers. In general, role conception was

characterized by malleability, pointing to the importance of 'social-interactionist approaches to journalistic roles', where 'Interactions with reference groups, perceptions of the broader political context and anticipation of the potential consequences of their reporting are key in informing the journalist about what tasks and objectives one ought to pursue in a particular situation' (2018: 176).

4   And also visual frames: in a study of the 'regimes of public visibility' of refugees in newspaper headline images in Greece, Hungary, Italy, Ireland and the UK during this period, Chouliaraki and Stolic note a similar form of ambivalent intersection in how 'public visualities perpetuate the refugee as either a sufferer or a threat' (2017: 1165). Examining the 'normative dispositions of responsibility towards refugees' in news images, a regime of 'visibility as biological life' massifies refugees in images of huddled bodies on creaking boats, and intersects fluidly with 'visibility as threat', often highly masculinized images of 'masses' of refugees on the move, an implicit threat to the social order. 'Visibility as hospitality', through images of pro-refugee protests and actions, disturbs the assumption that border politics is validated by 'popular passions', but in predominantly centring the actions of European citizens, perpetuates the ways in which refugees are 'acted upon' in a European drama (ibid: 1167–70).

5   The idea of Orientalism is associated with Edward Said's influential *Orientalism* (1978). Here it is used in a more general sense for the stock of exoticizing and essentializing images and forms of 'knowledge about'.

6   The video can be viewed here: www.youtube.com/watch?v=gy57O9ZMENA

7   The documentary can be viewed here: www.youtube.com/watch?v=xQcSvBsU-FM

8   I have written about these histories at length, as well as the narratives I have summarized here through the idea of 'reasonable aversion', in my book with Alana Lentin, *The Crises of Multiculturalism: Racism in a Neoliberal Age* (2011).

**4**

From 'hate' to 'like':
organized and
assembled racism in
a networked media
environment

# Introduction

The 'far-right' occupies an ambivalent space in European and western politics. Far-right parties and movements, some openly redolent of the fascist past, pose a renewed and often violent threat to the wellbeing of those racialized as alien to the nation. While the political nature of this violence is often downplayed in public discourse, the far-right is simultaneously sensationalized as the final locus of racism's persistence, where racism in postracial societies, as Barnor Hesse reminds us, is confined to the 'residuum' of the political extremes, 'a profound moral deviation from the western liberal and democratic ethos and ethnos' (2004: 10). Yet rather than viewing the far-right as a pathology, espousing values at odds with western democracy, it is more productive, Cas Mudde (2010) has argued, to approach far-right parties as a 'pathological normalcy', that is, as actors that radicalize existing attitudes and intensify political positions on such questions as immigration and national security within the contours of nation-state politics.

To this political ambivalence must be added the ideological and organizational heterogeneity barely contained by the category of the 'far-right'. Parties and movements of the far-right are shaped by reactionary positions on immigration and national identity, and cultivate racism as a 'mobilizing passion', but their politics and political differences extend beyond this. The 'newly-reconfigured right' in Europe, according to Liz Fekete (2016), 'takes in a range of authoritarian traditions, from social conservatism to fascism, from radical right-wing populism to those who continue in the tradition of Franco'. The full-throated chauvinism of the Trump presidency provided a platform for a diversity of movements to claim increased public space, from white nationalist and neo-Nazi movements, to 'neo-confederate' and Ku Klux Klan groups, to the highly mediated 'alt-right' network that, as Aaron Winter (2017) observes, has been able to 'mainstream white nationalism and fascism and make them part of popular culture, the media landscape and the national dialogue'.

While this multiplicity must be approached as emerging from divergent national traditions, far-right movements have always been influenced by, and often oriented towards, transnational exchange. This transnationalism is intensified and extended in important ways by connective media, and the platform and media integration that characterizes the 'hybrid media system' has provided important communicative pathways for far-right parties and movements. The digital media environment allows them to generate publicity and orchestrate intensive spectacles; to establish but also simulate scale and presence as movements; circulate misinformation and 'alternative' facts; integrate into news flows and public discourse dynamics, and build media operations that often skillfully navigate the media space provided by the accelerated and extended contemporary news cycle. Those movements committed to presenting themselves as 'not racist' are often adept at exploiting the discursive opportunities opened by the ambivalences of *debatability*. The study of the far-right and media has dominantly focused on the communication strategies of specific actors, particularly the expansive mobilizing and community-building dimensions of the internet. This chapter builds on these approaches, but moves on to argue that a focus on organized far-right actors must be complemented by paying attention to the transnational 'spreadability' of fascistic and racist ideas, memes, images, 'facts' and talking points in the circuits of connective media, translated and transposed far beyond dedicated sites of far-right communication and communion. This, in turn, means examining how corporate logics, technological affordances and public dynamics shape what particular actors can do, and what they can control.

## Situating the 'far right'

In recent years, far-right movements and radical right parties have flourished in the political crisis shaped by the precariousness and alienation of 'austerity' and neoliberal governance, the tensions caused by terrorist attacks and inevitably securitarian state responses, and the complicity of centrist parties in scapegoating people who migrate and seek asylum for this social insecurity and cultural anxiety. This flourishing encompasses electoral successes, a resurgence of far-right protest and street movements, and a related increase in violence and hate crime. Yet snapshot surveys of far-right activity easily lapse into dramatic narratives of the 'rise of the far-right' that obscure the dynamics and contingencies of particular political contexts and the historical, structural reasons for relative advances. The range of actors that normally feature in such snapshots is sufficiently diverse to require some more nuanced relational analysis than the umbrella category of the 'far-right' allows. The range of labels – radical right, extreme right, populist right, neo-nationalist right, neo-fascist right – employed in attempts to characterize such movements hints at both the sheer diversity of the 'far-right', particularly in transatlantic and transnational perspectives, and the range of theoretical frameworks and analytical emphases brought to bear on them. Across this diversity, Saull et al. provide a useful summary of what they term the 'definitional attributes' of the far-right:

The definitional attributes of the far-right relate to enduring political and ideological qualities as well as those social layers produced by capitalist development most drawn to the far-right style of politics. The key appeal is to 'the people' understood as a racially-defined *demos,* premised on a gendered social hierarchy and obscuring the class cleavages associated with capitalist development ... further, in appealing to a people through language and symbols that both reify and fetishize particular qualities and attributes associated with the cultural identity of 'the people', the far-right not only articulates those values and institutions that it sees as key to the identity of a people (e.g. race/ethnicity, culture rooted in fixed narratives and symbols, history, masculinity, etc) but it also seeks to erase and obscure those other qualities – notably the socio-economic – that are, arguably, central to the material and lived reality of concrete individuals within capitalist societies. (2015: 4)

Within these terms, various differences can be drawn out. One obvious distinction is between electoral parties and far-right movements – a distinction frequently captured in political science as a relation between the 'extreme' and 'radical' right: 'While extremism rejects democracy altogether, radicalism accepts democracy but rejects *liberal* democracy – that is, pluralism and minority rights' (Mudde, 2014: 98, original emphasis). The importance of this distinction notwithstanding, there is a significant literature that disputes the extent of the democratic transformation of radical right parties in their journey 'from the margins to the mainstream', and rejects any solid categorical divide between 'radical' and 'extreme'. This is because the far-right constitutes a 'polymorphous galaxy', where parties are frequently riven with factions and divergent and competing ideological influences, and exist in an increasingly transnational mesh of ties and relations to far-right movements, 'alternative' media networks, and cultural scenes (Mammone et al., 2013). Even where strong informal party/movement ties do not exist, the electoral success and public profile of 'populist' or radical right parties create a nurturing environment for far-right street activity (Fekete, 2018).

This taxonomy of 'extreme' and 'radical' underlines how an enduring question in the study of the contemporary far-right is its relationships to European inter-war fascisms, enduring not just because of differences as to what fascism is or might be today, but also because it inevitably raises debates as to what fascism *was*. 'Everyone', the historian Robert O. Paxton argues, 'is sure they know what fascism is. The most self-consciously visual of all political forms, fascism presents itself to us in vivid primary images' (2004: 9). One response to this spectrum of interpretation has been to seek to specify an ideal type or 'fascist minimum' – core ideological commitments and political characteristics – that allows for definitional comparisons. Michael Mann's *Fascists* (2004), a comparative study of fascist movements in interwar Europe, is critical of this approach, and of two influential schools of thought that tend to foreground idealism or materialism in explaining successful fascist mobilization. Broadly idealist accounts that focus on the mobilizing power of visions of national rebirth emphasize the power of ideas, but risk promoting an understanding of relatively autonomous beliefs abstracted from material conditions, and without an adequate account of power centred on the *nation-state*. Tilting too deterministically in the other direction, Mann argues, some Marxist accounts can tend to neglect fascist ideas for a generic account of fascism's counter-revolutionary emergence in a context of capitalist and imperialist crisis (2004: 17–18). Fascism, he states, 'was generated by a world-historical moment when mass citizen warfare surfaced alongside mass transition towards democracy amid a global capitalist crisis' (ibid: 374). An adequate definition of fascism must pay attention to this context, but also to fascism's values and organizational forms, to account for fascism as *'the pursuit of a transcendent and cleansing nation-statism through paramilitarism'* (ibid: 13, original emphasis).[1]

In a celebrated essay, Umberto Eco (1995) warns against post-1945 understandings of fascism that remain fixed on a mimetic resemblance to past movements, or that fail to accommodate how fascism as a political category encompasses contradictory elements and significant local variation. In outlining 14 features of 'ur-fascism', Eco argues that key elements – an integralist appeal to the unity of the people against internal and external threats; to the primacy of community over class conflict; to the necessity of strong leadership as an expression of shared will; to the self-evident weakness or corruption of 'elite-led' government – can be mobilized in different forms, but, crucially, in contexts where middle-class social frustration and humiliation are acutely amplified by economic crisis and a resultant weakening of political representation and institutional legitimacy.

The global economic crisis, from 2008, provided a significant if contextually differentiated boost to radical right electoral parties by deepening a sense of fundamental democratic crisis. Recent literature has explored a multi-faceted crisis of representative democratic systems, brought about through the competitive imperatives of economic globalization and the declining counter-power of organized labour (Crouch, 2004); the shrinking range and register of party political action and conceivable, alternative political projects and policy interventions in 'technocratic' societies, as well as decreased voter turnout and fragmenting party structures (Gilbert, 2013; Mair, 2013); the retraction of the state from the provision of public goods and infrastructure (McNally, 2011); the increased power of corporations and transnational financial agencies over public priorities (Mair, 2013); as well as the elite choreography of 'adversarial' politics in democracies that 'speak without listening' (Dean, 2009). Writing in this context, Alberto Toscano's (2017) 'Notes on Late Fascism' provides an interesting renewal of Eco's non-definitional, thesis-led approach. While emphasizing the Marxist starting point that fascism is fundamentally linked to capitalism and recurrent crisis, he emphasizes the 'intensely superstructural character of our present's fascistic traits', pointing to how analyses of the 'Brexit' vote and the Trump election that emphasize the 'revenge' of the 'white working class' cannot account for a 'fascism that is not reacting to the threat of revolutionary politics, but which retains the racial fantasy of national rebirth and the frantic circulation of a pseudo-class discourse'.

The study of the contemporary far-right, therefore, needs to combine this form of conjunctural analysis with a focus on the organizations and practices of particular political actors. Following the defeat of Nazi and fascist regimes at the end of the Second World War, historians of fascism tend to represent the post-1945 development of the European far-right in terms of party 'waves'. Camus and Lebourg identify four:

> The first, between 1945 and 1955, was characterized by its proximity to the totalitarian ideologies of the 1930s; it is often called 'neo-Fascist'. The second wave, which arose in the mid-1950s, corresponded to the movement of the radicalized middle classes. Their 'third wave', which a number of authors have called 'nationalist populist', arrived between the 1980s and 2001. And since September 11, 2001, the fourth wave has unfurled, a populist expression of the 'clash of civilizations'. (2017: 44)

The third wave is structured by the question of party/movement disso-ciation from or rehabilitation of the fascist past, with for example the electoral success of parties in Alpine and Nordic Europe in the 1990s characterized by a 'move away from overt neo-fascist discourse ... (to a) protection of – seemingly homogenous – national identities or a "mythical" homeland (*Heimat*)' (Wodak, 2013: 25). This period was also characterized by a significant investment by far-right parties in media strategy and discursive production; however the study of discourse must be accompanied by an analysis of *what parties and movements do and not just what they say* (Mammone et al., op.cit.). Taking internal devel-opments, networking in a wider far-right environment, and links with other parties, movements, and 'civil society' into account, the question, according to Mammone et al., is the extent to which far-right parties have undergone a 'process of genuine democratization' or whether 'their use of "new" mobilizing themes, their organizational cultures, their use of new media, tend to point to neo-fascist forms of modernization or adaptation to a multi-ethnic society' (2013: 3).

Thus, what is at stake is not simply whether 'the new radical right' is categorically democratic or anti-democratic, but the extent to and ways in which 'politically it performs a bridging function between an estab-lished conservatism and an explicitly anti-democratic, latently or openly violent right-wing extremism' (Minkenberg, 2011: 13). Without this emphasis on relations and interconnections within the organizational multivalence of the far-right 'family', and the critical emphasis on a 'bridging' relation between 'radical' parties and 'extreme' movements, it would not be possible to understand the political mobilization of par-ties of the 'fascist-autocratic right' (ibid: 14) such as the Greek Golden Dawn or German NDP, but also 'populist' parties such as the True Finns, which does not have roots in the anti-democratic fascist past, but does have ties with ultra-nationalist organizations. This chapter's analysis follows Enzo Traverso's (Traverso and Marin, 2017) characterization of the imbricated parties and movements of the European contemporary far-right as a 'post-fascist constellation', advancing nationalisms pri-marily focused on 'postcolonial immigration and Islam', but with diver-gent 'ideological matrices and origins' (a key divergence, for example, is the *public* importance different groups accord to the far-right's his-torically unifying antisemitism). While transnational interconnection is central in what follows, the starting point for understanding the US far-right must be in noting its differences, as it is largely comprised of anti-Black and anti-Semitic white nationalist groups with traditionally scant familial interaction with political parties – though in the Trump era, this has arguably changed (see Potok, 2017) – and overlapping but also somewhat autonomous anti-Muslim networks.

Radical right parties and the far-right milieu are the subject of an extensive academic literature and incessant media fascination, and thus this orienting sketch is inevitably very limited. Bearing in mind the relations and interconnections discussed above, this chapter considers political parties while primarily focusing on far-right movements online and their social media-enabled strategies within the hybrid media system. The next section develops a framework for this analysis by examining a political movement whose formation and political presence were heavily influenced not only by the conjunctural nature of the anti-Muslim racism discussed in the last chapter, but also by being one of the first movements to be closely associated with social media.

# Scavenging: the fusion of political and media logics

The history of the English Defence League is frequently narrated as beginning in 2009 with mobilizations against protests by the Al-Muhajiroun front group Islam4UK, at a homecoming parade in Luton for a British army regiment recently returned from the occupation of Afghanistan. In effect, these events provided a mobilizing opportunity for established networks of football hooligans and far-right activists, including some who subsequently became part of the EDL's original leadership. In a preface to *Angry White People*, Hsiao-Hung Pai's (2016) ethnographic study of the EDL, Benjamin Zephaniah situates the EDL in a continuum of racist street movements beginning with his experience of the National Front in the late 1970s. A neo-Nazi movement, it violently targeted people of Caribbean and South Asian backgrounds, predominant amongst them the children of post-war, postcolonial migrants then becoming adults, and challenging their social marginalization, institutional discrimination and exclusion from (white) understandings of Englishness and Britishness. For Zephaniah, it is the experience of racialized violence that gives coherence to this continuum, regardless of the shifting morphology of variegated political groups:

> When the racists were busy changing their names and public personas, the majority of their victims weren't concerned with what they were calling themselves … At various times we were being

told by the racists that their enemies were the 'Pakis', or 'Jamaican Yardies', or the 'Islamic fundamentalists', but whatever they say, whatever they call themselves, they have been attacking the same people on the streets, and we (those same people) still have to fight them on the streets. Nothing much has changed. (2016: loc 113)

Zephaniah's collective invocation – 'We, the same people' – recalls a critical aspect of anti-racist mobilization against state racism, workplace discrimination and far-right groups in Britain during this earlier period; the cultivation of a collective and resistant Black political identity. Shaped by an awareness of the shared experience of colonialism, it was a 'way of referencing the common experience of racism and marginalisation in Britain ... among groups and communities with, in fact, very different histories, traditions and ethnic identities' (Hall, 1989: 441). While the subsequent fracturing of political blackness is a complex story (see Ramamurthy, 2013; Virdee, 2014), his sense of continuity is also reflected in how the EDL was confronted by broad-based coalitions of working-class community groups, anti-racist movements and trade unions (see Pai, 2016). Zephaniah's insistence on the experience of racialized violence is important, as it often recedes from view in social science devoted to the political analysis of categories and gradations within the far-right. Yet nothing much can change and still change significantly. In *The Muslims are Coming!* (2014), Arun Kundnani describes a video posted on YouTube in September 2009, announcing the formation of the EDL. In a disused warehouse, 20 men in balaclavas stand to attention while one reads a statement, and another sets fire to a Nazi flag. The burning of the flag dramatically underscores the message of the text; the EDL is not a far-right group, but one opposed to Islamic extremism:

Behind the men hang placards with the slogans 'Black and white, unite and fight' and 'We support Israel's right to exist'. After the spectacle of the flag burning, the camera zooms in on section of the EDL members to demonstrate from the skin colour of their forearms that this gathering includes black men as well as white. In the description that accompanies the video on YouTube, a supporter has written: 'How anyone can call this group far right fascist Nazis is beyond belief. Since when were Nazi groups multi-race? It's not racist to oppose Islamic Extremism!' (2014: loc 4336)

The appropriation of the slogan 'Black and white, unite and fight' is as striking as the burning of the Nazi flag, as their symbolic use lays explicit claim to the broad anti-racist tradition that Zephaniah draws on in writing against the EDL. Not only is the EDL 'not racist', but it is also building a multi-racial coalition to oppose an oppressive ideology, with 'Islamism' replacing Nazism as the contemporary threat. It is not difficult to find evidence to puncture the EDL's progressive claims: from attacks on 'Muslim-looking' people and the fascistic targeting of trade unionists (Fekete, 2012: 11–12), to public calls for the collective punishment of the 'Islamic community' (Kundnani, 2014: loc 4396). Its short history was also punctuated by scandals that undermined its not-racist brand; despite the high-profile presentation of its LGBT, Jewish and Sikh Facebook-page based 'divisions' as alibis to its anti-racism, its Jewish Division leader resigned due to antisemitism and extreme-right links within the movement (Meleagrou-Hitchens and Brun, 2013: 13).

However, it would be a mistake to interpret these historically resonant dimensions of far-right activity as evidence of the mask slipping to reveal a 'traditional' far-right racism underneath. The EDL's overt opposition to 'Islamic Extremism' stands in a complex post-war history of far-right continuity and reinvention. The continuity, as Zephaniah insists, lies in the boots on the street; mobilization against racialized minority communities held to constitute a 'threat to the unity and order of British society' (Solomos, 2013: 127). However, the prevalence of political appropriation in the EDL's self-presentation is equally important. The EDL's origin story is one of opposing Islamic extremism, and it rallied extensively after the murder in Woolwich in 2013 of Lee Rigby, an off-duty British soldier, by two attackers claiming, in explicitly political terms, to be avenging the 'daily killing' of Muslims by the British army (Shabi, 2013). (On Facebook, its supporters, measured in 'likes', increased from 25,000 to over 100,000 within days of the attack; see Ramalingam and Frenett, 2013.)

In the 'counter-jihad' imaginary, such violence is understood as teleological, as religiously derived and inspired by Islam. As 'Islam' is framed as a homogenous and totalizing political-religious system, 'Islamic extremism' can be located as an existing or potential threat in *any* public symbol, social referent, or cultural practice. These visions of a future *Eurabia* are combined – as the EDL's flagging of the putative cultural diversity of its membership indicates – with a wider appropriation of a legitimating repertoire of gender equality, LGBT rights and free speech – values now held, as the last chapter discussed, to characterize an upgraded 'unity and order of British society', and exclusively threatened by an un-integrated enemy within. The EDL thus built on an established politics of a 'cultural differentialist' defence of an embattled indigenous culture, but one fused with the more recent possibilities presented by what Arun Kundnani describes as the 'displacement of the war on terror's political antagonisms onto the plane of Muslim culture' (op.cit.: loc 180).

This kind of fusion, because of its evident opportunism, is frequently treated as a patently artificial construct, bound to collapse under the weight of its contradictions. This is a profound misunderstanding. John Solomos and Les Black describe post-war racism as a 'scavenger ideology, which gains its power from its ability to pick out and utilize ideas and values from other sets of ideas and beliefs in specific socio-historical contexts' (1996: 18–19). The idea of scavenging unsettles the idea that racism can be understood as a set of Russian dolls, with the 'real racism' of neo-Nazi and overtly supremacist movements nestled at the ideological core of an unpacked EDL. Rather, the racism of the EDL must be understood as a responsive field of continuities, affinities and tensions, wherein the defence of liberal values is mixed and mashed up with the racialized rhetoric of an imperiled 'white working class' as well as the 'two minutes to midnight' genre of the 'counter-jihadist' defence of 'Western civilization'. As Ghassan Hage argues, anti-racist scholarship often focuses on the 'interpretative/intellectual sins' of racist actors, whereas 'the performativity of racists statements and more obviously racist practices ... is what is most important to the racists themselves' (2015: loc 3070).

What then, does the EDL's 'scavenging' suggest for a broader analysis of far-right media activity? Firstly, as Kundnani's positioning of the EDL in relation to the 'war on terror' suggests, 'scavenging' requires us to pay attention to the persistent relationality between the 'far right' and the broader political culture. Scavenging can only take place on a field that has been prepared in advance, and the degree to which 'forces and processes from within the political and social mainstream' provide legitimating structures and spaces for the far-right is a recurring question in political and discourse analysis (Kallis, 2015: 8). Secondly, by underlining how the apparent contradictions and inconsistencies in the EDL's confluence of ideological and affective flows are of limited political importance, it allows us to approach the question of *ideological reproduction* within evolving socio-political movements. There is no contradiction, as Hage's argument suggests, between the ideological commitment – and in many instances, also intellectual work – that characterizes far-right activism, and the contingency and opportunism of scavenging. The loud anti-Muslim racism of the 2000s emerged from the anti-immigrant racisms of the postcolonial period, but as the variegated EDL repertoire suggests, it exceeds and transcends it. Scavenging is at work in the extraordinary speed with which it was sutured to the identity of existing movements, informed the formation of others, and as the prevalence of anti-Muslim rhetoric to anti-immigration politics in Poland, Hungary and the Czech Republic during the borders crisis attests, took virile political shape in countries with no significant 'Muslim' presence (Kavan, 2016; Narkowicz and Pędziwiatr, 2016).

As the centrality of Facebook to the EDL suggests, this ideological reproduction takes place across the interactive platforms of connective media and through the 'political rituals of social media' (Highfield, 2016) – surveillance of breaking events, commentary on news stories, sharing of 'alternative' sources, circulating screenshots, meme production and adaptation. Thirdly, therefore, the shaping importance of digital media spaces to this ideological reproduction suggests that to scavenge is also to engage in *bricolage*, that is, to combine and fuse diverse sources and materials together into contingent and mobile forms. If *bricolage* is what Deuze (2006) terms a 'principal component' of digital culture, the scavenging, remixing and circulation of vast reserves of digitized 'racial debris' – and the ways this shapes processes of collective meaning-making, 'knowledge' dissemination and tactical media intervention – is critical to far-right activity online. Thus, ideological reproduction cannot be separated from internet dynamics and the shaping affordances of connective media platforms, particularly in giving protean shape to the transnational formation of racist imaginaries and mobilizations.

The next sections initially zoom backwards in time from the EDL, to sketch out the established affinity of the far-right with 'new' technologies, and then forwards to focus on social media tactics that make the EDL's battery of Facebook pages seem positively quaint.

# Masters of the Web: Researching the far-right online

## Uses and gratifications online

The – putative – anonymity of computer-mediated communications, and the possibilities of online engagement for the cultivation of 'virtual communities', were influentially theorized in the 1990s in relation to expansive possibilities for human subjectivity in cyberspace, from explorative forms of self-making, expression and play to transcending the physical limits and social regulation of the gendered body and the disciplining constraints of race (see Athique, 2013: 71–5). Of course, understandings of 'offline/online' interrelations, particularly in relation to the ubiquity and mobility of social media, have become far more complex. Nevertheless, because of this legacy, it is common, in accounts of the enthusiastic internet adoption of the far-right, to position their activities as the 'dark side' of the participatory dimensions and emancipatory potential of the web, despite the fact that communication technologies, while not neutral, are not 'automatically political' and are 'generally under-determined' (Couldry, 2010: 141). Because the internet is so often thought of in terms of unprecedented change, the ways in which it also provided enhanced forms of continuity are often underplayed; part of its immediate attraction to the far-right was the expansion of established forms of extreme right publishing – including 'underground' magazines, books and newsletters (see Camus and Lebourg, 2017) – and for consolidating and expanding those networks active through shortwave or 'ham' radio broadcasting (Downing and Husband, 2005: 63–5).

Berlet and Mason (2015), for example, credit the German-born, US-based National Socialist George Dietz with launching a 'new era of white supremacist organizing in cyberspace' in 1983 when he launched an electronic bulletin board (EBB), celebrating its innovation as a mode of evading 'Jewish control' of the media system. Dietz was the publisher of the *Liberty Bell* magazine, and the coordinator of Liberty Bell Publications, a mail order service for the distribution of American and European anti-Semitic and supremacist publications. Computer networking promised a more efficient and expansive circulation of racist materials, as well as a way of providing race-hate publications to contexts such as Canada, where many such materials were proscribed. At the same time, a central priority of the move to develop EBB networks was movement security and coordination. Dietz was influential in the subsequent establishment – with the Klansman Louis Beam, who saw online bulletin boards as critical to his praxis of cellular 'leaderless resistance' – of the Aryan Liberty Network, which aimed to support decentralized organizing and action that was less vulnerable to state surveillance and infiltration (Berlet and Mason, 2015: 26–8). Similarly, by the early 1990s German neo-Nazis had established not only the 'Thule network' of bulletin boards but also 'electronic mailboxes' to share encrypted information about activities, at a time when the German state was under pressure to respond to a string of lethal attacks by neo-Nazis on asylum-seekers (Cowell, 1995).

This early drive to network subterranean 'resistance' underlines the stark fact that many groups under discussion are actively and violently involved in prosecuting 'race war': defending 'white/Christian/ European identity and heritage'; combating 'Cultural Marxism, feminism and identity politics'; and resisting 'the immigrant/Jewish/Muslim takeover'. This means targeting those racialized as threats to the race/ nation/civilization, and those who stand against their mobilizations.[2] For that reason, the dominant approaches in research have been aimed at gauging the scale and dynamics of online activity by particular movements, and assessing the role of the internet as a real and potential mobilizing force – for ideological indoctrination, recruitment, propaganda dissemination, and potentially, coordinating forms of violent action.

Until recently, the preponderance of research in this field has concentrated on the far-right in the US (see Caiani and Parenti, 2013: 8-11). 'White nationalist' movements, the historian of the 'alt–right' George Hawley (2017) argues, emerge in a context where 'white supremacy was formally institutionalized throughout most of American history'. White nationalist groups cannot therefore be explained away either as a pathology or an epiphenomenon, making it important, in examining the emergence of white racial movements during such periods as the Reconstruction or Civil Rights era, to 'disaggregate those groups and individuals throughout American history that were white nationalist and white supremacist in a general sense – that is, they accepted the views on race that were common at the time – from those that treated race as their primary concern'. While the periodically insurgent Ku Klux Klan has left a 'deep imprint' on public consciousness, the post-1945 history of movements, Hawley demonstrates, is of periods of temporary mobilization followed by implosion and disarray. While many active groups embrace the 'dark net' as a more secure organizing space (see Bartlett, 2014), an immediate benefit of the internet for such fragmented and generally small movements has been the manifestation of presence, and the exaggeration of scale and reach.

Consequently, several monitoring groups attempt to *quantify and map online activity*. The Southern Poverty Law Centre, for example, has monitored white supremacist and 'hate group' online activity in the US since the early 1990s, and integrates this monitoring into its production of annual 'hate maps' that spatially quantify the ebb and flow of 'active' Ku Klux Klan, Neo-Nazi, White Nationalist, Racist Skinhead, Christian Identity, Neo-Confederate and Anti-Muslim groups (with the latter increasing by 197% between 2015 and 2016; see SPLC, 2016). The difficulty with relating movement configurations to web monitoring, Foxman and Wolf note, is that 'there are dozens of groups … with overlapping memberships, parallel agendas, and sometimes shared leadership rosters. From time to time, these groups fold, merge, splinter or rename themselves' (2013: loc 186).[3]

Informed by an awareness of the sheer utility of online spaces to the far-right, the dominant research orientation in the field has arguably been a *functionalist assessment of the organizational uses of the internet* and networked media. In a review of research between 1995 and 2011 on the overlapping groups of the US 'white power movement' – 'the Ku Klux Klan, Aryan skinheads, neo-Nazis and Christian Identity groups' – Chris W. Hale argues that while the precise numbers of groups and activists operating online is impossible to estimate, the general uses of online spaces are by now well-established. The web effectively decimates costs of entry into media-making and dissemination, and thus *information-sharing* of ideological tracts, banned materials, and operational manuals is facilitated with reduced legal and political risk to the distributors. *Fundraising* is also made simultaneously more extensive and more efficient, allowing organizations to utilize various pay online options while also selling 'merchandise'. While an online presence alone will not sustain a movement with political goals, the plethora of spaces in which active recruiters can deploy net-specific strategies of engagement ensures that *social networking and recruitment* is arguably the key function. The fourth major use, *publicity*, is discussed in the next section. Hale finally identifies *risk mitigation*, predicated on the affinity between decentralized and fragmented 'groupuscles' and the organizational logic of the internet (2012: 347–52; see Caiani and Kroll, 2015, for a more recent comparative study). The attention given to functions and uses has been complemented by forms of *network analysis seeking to analyze online connections between far-right actors*, primarily by taking a sample of influential group websites as nodes and mapping all forms of ties and links between them and other sites. Val Burris et al.'s study of 'white supremacist networks' makes clear that a structure of internet links cannot be taken as 'a meaningful representation of the white supremacist movement as it exists outside of cyberspace', and that while some links may represent formal or durable connections, more often linking practices 'are simply an indication of ideological affinity or common goals and interests' (2000: 16).

## Communities, together alone

The idea of a 'persistent dynamic community' introduces a final major area of research for consideration. Functionalist emphases on the organizational and communicative advantages of websites were complemented from the late 1990s onwards by studies that took the interactive and networking affordances of community forums and message boards as sites of *identity work*. For often dispersed or clustered individuals in small and fragmented movements, the increased variety of participative venues provided not only information, but also forms of belonging and negotiated collective identity. A recurring site of study has been the website Stormfront, established in 1995 on a dedicated web hosting service by the white nationalist Don Black and widely hailed as the first 'hate site' on the internet. Under its banner of 'white pride worldwide', Stormfront's discussion forums became hugely popular both in terms of comments posted and registered users – it claimed 300,000 registered users in 2015, though studies show that the vast majority of its accounts have generally been inactive (Bowman-Grieve, 2009).

Regardless of active use levels, the SPLC (2014) branded the site the 'murder capital of the internet' as its users have been 'disproportionately responsible for some of the most lethal hate crimes and mass killings since the site was put up'. In her study of the website's varied subject threads, the central drive of community maintenance, Lorraine Bowman-Grieve argues, is the cultivation of 'discourses of support' that 'provide the necessary justifications, validations, and encouragement that may in time function as a catalyst for further involvement or action in support of the movement' (ibid: 996). Yet while never losing a focus on the ways in which such sites provide important formative experiences for so-called 'lone wolf' racist murderers, the cultivation of community extends beyond this. In a study of the Dutch Stormfront site, threads dedicated to 'offline activism' were far less popular than threads that facilitated 'affect-laden relationships' between members who saw the chat spaces as sites of compensation for their 'offline stigmatization', and of recognition for extreme right identities they could fashion through discursive interaction (De Koster and Houtman, 2008).

Nationalism is both convinced of its own 'ethnic genius' and suffused with a sense of victimhood, of being threatened or historically wronged (see Appadurai, 2006). White nationalism produces a heightened sense of this victimhood, Sara Ahmed (2014) argues, through a powerful inversion of the terms used to position far-right movements as 'hate groups'. In a reading of material from the Aryan Nation website, she notes how such groups 'declare themselves as organisations of love on their websites'. That is, hatred of the racialized Other is not a root but a reflex; hatred is an inevitable response to the agent that portends imagined decline or subjugation, because in corroding the object of the love – the race-nation – they threaten 'not only to take something away from the subject but to take the place of the subject' (2014: 43). Across the ideological diversity of the far-right, this legitimating structure of feeling is pronounced, and it fuses productively with the scavenging dynamics of the internet; *evidence from somewhere* can always be found, and linked and shared, and dissected for what it says about impending demographic catastrophe, or Jewish control, or Muslim takeover, or multicultural treachery.

Writing in 2002, Les Back notes how for fractious yet interconnected movements 'the rhetoric of whiteness becomes the means to combine profoundly local grammars of racial exclusion within a trans-local and international reach that is made viable through digital technology' (2002: 633). As Back argues, the transnational framework of the internet serves to enhance anti-Semitic 'international conspiracy' theories, but, more broadly, it facilitates a flexible logic of particularization:

> Through the processes of substitution the image of alterity can take on different forms depending on local circumstances, i.e. Turks in Germany or black people in America. However, representations of particular racial minorities within this international framework are commensurable with each other, in that, depending on circumstances, they can be substituted without changing the wider structure of this trans-local racist culture. In this sense the Other is designated as a social contaminant in both the racial body and the virtual body politics. (ibid: 639)

Back's analysis demonstrates that the generation of discourse is integral to the construction of community, but that it also exceeds this, leaking out into the wider informational environment from sites, such as Stormfront, which are well-known and highly accessible, and indexed to search engines. As such, his argument provides a path for moving on from 'Web 1.0' analysis, as it preempts the generativity of social media circulation in a number of ways. Discursive diffusion is accelerated and expanded in the 'sharing and spreading' logics of social media platforms, as is the scavenging that Back identifies as critical to transnational processes of communication (though in practice transnational audiences and interaction may be quite limited; see Froio and Ganesh, 2018). The internet archive of far-right material provides expansive access to very particular forms of 'racial debris', revitalizing historical artefacts, theories and images through their circulation and contingent recombination. His analysis emphasizes the need to examine how 'racist ideas and values are expressed through particular cultural modalities' and aesthetic practices, an insight that is vital to understanding the proliferation of racist discourse in the intensely visual and self-referential forms of contemporary social media culture. Understanding the far-right in a networked media context, therefore, involves paying attention not just to what they say and do, but also to the formative dimensions of digital infrastructure, the informational environment, and online cultures (Klein, 2017: 5–6).

# Social media: presence and proliferation

## Digital space, political assemblage

The category 'social media' is comprised of interconnected 'platforms' that can be approached as particular types: 'social network sites' that foreground networked interpersonal contact and content sharing, and 'user-generated content' sites that facilitate media and cultural activity (Van Dijck, 2013: 8–9). These distinctions, José Van Dijck demonstrates, diminish in practice as sites incorporate each other's dimensions while seeking to build a particular niche within a mutually constitutive 'online structure where each single tweak affects another part of the system' (ibid). Any attempt at definition, Graham Miekle argues, 'must acknowledge the whole complex of technological, economic, industrial, social and cultural developments that are caught up in the term "social media"' (2016: 6). His definition – 'networked database platforms that combine public with personal communication' – emphasizes *networks* as technological systems that are adopted and adapted; *platforms* as corporate services that commodify the information generated by user interactions into valuable *databases*; and *public/personal communication* that vastly extends forms of mediated interaction through the imbrication of the 'public space of the media industries and the personal space of the individual response' (ibid: 6–23).

The 'always-on' dynamics of these convergent platforms and practices provide deeper, accelerated forms of connectivity that enable far-right movements to integrate more fully into the public sphere, paradoxically through the media ecosystem dynamics most often associated with public fragmentation. Yet to analyze how this occurs requires approaches that transcend a focus on the uses of 'new technologies' by particular actors. The term 'connective media', Van Dijck argues, is analytically preferable to 'social media', as the latter term has a corporate valence that emphasizes human connectedness at the expense of the forms of 'automated connectivity' that 'direct human sociality' (op. cit.: 13). In their work on what they call the 'Digital Golden Dawn', Siapera and Veikou (2016) follow a similar logic. They are critical of functionalist approaches that focus on the actions and connections of the far-right online without paying sufficient attention to the dynamics of *assemblage*. That is, online formations are produced not just through networked action but also in a digital-material nexus. Here, the specific affordances of social media platforms, the algorithmic logics shaping content flows, the multimedia possibilities of convergent media forms, the terms of service of private companies and the technological interfaces employed by users generate mutually formative relations.

Golden Dawn, which is dedicated to a Greek 'national rebirth', is an openly fascist party engaged both in street action and electoral politics, and a regular perpetrator of violence against those racialized as migrants, and political opponents (see Halikiopoulou and Vasilopoulou, 2015). Yet while it is an organized political and social force, 'Digital Golden Dawn' can never simply be a representation or approximation of Golden Dawn, online, with the official website as the central node. Rather, it is an assemblage that emerges in a digital media space shaped not only by these techno-social conditions, but also by the responsive interaction of a wide variety of actors. These include the interventions of social media corporations, the counter-strategies of anti-racist actors and the counter-responses to them, the initiatives of 'official' and 'unofficial' supporters in multiple interactive spaces, the national and transnational legal context of communication and varying degrees of expressive latitude or content moderation applied across different platforms, and so forth. This approach, they argue, 'has the important implication of considering the Golden Dawn not as a pre-constituted actor, but as a dynamic assemblage of disparate parts. This shifts the focus towards the generative element of the assembling together' (Siapera and Veikou, 2016: 55).

This approach has applicability beyond the example of Golden Dawn, as it draws attention to the increasingly constitutive nature of connective media to far-right formations, while also emphasizing their contingency. While Twitter and YouTube are discussed subsequently, the rest of this section develops this approach by considering the multi-modality of Facebook pages as 'movement pages'.

## Facebook: between community and public

Facebook pages are the social media form that most directly extends the functions of a website, while diminishing the costs of web hosting. They can potentially act as sites for movement mobilization, and thus group-building, and also instantiate a public presence and image. This extensionality, however, does not automatically result in extended reach or influence. Personal Facebook profiles are sustained through processes of verification and archiving, and thus take shape as a 'repository of self- and other-provided data' (Ellison and boyd, 2013: 154). Movement, campaign issue or event pages are different, as they are 'not permanent but exist in an interactive process of creation, deletion (due to violation of Facebook's terms of use) and recreation' (Farkas et al., 2018: 5). When this contingency is activated by different kinds of movements, integrated into wider communicative action, and leveraged to secure or amplify a political identity, it throws up very different dynamics and results.

For parties and movements with an established social base, Facebook proliferation is not an uncomplicated good, as there is frequently a tension between movement mobilization and managing an acceptable public presence. While far-right websites have managed this tension through moderation and profile registration, Facebook pages are much harder to moderate and restrict communicatively (even the use of closed groups and open pages does not resolve the need for the labour of moderation). The amplification of presence provided by social media is also shaped by the nature of the movement in political context. This is in part a question of the centralizing drive of radical right parties versus the diffuseness of extreme right movements, but not only, and not always. The Front National (FN), for example, was the first French political party to establish a website, and in 2006, to create a virtual office in Second Life and establish a Facebook page (Hobeika and Villeneuve, 2016). Yet much as the party has been characterized by a tension between the significant effort required to position it as a potential 'party of government' while also 'throwing red meat' to its traditional post-fascist constituency, its online assemblage is fraught. As Gimenez and Voirol demonstrate, the mesh of FN-supporting

Facebook groups that serve to 'liberate racist speech' eventually became a public relations problem for the 'smooth image of a political party in search of institutional respectability' (2017: 17). For Golden Dawn, however, this proliferation and turnover of Facebook pages became essential to their digital presence after Greek anti-racist groups began mass reporting Golden Dawn activist profile and party pages, and Facebook removed them. Members and supporters responded by creating more closed groups and broader 'patriotic' pages that are not overtly connected to the party, and advertising new Facebook pages directly through the party website (Siapera and Veikou, 2016: 14–15).

While Facebook provides an important space for new political formations, the dynamics and tensions experienced by established parties do not automatically dissolve as a consequence of their substantively taking shape through digital networking. The capacity of 'spreadable' Facebook page activity to allow nascent movements to suggest a scale of activity and public presence far beyond their material resources or active memberships has encouraged a trend towards 'memetic' or modular movements. The EDL and Dresden-originating Pegida (Patriotic Europeans Against the Islamisation of the Occident) acted as attractive recent templates, prompting moves to establish national chapters in other countries with Facebook pages as the central focus of publicity and recruitment. The political response to the 'refugee crisis' intensified this trend, as 'the events of 2015 saw the emergence of a variety of new organisations engaged in extra-parliamentary activities and hybrid forms of mobilisation, paving the way for the development of a broad, European anti-immigration movement' (Castelli Gattinara, 2018: 272).

The Soldiers of Odin (SoO), for example, were established in Finland by a known neo-Nazi, and became a key presence in what Oula Silvennoinen (2016) termed a 'fragmented field of would-be capitalizers' seeking publicity during the 2015 border crisis. They launched street patrols in several cities, presented as 'protecting' a vulnerable society from refugee crime and, in particular, 'rampant' sexual violence. While this tactic of 'stepping in' to protect the nation when the state has 'failed' to has a clear fascist genealogy, the group attempted to marry this putative civic responsibility with the not racist/anti-racist discourses central to contemporary Islamophobia, providing a potential template for transnational translation. During 2016, even as the level of street mobilizations in Finnish cities faded, SoO claimed 'national chapters' in 20 countries. While copycat street patrols were held in several countries, in most instances this organizational claim depended on the existence of Facebook pages, counting 'likes' as membership, and positioning the pages as sites for tapping the cross-current of anti-Muslim and anti-refugee online comment and re-posts from established sources. (At the same time, given the importance of style and symbolism in far-right youth culture [see Miller-Idriss, 2018], the distinctive brand of hoodies and merchandise, and the ease with which it could be adapted to national colours, undoubtedly also drove interest and activity.)

A Facebook group network analysis of activity within the Canadian movement depicted a diverse set of regionally dispersed, Facebook-page-based groups, with some heavily overlapping with existing white supremacist groups – a pattern in common with the US – and others actively distancing themselves from these fellow chapters. The extent to which the Canadian chapters should orient towards the 'global move-ment', relate to the open racism of the Finnish movement, and manage overtly racist material on public Facebook pages caused further tensions (Veilleux-Lepage & Archambault, 2017). In his study of the Swedish branches of SoO on Facebook, Mattias Ekman examines how this ten-sion came to inform the 'self-mediation practices' of the group. Given Sweden's proximity to Finland, Swedish groups formed rapidly in 2016, conducting patrols in various cities while flagging 20 local chapters on Facebook. That most 'offline' political activity had ceased by later that year emphasizes, Ekman argues, 'the volatility and temporality of socio-political activities centred on networked communication – in contrast to more traditional forms of grassroots mobilization and organization building' (2018: 6). Nevertheless, their open Facebook pages were mod-erated to tone down 'open' racism, and posts mainly provided accounts of activities and statements rejecting all allegations of being a racist organization (a strategy undermined when *Aftonbladet* journalists infil-trated closed leadership groups and published extracts from blatantly racist conversations [ibid]).

Therefore while this memetic movement-building through Facebook can heighten the sense of trans-local togetherness examined by Les Back, and bolster the affective masculinity that Ekman regards as cen-tral to SoO group-building, there remains a recurring tension between identity work and managing a public presence. Online participation involves an invitation to construct a collective (white, 'European') iden-tity, and promises a form of uninhibited discursive enjoyment, partic-ularly as online discourse is structured as a space free from 'political correctness' and 'self-censorship'. Movement-building also requires a political determination to be perceived as 'not-racist' – a calibration, as the SoO case shows, that not only requires ongoing labour but that also varies in its emphases contextually. In a hybrid media system, the Facebook page is also inevitably a media source and representative artefact, and demands the maintenance of a reflexive sense of a wider public horizon. However, this tension is dissolved when we consider how far-right discourse circulates in social media, beyond movements and specific sites.

## Facebook: right-wing proliferation and racist assemblage

Facebook is the central 'platform' of the 'sharing industry', where, as Miekle summarizes:

> Users of social media now share ideas, information, meanings – and noise – through networks of mediated sociality. Communication through social media is an unfinished process of circulation and connection, of relationships and associations. Each new link, like and share opens up different kinds of connectivity and different possibilities for meaning, and each makes possible different trajectories for further circulation to still other people. (2016: 50–1)

'Sharing' is social, and also commodified by the social media platform, and enabled and shaped by its technological affordances (i.e. the option to like/share/comment) and algorithmic structures. Under these conditions, it is imperative to pay attention to the ways in which far-right 'ideas, information, meanings and noise' spread through corporate social media networks in ways that exceed the presence and agency of movements. While 'fake news' and disinformation, are now somewhat spectacularly associated with the speed and multiplicity of digital networks, pre-social media, far-right actors were quick to recognize how the web's search architecture would drive traffic to various forms of misleading and disguised sites. Jessie Daniels' sustained work on 'cloaked websites' – sites that 'conceal authorship or feign legitimacy in order to deliberately disguise a hidden political agenda' (2009: 660) – revealed a versatile repertoire of strategies. The Holocaust denial site *The Institute for Historical Review* and the racialized chattel slavery denial site *The American Civil Rights Review* adopt an institutional sensibility, pseudo-academic gravitas, and the language of civil rights discourse to encourage browsing readers to approach them as reputable sources.

Perhaps the most notorious 'cloaked site', 'martinlutherking.org' featured prominently in Google rankings, Daniels argues, because the idea of registering the domain name 'relatively early in the evolution of the web was a shrewd and opportune move for advocates of white supremacy, in part because it claimed the web presence of a civil rights leader, and because top-level domains ending in ".org" are widely perceived as credible' (ibid: 672). Cloaking, therefore, is not solely a discursive or design strategy, but a result of how search engines have come to shape the distribution of knowledge, allowing systemic processes of disinformation and cloaking that Klein (2012) describes as 'information laundering'. Further, 'cloaking', Daniels argues, emerges in a context where significant resources were invested in a broader 'reinforcing system of knowledge' on the US political right, comprised of think-tanks, pundits, writers and 'astro-turfed' institutes whose purpose is a 'version of postmodern, radical deconstructionism' (op.cit.: 675). At first glance, this conclusion may seem counter-intuitive, and markedly at odds with far-right anxieties as to 'Cultural Marxism' and 'gender ideology'.

In *Infoglut* (2013), Mark Andrejevic sketches out a sustained account of this intersection of informational conditions and political malleability. A consequence of abundant mediated information is not just the problem of volume and multiplicity for, say, trying to research an issue. It is also the haunting of an unsettling reflexivity, the knowledge that it is never possible to be fully informed, and a 'recognition of the constructed and partial nature of representation' (2013: 3). This media terrain disrupts an established assumption about the relation of information and power, which is that, in few-to-many media systems, information gate-keeping ensured (some form of) ideological control, implying that any challenge to 'dominant interests relied at least in part on challenges to the dominant understandings of the world upon which they depended' (ibid: 5). However, conditions of information surfeit multiply evidence, data and versions of reality to an extent that renders preferred historical or social accounts relative to each other. This, Andrejevic argues, is producing new forms of control, as 'such forms of narrative multiplication have become a hallmark of the media strategy of what might be described as the postmodern right for handling political debates that they appear to be losing, such as that over climate change' (ibid: 6). The debatability of racism is similarly intensified – why should this account of what constitutes racism be believed over these other available versions?

Farkas and colleagues' (2018) research on fake Islamist propaganda on Facebook extends Daniels' research on cloaking for a context where sock-puppeted pages can flourish through a combination of the site's page architecture, which allows page administrators to remain anonymous, and the laundering dynamics of Facebook-user engagement and sharing. Their study examines Facebook pages set up as fake 'Islamist' profiles, gleeful stereotypes whose remarkably candid posts seemed to confirm every racialized fear as to the Muslim/migrant drain on the welfare state, their take-over of the nation, and derision for the multicultural naivety of their Danish 'hosts'. Unlike the often significant labour involved in cloaked sites, these Facebook pages were deliberately ephemeral, aimed at provoking an intensive cycle of reaction, as outraged Danish user responses prompted their networked sharing, political reaction, and eventually media and activist investigation:

> First, the Facebook pages were created in a manner that disguised them as representing radical Islamist identities through symbolism, text and imagery. Second, the pages were disseminated through hateful and aggressive posts antagonistically directed at the Danish people and state. Third, users reacted to the posts with comments and shares without questioning the pages' authorship. Fourth, the Facebook group Stop Fake Hate Profiles on Facebook acted by contesting the pages' authorship and reporting them to Facebook. Fifth, Facebook deleted the pages due to violations of their content policies. (Farkas et al., 2018: 7)

As Farkas et al. point out, there is no way of telling whether the authors of these fake profiles have connections to far-right movements or not. They flare and vanish, pointing to how ephemeral digital spaces act as sites for the dissemination and recontextualization of far-right talking points, imaginaries and narratives, beyond movements. The start of Chapter 1 referenced an 'I'm not racist, but' moment when Laura Huhtasaari, an MP for the right-wing nationalist True Finn Party, was revealed as a member of a closed Facebook group 'The racist background of rapists that hide in bushes'. While the group undoubtedly had members from the rash of anti-immigration groups that mobilized around the 'refugee crisis', its primary function, arguably, was as a kind of discourse laboratory, a space where racial debris can be scavenged and assembled into relations and affinities, presenting accumulated evidence, from here, there and everywhere, of the problem of racialized populations. Racism must be studied relationally, Goldberg argues, because 'racial ideas, meanings and exclusionary and repressive practices in one place are influenced, shaped by and fuel those elsewhere' (2015: 254). In the discourse laboratory, this relationality is digitally curated and accelerated, and it is not possible to sift through this eclecticism, through the accumulation of posts, memes and links, of *digital debris*, to locate a foundational racism that renders this bricolage coherent. In the logics of assemblage, the bricolage is the racism; the colonial primitive, the migrant as social enemy, the Muslim as invader, virile blackness as the threatened castration of whiteness – these stereotypes and projections sustain each other relationally and dynamically. It is *fluency*, once more, this time flowing through the discursive diffusion and scavenger-like accretion of the 'sharing and spreading' logics of social media. And, as the concluding discussion examines, the form of fluency found on an obscure Finnish Facebook page can be ventriloquized at a far headier scale of political activity.

# Ikea racism: assembling Sweden

Speaking in Florida on the 18th of February 2017, Donald Trump pledged to keep the US safe from refugees, and pointed to catastrophes unfolding elsewhere as his justification: 'We've got to keep our country safe. You look at what's happening in Germany, you look at what's happening last night in Sweden. Sweden, who would believe this? They took in large numbers, they're having problems like they never thought possible.' The claim elicited journalistic puzzlement and a scornful response from some Swedish politicians to the clear intimation that a terrorist attack had taken place. The next day, Trump tweeted a clarification; he had been referring to a Fox News programme 'concerning immigrants and Sweden' that had aired the night before his speech. This was a reference to an interview, on Fox's *Tucker Carlson Tonight*, with Ami Horowitz, introduced as a 'documentary film-maker' who had been investigating 'how Sweden became the rape capital of Europe'.

A few weeks later, Yochai Benkler et al. (2017) published the results of a study of 1.25 million stories posted online between April 1st 2015 and the Presidential Election of November 8th 2016. Dismissing excitable speculation as to 'external disruption explaining (Trump's) unanticipated victory', their study proposed a mapping of a hyper-partisan, 'distinct and insulated media system' that impacted on the wider media terrain in particular ways. Their map of Facebook and Twitter news-sharing patterns positioned Breitbart News at the centre of an internally coherent right-wing media system and 'knowledge community', a clustering of relatively new media titles and platforms comprised of recognizable channels such as Fox News, and a plethora of online-only actors. A key dimension of what they termed this 'altered media ecology' is patterns of 'asymmetric attention' – while 'progressive' new outlets did not feature in the hyper-partisan media sphere, Breitbart and related outlets were widely discussed, linked and responded to in liberal media discourse and journalism. While this coverage was critical, they argue, it granted significant agenda-setting power as

> ... it nonetheless revolved around the agenda that the right-wing media sphere set: immigration. Right-wing media, in turn, framed immigration in terms of terror, crime, and Islam ... Immigration is the key topic around which Trump and Breitbart found common cause; just as Trump made this a focal point for his campaign, Breitbart devoted disproportionate attention to the topic. (ibid)

It was these synergies, they note, that have 'created an environment in which the President can tell supporters about events in Sweden that never happened'. Trump's Sweden moment requires two lines of explanation. The first is the particularization of the 'hybrid media system' that Benkler et al. describe: a network of ideological exchange that operates coherently across scales and forms of media activity, despite internal political diversity and levels of economic power. The second is the racialized imaginative geography of 'Sweden', a mythology that circulates across genres and scales of right-wing media production. This concluding section works back from Trump's utterance and traces the discursive assembly of 'Sweden' through this altered media ecology. This provides a partial but instructive picture of the density, diversity and convergence of digital 'far-right' media activity in a transnational, cross-media platform milieu, one marked by political differences and varying scales of media activity, and also by collaborations and elective affinities. Sifting through the connotations actively attached to 'Sweden' illustrates the scale of the 'creative labour' being invested in producing 'forbidden knowledge' about racialized populations. This 'knowledge' trickles down and trickles up, and Trump's original point of reference is a useful starting point for mapping these conduits and connections.

Fox's *Tucker Carlson Tonight* programme is one of the most popular programmes on Fox News, the most-watched cable news channel in the US. As Carlos Maza of *Vox*'s news analysis programme *Strikethrough* notes, from 2016 onwards Carlson earned public praise from former Ku Klux Klan 'grand wizard' David Duke, and the so-called Alt-Right's Richard Spencer, for his 'open-mindedness'. For Maza, this affinity was the result of Carlson's willingness to discuss the problem of immigration *tout court*, rather than the more euphemistic target of 'illegal immigration', and to connect the 'problem' not just to crime, but also to a soft-focus *ethnopluralism* that emphasizes the inevitability of conflict between 'European culture' and 'the inferior cultures those immigrants are bringing' (Maza, 2017). This provides a mediated opportunity structure for the inclusion of more radical voices, a process of what could be termed 'cite right' validation that is pronounced within relations of 'moderation' and extremism in the ecosystem. Ami Horowitz, the director of the predictably titled 'Stockholm Syndrome' documentary, fits this profile, telling Carlson that while Sweden sees itself as a 'humanitarian superpower', he was prompted to make his documentary because, after Sweden's 'open door' approach to the 2015 refugee crisis, there was an 'absolute surge in gun violence and rape in Sweden'. 'Aah', Tucker sighs, 'The masochism of the west knows no bounds'.

A fact-check on the documentary by the *TheLocal.se* documented a string of unfounded and erroneous claims in the documentary, and two police officers interviewed in the documentary told *Dagens Nyheter* that their answers, which seemed to suggest a link between an increase in crime and refugee numbers, had been edited unscrupulously (Oltermann and Helmore, 2017). Defending himself from criticism, Horowitz was interviewed in December 2016 on *Breitbart News Daily* by Raheem Kassam, formerly of the openly anti-Muslim right-wing thinktank The Henry Jackson Society, then senior advisor to Nigel Farage of UKIP, before becoming editor of Breitbart UK. This shifts the focus swiftly to the 'central node' of Benckler's 'altered media ecology'. A 2017 report on Breitbart by the monitoring organization Hope Not Hate stated that 'Breitbart is not a news website or a media outlet in any ordinary sense and its staff are not mainstream journalists. Breitbart is a political project, with a specific political agenda, staffed by willing propagandists' (2017: 3). Founded in 2007 by Andrew Breitbart, Breitbart News Network began as a 'pro-freedom and pro-Israel' news site that attracted mainstream attention through a series of dubious undercover political 'stings'.

While David Neiwert argues in *Alt-America: The Rise of the Radical Right in the Age of Trump* that 'there was often an ugly racial undertone to the stories Breitbart promoted' after the death of Breitbart and the appointment of Steve Bannon as executive chairman, 'Breitbart began specializing in coverage that supported white-nationalist narratives about black criminality and the supposed "threat" of immigration' (2017: loc 3850–70). News about Sweden became oddly central to this narrative push. In 2017, the year of Trump's Nordic epiphany, Breitbart published 34 stories with headlines proclaiming the problem of immigrants in Sweden. In the *Breitbart Daily News* podcast of January 19th 2018, Kassam boasted that 'we have a bureau of a half a dozen people over in the United Kingdom and 16 of our biggest stories this year have been about Sweden'. After criticism of Trump's reference, Breitbart published 'Ten incidents in ten days that prove that Trump was right about Sweden' by Chris Tomlinson, a Breitbart London 'journalist' and 'member of the "Archeo-Futurism" Facebook group, an "alt-right" online hub dedicated to the radical creed of New Right white supremacist Guillaume Faye' (Lowles, 2017: 22).

Breitbart was not alone in seizing on Trump's reference. 'Tommy Robinson', former leader of the EDL, posted a similar defence in a video on February 22nd 2017 entitled 'Sweden self-destructs for diversity', featuring a critical reading of 'the fake news hysteria of the left-wing media'. Robinson, since 2017, has styled himself as a journalist, hosting the 'Tommy Robinson Show' on Rebel Edge. Rebel Edge is a spin-off of the Canadian far-right platform Rebel Media, established by a 'conservative' writer and activist, Ezra Levant, in 2015, and promising, inevitably, 'the other side of the story'. Spinning out from Fox to Breitbart to Rebel Media focuses attention on other scales of media activity within the 'altered media ecology'; the success of cross-media ventures that have thoroughly integrated corporate social media platforms into their dissemination infrastructure and audience/user mobilization. Rebel's media content has free and 'premium' levels that can be accessed through its website and YouTube channel (which has 907,000 subscribers). Its funding is therefore sourced not only through YouTube advertising revenue, subscriptions, and soliciting donations from wealthy benefactors, but also through an email list drive and the setting up of often astroturfed single-issue websites – such as thetruthaboutrefugees.com – that promote petitions and seek donations for specific 'solidarity' actions (Ling, 2017).

Jared Holt, a researcher with the monitoring group Right Wing Watch, has described Rebel Media as an 'alt right safe space' (2017), in that it provides legitimating opportunities through features and interviews to figures further to the right, while also having nurtured journalists who have then departed to become far-right 'independent journalists' and YouTube celebrities. Possibly the best known of these is Lauren Southern, who, in her Rebel Media show 'Stand Off' on June 24th 2016, used as a studio backshot a screen grab from the 'fake news' aggregation site *Speisa*, touting the story 'Sweden to become a Third World Country by 2030, according to the UN'. This, she argued, proved that 'Immigrants to Europe differ from native Europeans in ways that are much more significant than just skin colour. And no matter how much the left deny it, this change is creating deep issues for European culture'. Southern's ethnopluralist fatalism echoes Tucker Carlson's, but her comments were aimed at, again, opening space further rightwards.

Her guest was Martin Sellner, spokesperson for Generation Identity, the attempted pan-European movement based on Génération Identitaire (GI, the youth wing of the French extreme right group Bloc Identitaire). For Southern, 'new' Identitarian movements have not only 'emerged with the aim of reinvigorating European culture', but also as nationalist ventures that can avoid 'succumbing to the racism and fascism of past European nationalist groups'. While the political-theoretical genealogy of these French movements in relation to fascism is complex, GI's political practice encompasses direct, racist action against mosques and attacks against migrants, most notably at the Calais refugee camps (Fekete, 2018). Further, the transnational attractiveness of identitarianism owes much to the malleable ways in which its (racial) separatism intersects with 'Alt-Right' white nationalism as an 'identity politics for white people', committed to the idea of an integralist 'ethnostate' and obsessively focused on 'mass immigration' as a demographic and cultural threat (Hawley, 2017: 59–60). Identitarian groups have proven quite adept at fashioning media-oriented forms of activism, and it is here also that the prevalence of activist-journalists and podcast/vlog pundits becomes most pronounced. Figures like Southern, who left Rebel Media for her own YouTube channel of 519,000 subscribers, are not formally aligned with any one group, but create social media space for, and in turn gain audiences from, wider movements and ideological milieux.

Casting a wider net in the social media-enabled ecology draws out further dimensions of Sweden's fantastical utility. As Trump's rhetoric makes clear, what stabilizes 'Sweden' as a site of projection is that it can be inserted into a particular narrative of crisis, causality and counsel – 'look at the multicultural madness happening there, it's not too late to stop it happening here'. This logic forms the basis for the Twitter account 'Peter Sweden', which is run by a British national resident in the UK, but which, in pretending to be reporting from diversity's ground zero, performs the role of politically reluctant witness to socio-cultural dissolution. This reality must be witnessed as it is being denied by the very elites that have provoked the crisis through their liberal naïveté and disastrous immigration and multicultural policies. It is this performance of dissident truth-teller that accounts for the persona being regularly tweet-quoted on popular conspiratorial sites such as Info Wars and Gateway Pundit (Mast, 2018).

This gesture of global surveillance has varying intensities. It provides a form of not-racist legitimation, a way of talking about 'problem populations' based on the evidence of social disintegration and cultural loss *just over there*. It can also be reproduced, however, by conspiratorial narratives animated by overtly racist fantasies. Red Ice Radio, which simulcasts from its website and YouTube, is a fixture in Sweden's historically highly developed, professionalized and differentiated far-right media scene (Arnstad, 2015; Ekman, 2014, 2018). Broadcasting in English, it also situates itself as a dissident voice seeking transnational solidarity. Its June 26th 2017 edition, 'Nordic News: the genocide of the Swedes', salutes its audience from 'Sweden, the canary in the multicultural coalmine'. Here, the failed experiment of 'importing a low IQ third world population' is not a product of 'pathological altruism' but rather a 'globalist' (UN/American/Jewish/Soros) plot: an advanced instance of the resurgent idea of 'white genocide', or, in the conspiracy-amenable variant associated with the French 'identitarian' writer Renaud Camus, the 'great replacement' of indigenous European populations. It is by linking these intensities of expression that the 'cite right' dynamic of the ecosystem produces ideological affinities, but this cascade is also bolstered by a media sectoral logic:

The punditry faction of YouTube, much like cable news, thrives on collaboration and guest appearances on other pundits' channels. These right-wing YouTube commentators believe that by bolstering one another they can break through 'fake news' mainstream media narratives and spread their own flavour of political analysis. The most extreme of these commentators will identify YouTube pundits slightly closer to the center-Right than them, and appear on their programs to share their viewpoints. They then use this access to a larger platform to recruit more people to their own pages, where they espouse extremist views with even less restraint. (Holt, 2017)

Given the translatability of these imaginaries, it should come as no surprise that fantasy Sweden is also assembled within Nordic and Swedish far-right networks, and that while it was amplified by the focus on Sweden's response to the 'refugee crisis', it long precedes it. Two of Anders Breivik's most important citations focused relentlessly on the dystopia-next-door as Norway's endarkened future; the blogger 'Fjordman', and Bruce Bawer, who wrote *The New Quislings: How the International Left Used the Oslo Massacre to Silence Debate About Islam* (2011), and wrote in a similar vein for *Frontpage Magazine* in 2013 as to 'Sweden's March into Oblivion: The Fruits of Denial'. These interventions find an audience of users that also co-produce the imaginary through comment, blogging and memes. In a study of the remediation and circulation of an image of a Swedish woman taken after she has suffered a violent attack, Karina Horsti demonstrates how the image was shared and reproduced through Nordic far-right and counter-jihad blog networks within an 'Islamophobic rape frame', and despite the wishes of the woman in the photo. Her analysis emphasizes the importance of visuality to its circulation, as the photograph circulated first as 'evidence' and then as a meme template that allowed different narrative additions, such as '"Muslim Rape, Feminist Silence" with the sub-text "Victim of Muslim gang rape in Sweden"' (2016: 10).

That 'Sweden' has stuck to the decontextualized image as it circulates, Horsti argues, is significant, as it opens out a critical valence of the fantasy projection – Sweden is imagined as 'feminist and white' (ibid). That is, it is not just that Sweden is constructed as a gendered racial imaginary, where the nation, like the female body, is vulnerable to violation and in need of the protection of 'white border guard masculinities' (Keskinen, 2017). 'Sweden' is not just feminized, but also *feminist*: sexually liberated, insufficiently dependent on white masculinity, in thrall to multiculturalism and the exotic Other, and thus complicit in its own violation. The generativity of 'Sweden' cannot be understood without centring the gendered politics of white nationalism; and the specific antagonism towards feminism, blamed as a prime driver of social re-engineering, accounts for the disturbing co-dependency of protectionist and punitive desires – 'our women must be protected, but feminists are asking for it'.

In assessing Trump's utterance, therefore, it is significant that he reproduced a racializing trope[4] that has been cultivated and circulated within an expansive, transnational, cross-media right-wing milieu. It is a scene that not only intersects with and amplifies a variety of movements, but that also transcends them, to incorporate emerging forms of punditry and political celebrity, and entrepreneurial media ventures and collaborations. This media ecology must now be seen as an enhanced political structure for the transnational far-right, one that is connected to and motivated by movements, but which, through the scavenging and laundering of digital debris in and across platforms and discursive spaces, must be approached as integrated to and influential within a 'hybrid media system' in ways that both transcend and evade movement logics and practices.

# Endnotes

1   For Mann, understanding fascism as an 'essential if predominantly undesirable part of modernity', characterized by a range of contextually variant doctrines and practices, particularly with regard to Nazism, but also between and within Italian, Spanish, Austrian, Hungarian and Romanian fascisms, requires paying attention to (a) *Nationalism*: a commitment to an 'organic' or racially understood nation whose unity is threatened by outside influences and ethnic/ideological/degenerate 'enemies within', (b) *Statism:* both as the idealization of state power and as an 'authoritarian corporate' political form capable of resolving economic, social and 'moral' crises, (c) *Transcendence*: of class conflict, liberal weakness and capitalist contradiction through the unity of the nation, (d) *Cleansing*: of political opponents and racial 'aliens' that threaten the organic unity of the nation-state, (e) *Paramilitarism*: where violence is celebrated as an expression of the popular will and as a mode of delegitimating the legal and democratic order (2004: 13–17).

2   As I began writing this chapter, Jimi Karttunen died after being assaulted by a member of the neo-Nazi Finnish Resistance Movement in broad daylight in downtown Helsinki; as I revised it, Heather Heyer was killed when a white supremacist smashed his car into an anti-racist protest in Charlottesville.

3   While websites were taken as a relatively stable unit of analysis for a period, the methodology of The Hate Directory project, for example, had expanded by 2008 to document not only 'hate sites' but also file directories, blogs, listservs, usenets, online radio and podcasts, chat programs (such as IRCs, internet relay chat) and dedicated web hosting services (Margolis and Moreno-Riaño, 2016: 78). When social media pages are added, it is possible for a body such as the Simon Wiesenthal Centre to offer, in their 2014 *Digital Terrorism and Hate* report, a figure of 'over 30,000 websites, online forums and social networks'. This diffusion of ephemeral sites, pages, groups and identities on social media platforms further complicates the relation between mediated engagement, mobilized action and political outcome, and particularly so where what is often misleadingly termed 'lone wolf' violence is characterized by immersive but erzatz online socialization (see, for example, investigations into Dylann Roof's digital interactions; Siegel, 2015).

4   It is important to note how this imaginative focus is, inter alia, also a product of Swedish politics. The subtitle of Allan Pred's brilliant study *Even in Sweden* (2000) is *Racisms, Racialized Spaces, and the Popular Geographical Imagination*, precisely because of the political significance of 'the telling and re-telling of symbol-laden stories about particular concrete-laden spaces'. Husby, Rinkeby, Rosengård and other urban spaces have been framed over decades as the fearful ghettoes of the neoliberal imagination, formed not through inequalities but through the self-segregation favoured

by unruly multicultural subjects. For example, when young people in the Stockholm suburb of Husby rioted in 2013 in response to police violence, the then Prime Minister Fredrik Reinfeldt called for 'respect for Swedish law and Swedish police'. The identification of the 'no-go zone' or internal borderland recurs across contexts and precedes the transnationalization of this discourse discussed above: the Parisian *quartiers populaires* racialized as 'lost territories of the republic'; or Bradford traduced as a failed city of 'parallel communities'; or East Helsinki racialized as a 'future Malmö'; or parts of Amsterdam and Rotterdam de-territorialized as 'dish cities' or 'sharia zones'. In keeping with the integrationist and domopolitical anxieties discussed in the previous chapter, these sites are always invoked as evidence of the 'problems of immigration' regardless of their sociological realities.

# 5

## Hate speech, free speech and media events

# The recursive and the real

Public debate concerning racism almost invariably features some form of controversy over the nature and legitimacy of public expression. Ideas such as offence, harm and injury have been emphasized in public culture in an attempt to capture the unsettling, humiliating and often dehumanizing impacts of being targeted by racist and discriminatory speech. The urgency and complexity of these notions have been ratcheted up by the extensive opportunities provided by connective media for organized and ambient racist harassment and expression, and the new range of regulatory and ethical questions raised by the generativity of these platforms in extending the scope and range of racialized abuse. At the same time, the sense that 'something must be done' about the extent to which digital media culture is awash with weaponized racial debris has reinvigorated vexed and often polarized discussions about the politically foundational and culturally privileged status of free speech. These debates are ferociously normative, but the question 'What ought to be done?' activates often radically different understandings of freedom, the public sphere, the consequentiality of communication, the importance of power and the nature of the 'political subject'. To open these tensions out in introduction, let's return to a key example from Chapter 1.

Writing just days after the attacks on *Charlie Hebdo*'s office in Paris in January 2015, the philosopher Brian Klug responded to what he saw as a prevalent conflation; not only that the attacks constituted an assault on free speech, but also that the paper's putative commitment to insulting *everyone* embodied something particularly vital to a defining European tradition of free expression. Klug situated a 'thought experiment' in the Place de la République in Paris, during the million-strong 'Republican march' held on the 11th of January to honour the victims of the attacks, and to express support for free speech. How would people have responded, he wondered, standing there with their '*Je Suis Charlie*' badges, if somebody turned up with a badge that said '*Je Suis Chérif*' (Kouachi, one of the killers)? What if the interloper was also carrying 'a placard depicting the editor of the magazine lying a pool of blood … saying "You really blew me away" or some such witticism'? How, Klug asks, would the crowd have responded – with laughter, or an appreciation of the 'gesture as quintessentially French', or applause for the stunt as a heroic example of 'standing up for liberty and freedom of speech'? Or would they have been offended, hurt, angry, and in some cases prepared to physically attack an interloper mocking a *communion* of solemnity and grief?

Klug's thought experiment is barbed, but its point, he argues, is not to accuse people expressing grief and solidarity of hypocrisy. Rather, it is to insist that this is only hypocrisy if one is 'committed to the proposition that there are no limits to freedom of expression; no subject so sensitive, no symbol so sacrosanct, that it cannot be sent up, sneered at and parodied, consequences be damned'. People who have turned 'the victims of a horrific assassination' into 'heroes of free speech' may see themselves as committed to this idea, but the jagged insensitivity of the thought experiment illustrates that 'they too have limits. They just don't know it'. Klug's conclusion that this abrupt swing from universalist certainty to contextual outrage is evidence that 'people don't know their own minds' is, on a first read, somewhat unforgiving. But his thought experiment drops us, immediately and abruptly, into the layered messiness of how free speech controversies are usually lived and played out.

John Durham Peters argues that to call for free speech 'is always an intervention in, and not only a statement about the world' (2008: 275). Public discussion of free speech, he argues, inevitably acquires a 'recursive character', because public controversies that pivot on the meaning, validity or impact of speech become as much, if not more, about the status of the principle itself as the primary substantive issue. This recursivity favours 'meta-debate' about free speech, often eliding what is substantively at stake in a disagreement or conflict. Klug's thought experiment is designed to break this recursive loop, as it forces the question as to what kinds of speech, and what kinds of freedom, are concretely at stake in this scenario, and in this context? Posed in this way, most people, arguably, would have little difficulty in recognizing free speech as a fundamental political right while also evaluating the salience of context, and deciding to argue for or against *balancing* the free speech of the provocateur with such considerations as public order, respecting the dead and the grieving, or preventing a racist backlash. The key shift the experiment demands is from invoking an abstract principle to making situated arguments for, against and about it. And this set of evaluative arguments about the status and remit of free speech rapidly produces another level of difficulty – what, if anything, should be done about 'offending' or 'harmful' speech, and what agent, if any, should be the one to act?

In a general sense, many debates about racist expression and free speech reproduce Klug's experimental dynamic, with – often abstract – declarations of support for free speech confronted with situated arguments as to how the speech of some can silence and also endanger others in unequal and racially stratified societies. In heavily mediated environments, these debates encompass 'speech' across very different sites, platforms and contexts, and involve complex scales and processes of regulation, from the moderation policies of comment threads, to broadcasting codes, to national and international law on speech governance. The purpose of this chapter is primarily to embrace the messiness of contemporary debates about free speech and hate speech. It is not directly concerned with the question of legal regulation or sanction, but rather with sifting through the conflicting understandings of freedom, power, communication, context and subjectivity that speech controversies routinely animate in public culture.

It does this in three stages, the first focused on hate speech and free speech in theory, the second on free speech in the world, the third on hate speech in practice. The first two are based on case studies, one semi-fictional, the other all too real. The semi-fictional focus stages a public controversy that, in seeking to answer the question of whether a poster should be publicly displayed or not, puts a range of theoretical and normative arguments about freedom of speech and hate speech in dialogue, and conflict, with each other. The subsequent section turns to the fraught aftermath of the attacks on the *Charlie Hebdo* offices and other locations in Paris in January 2015, events which precipitated an extraordinary debate about what constitutes the nature of freedom of speech in racialized societies. This analysis moves from the theoretical and normative focus of the first section to examine how multiple, overlapping understandings of freedom of speech were generated by these attacks, with often quite divergent issues at stake according to the media space and political context. The final section returns to the question of hate speech, and discusses its conceptual and political adequacy to the circulation of racist material through social media platforms.

# Hate speech versus free speech, and beyond

## Hate speech twinned with free speech

'A recurrent challenge for present-day democratic plural societies', Marcel Maussen and Ralph Grillo argue, '… is the negotiation of the boundaries of legitimate speech and the subsequent monitoring and protecting of these boundaries' (2013: 174). This negotiation is primarily conducted through the juxtaposition of free speech with hate speech, where free speech 'constitutes one of the essential foundations of a democratic society and it is applicable not only to "information" and "ideas" that are favourably received or regarded as inoffensive or as a matter of indifference but also those that offend, shock or disturb the state or any sector of the population' (ibid: 175). It is important, before exploring this juxtaposition further, to recognize that for all their capacious normativity, debates about free speech tend to occur in relation to very particular questions. In general, there is little difficulty in accepting that free speech is nowhere absolute, and everywhere and everyday regulated in a thicket of ways. 'Speech' is regulated by legal frameworks that, with some exceptions, rarely feature in discussions about the limits of free speech – laws on perjury, libel, slander, incitement and privacy; through the delimitation of private property in regimes of copyright, patenting and intellectual property; and acts such as criminal solicitation and insider trading.

Speech occurs in particular settings and relationships, and is thus also regulated by institutional provision, constrained through the disciplinary force of social convention, moral weight and interpersonal reflexivity, mediated by communicative infrastructures, gatekeepers and formats, and amplified or marginalized by political processes and dominant power relations (hence the emphasis in the political economy of media on questions of ownership and access – issues which are rarely integrated into normative debates about freedom of expression; see Freedman, 2014). Free speech, in effect, does not signal a general resistance to the regulation of speech and communications, but demands special consideration and protection for political expression, or as Maitra and McGowan put it, 'a principle of free speech consists in a presumption of liberty in favor of speech' (2012: 3).

Klug's thought experiment takes place in a public square. It is both a real place in Paris and a key site of the modern imagination, a space that brings a public into being (the event was a march for 'national communion'), and that provides the stage for an (imagined) speech act that is political *because it is intended to mean something for an audience.* Klug's protagonist does not actually *say* anything. But by being there, by wearing his badge and holding his placard, he performs speech acts; that is, he communicates a belief or attitude to others through a mix of communicative modes. 'Speech' is not just about speaking, and the freedom to speak is not the same as free speech. Klug's interloper could perform his routine to the bathroom mirror or to a select group of friends, and thus speak freely. It becomes a question of free speech through publicity; it is exercised in a particular *type* of context, intended to communicate propositions to an audience, and therefore protected as a 'public right' not limited to 'a subgroup or élite'. As such it is identified with a class of acts – such as freedom of the press, freedom of assembly and association – that seek protection in law and political practice, and thus grounded in a 'wider, liberal value system' (Haworth, 1998: 10–12).

This presumption of liberty in favour of speech is a critically important value, but one that should not lead simply to a reprise of what John Durham Peters characterizes as a 'heroic version of the liberal story about free speech (that) continues to define much popular and academic thinking about the relation of democracy and communication' (2005: 14). To be wary of this celebratory narrative is not the same as not supporting free speech – in fact, part of my argument is that the political defence of free speech is undermined by investments in this seductive, teleological mythology. Given this contemporary fetish for what Sindre Bangstad (2011) has termed 'first amendment absolutism', nuanced discussion is thus often resolutely interpreted as weakness on a point of principle. These stylized forms of absolutism often rely on aphoristic understandings of freedom of speech that neglect, as Alan Haworth argues, how free speech principles have been hewn from political and philosophical arguments, and that arguments about free speech today must also 'derive the conviction they contain from the realistic assessment of actual political events. They do not rest on invocations of abstract philosophical principle' (1998: 50). Similarly neglected are 'thicker histories of free speech' that account for the historically conditioned positions taken by different political actors on the question of speech in situated political struggles (Goodman, 2015). Further, by failing or refusing to take account of how racism distributes power, meaningful communicative access and public legitimacy, these thin renditions of the heroic narrative risk functioning as little more than 'an *idealizing* abstraction that abstracts away from the crucial realities of the racial polity' (Mills, 1997: 76, original emphasis).

On the other side of the conventional equation of 'free speech *versus* hate speech', the story of 'hate speech' cannot be told with such normative assurance, because its emergence as a concept is predominantly as a contingent and tentative qualification of free speech, an attempt to valorize the value of free speech and recognize the *harm of some speech*. But what harm is caused, how speech inflicts or precipitates it, and what ought to be done about it in terms of regulation or response, is the subject of intensive normative, legal and regulatory debate. Working with the idea of hate speech, as Stanley Fish (2012) points out, demands accepting that 'there is no generally accepted account of (1) what hate speech is, (2) what it does (what its effects are) and (3) what, if anything, should be done about it … (these questions are unanswerable) … because hate speech is a category without stable content'. Maussen and Grillo offer the elements of a definition:

> Commonly, three essential features are seen as defining such speech: it is directed against a specified or easily identifiable individual or, more usually, group of individuals based on aspects of their (core, non-voluntary) identity; it stigmatizes the target group by implicitly or explicitly ascribing qualities widely regarded as highly undesirable; and because of its negative qualities, the target group is viewed as an unwelcome presence and a legitimate object of hostility. (op. cit.: 175)

From a broadly liberal perspective this instability constitutes an unacceptable form of conceptual inflation, and potentially, as Kenan Malik argues, 'a way of making certain ideas illegitimate without bothering politically to challenge them' (2012: 81). For others, this lack of agreed definition is actually a strength, as the idea of 'hate speech' is not solely a legal concept or an attempt at socio-linguistic categorization. It is also an interventionist idea, a way of challenging the public legitimacy of racist speech, one that has attained contingent and strategic utility for intervening in situations where racist rhetoric, images and narratives compound the ways in which racialized or stigmatized groups are politically framed and socially situated as objects of suspicion and hostility. As such, it provides an ambivalent way of intervening in conditions of *debatability*; while the force of the idea of hate speech pushes back at the relentless relativization and denial of racism, it also risks reducing racism to manifestations of overt hate, *in and as particular kinds of speech acts*.

The aim of this section, therefore, is to draw out the complexity and tensions at stake in these debates, beyond simply providing another rendition of either the heroic or tentative story. It proceeds by borrowing a scenario from Jeremy Waldron's *The Harm in Hate Speech* (2012), where his general concern as a legal scholar is with arguments as to when and how liberal democracies should use their legislative apparatus to intervene in the dissemination of 'harmful' speech and communications. The question of the regulation of harmful or discriminatory speech, or censure for it, is a key fault line between advocates of the notion of 'hate speech' and broadly liberal objections to it. This section concentrates on a scenario that Waldron used to introduce his book's central arguments, and engages with it as a heuristic device to bring a diversity of positions into dialogue and antagonistic relief. Focusing on questions of communication, consequentiality, and political subjectivity, this exercise puts his position into dialogue with ideas and arguments from two further positions, or more accurately, composite forms of critique drawn from literature and writers that can be broadly categorized as 'liberal' and 'race critical' scholarship.

## The scenario

> A man out walking with his seven-year-old son and his ten-year-old daughter turns a corner on a city street in New Jersey and is confronted with a sign. It says: "Muslims and 9/11! Don't serve them, don't speak to them, and don't let them in". The daughter says, "What does it mean, papa?" Her father, who is Muslim – the whole family is Muslim – doesn't know what to say. He hurries the children on, hoping they will not come across any more of these signs. (Waldron, 2012: 1)

Waldron's scenario is a thinly veiled reference to the 'anti-jihad' campaign by the American Freedom Defense Initiative (AFDI) – a front group for Pamela Geller's hate group Stop the Islamisation of America – that placed paid advertisements in subway stations and on buses in New York, San Francisco and Washington DC, in some cases only after court orders forced transport authorities to do so in respect of AFDI's First Amendment rights to unfettered public discourse, that is, speech acts constitutionally recognized 'as appropriate ways to influence the formation of public opinion' (Post, 2012: 12). Waldron abstracts his account to allow him to construct a normative dilemma uncluttered by too much contextual detail. 'What', he asks, 'is the point of these signs?'

## The message

Every delineation of acceptable speech or hate speech involves (an often tacit) theory of communication. In Waldron's argument, the signs send out two interlocking messages. The first is to those who, as Muslims or 'Muslim-looking' people, are the *targets*, those who can be made a subject of the imperative demand of the message. To them,

Waldron argues, the sign says, 'Don't be fooled into thinking you are welcome here. The society around you may seem hospitable and nondiscriminatory, but the truth is that you are not wanted ... '. Hate speech is generally interpreted as derogatory public discourse that targets 'racial and ethnic minorities' (gender is conspicuously absent from definitions of hate speech that have been forged in the legal-historical context of post-fascism and 'ethnic minority relations' in Europe; see Bleich, 2011). Yet as Waldron makes clear, the addressee of the message is *also* the non-Muslim, specifically the 'silent majority' that is both constructed and spoken for through the integralist projection of far-right discourse. For those who are asked to recognize themselves in this position, the advertisement is an invitation: 'We know some of you agree that these people are not wanted here. Know now that you are not alone.' Waldron's focus, then, is not only on how the message performs this dual interpellation, but also on that the 'point of hate speech ... is to make these messages part of the permanent visible fabric of society' (op. cit.: 2–3).

A 'classic liberal' approach to the message may initially assess whether the ads constitute an incitement to violence, as the concept of hate speech is generally regarded as meaningful only when it describes a speech act that generates some form of 'imminent threat' against those targeted by the speech – a threshold that raises complicated questions of intentionality, interpretation and contextual relations, questions rendered even more complex by the real-time spatial networking of connective media. Because it is in part a legal concept that can result in speech restriction or prosecution, much hinges on the kind of 'threshold-seeking' question asked by Michael Herz and Peter Molnar: ' ... at what point does condemnation, insult, or disdain cross the line to become a message of persecution, inhumanity, degradation, or whatever other term one uses to identify what is substantively beyond the pale?' (2012: 3).

The metro ad certainly constitutes 'condemnation', but to argue that it crosses this threshold to become a 'message of persecution', it might be argued, gives too much weight to the intended interpellations of the message. It imbues the content with what Eric Heinze terms 'rhetorical consequentialism' – the verbal assertion of causation as so likely that it does not require some form of empirical evidence of a relation between speech and action (2016: 155). The problem with this, Kenan Malik argues, is that it comes to depend on one of Communication Studies' most discredited paradigms – an 'effects like' understanding of mediated communication that not only flirts with crude behaviouralism, but also blurs the relation between human agency and moral responsibility:

> Racists are, of course, influenced by racist talk. It is they, how-ever, who bear responsibility for translating racist talk into racist action. Ironically, for all the talk of using free speech responsibly, the real consequence of the demand for censorship is to moderate the responsibility of individuals for their actions. (2012: 85)

Therefore, the sign constitutes an exercise in free speech that cannot be banned simply because of its content, whereas if people were to act on that content and – for example – 'deny them service', their acts would contravene existing legal provisions on discrimination. Beyond this point, the specific content of speech, the message, is of diminish-ing importance for free speech positions that embrace ideas of 'content neutrality' or 'viewpoint neutrality' (see Eckert, 2010), but it is a more complex proposition for *consequentialist* arguments, that is, reasoning that makes instrumental claims for the benefits of free speech and the free flow of ideas to democratic viability and the pursuit of knowledge. A liberal 'classic defence' response to Waldron would certainly dis-tance itself from the prejudice of the advertisements, and might clarify that it could not be regarded as a Millsian 'exercise (of) the liberty of thought and discussion' that advances knowledge and understanding (see Haworth, 1998: 24–32; though it should not be discounted that an adversarial response to it could support the 'pursuit of understanding' – as David Cole [2012] argued in response to Waldron's scenario, 'such speech may generate responses by both neutral observers and respected leaders of the Muslim community that will both produce a better under-standing of that community's culture and correct misleading statements by extremists').

However, the *offensive character* of the message does not justify it being censored or censured, because if democracy depends on the participation of citizens, then it is freedom of speech, protected from coercion and suppression, that underpins that participation. To interfere with free speech is to undermine the very character of democracy, and is open to the charge of arbitrary authority or a presumption of infalli-bility. For the state to interfere in order to suppress problematic speech is to invite a 'slippery slope' towards greater intervention, ultimately allowing the suppression of, for example, political dissent, and in an unintended irony, minority opinions. Any claim for particular forms of speech to be censored or managed increases the legitimacy and power of the state to abrogate powers to define the limits of acceptable political discourse, with consequences for political freedom. Concomitantly, free speech, as it throws up unorthodox ideas and unpopular opinions, is our best hope of accessing truth and generating knowledge: ' ... by saying what we think, and by attending to the opinions and reactions of others, we, as a society, are more likely to form true (and better justified) beliefs' (Maitra and McGowan, 2012: 2).

Theories critical of liberal toleration counter that the idea of hate speech proposes, at its most fundamental, that communication is a form of action – it does something in the world, and does something to people in that world. In communicative terms, therefore, definitions of hate speech combine a number of the following components: the *content* of speech; the (written or oral) *tone* of speech; an evaluation of the *nature* of that speech; the (individual and collective) *targets* of that speech; and the potential *consequences* or *implications* of the speech act. Given that prejudice, as Judith Butler notes, 'neither begins nor ends with the subject who speaks and acts' (2009, quoted in Yanay, 2012:10), critical approaches to 'hate speech' are distinguished by their emphasis on how speech acts may derive their force structurally and relationally within societies shaped by histories of racialized violence, exclusion and hierarchy.

Writing in the US during the 1980s to 1990s, the critical race theory associated with legal scholars such as Mari Matsuda, Kimberlé Crenshaw and Richard Delgado confronted 'First Amendment absolutist' permissiveness with regard to racist hate speech (Downing, 1999) by examining how racist speech can encompass – in the terms of J.L. Austin – both *illocutionary* and *perlocutionary* acts. That is, speech may *act to* subordinate, or *cause* subordination, because the message of racist speech is less an 'argument' than a ritual reinstatement of racialized arrangements produced by histories of violence and oppression. Thinking of speech relationally and contextually, Matsuda argues, produces an understanding of hate speech as communication that has a message of racial inferiority, is directed against a member of a historically oppressed group, and *as an act* is persecutory, hateful and degrading (1993: 36). Thus, perspectives from 'race critical scholarship' (Bhattacharyya and Murji, 2013) may welcome Waldron's recognition of the situated power relations invoked by the message, but argue that a full reckoning with its significance involves starting from examining how the 'visible (and invisible) fabric of society' is striated with racialized relations of power, legitimacy and possibility. It could point to how his abstracted scenario neglects how the message of the billboard is rendered coherent and potent by the ways in which the 'war on terror' has positioned 'Muslim culture' as a source of potential violence and dis-integrating difference, and therefore an object of widely sanctioned political and cultural suspicion before the sign was erected (see Kundnani, 2014).

It is not just that the opportunistic campaigns of groups such as the SIOA have emerged from the mainstream legitimation of anti-Muslim racism discussed in previous chapters, but also that the message of such a billboard takes on meaning through its circulation in what Sara Ahmed terms an 'affective economy of hate', where 'signs increase in affective value as an effect of the movement between signs: the more signs circulate, the more affective they become' (2004b: 45). Ahmed's model of economic exchange and flow is designed to complicate – but not minimize – how we think about hate as expressed in a relation between 'message' and 'target'. The father and his children are interpellated by the message, but hate is produced as an effect of its circulation in a context where it is already sanctioned materially and ideologically: ' … figures of hate circulate, and indeed accumulate their affective value, precisely insofar as they do not have a fixed reference' (Ahmed, 2004b: 47). In other words, the advertisement cannot be interpreted solely as a discrete text or singular message, but as having an exchange value, as having accumulated significance in what Moustafa Bayoumi describes as the 'War on Terror Culture that is continuously reflected and reinforced across American society' (2015: 16).

## The consequence

Waldron grounds his treatment of consequence in particular conceptions of social life and the public good, and in so doing undercuts the argument that harm requires definitive causal evidence to be treated as a meaningful injury. He is dismissive of the argument that those targeted should 'just learn to live with it'. Not only does this assume that they must pay a price to defend freedom of speech – a cost that will never be incurred by those not targeted – it also neglects that other public goods are risked by accepting the 'visibility' of these messages. The first is what he terms a *public good of inclusiveness*, which is dependent on everyone accepting that 'the society is not *just* for them; but it *is* for them too, along with all of the others'. To insist that harm is not caused by the corrosion of felt security is to ignore how hate speech acts as an 'environmental threat to social peace' (2012: 4).

Secondly, Waldron turns to the notion of dignity, which in this argument entails a person's 'social standing, the fundamentals of basic reputation that entitle them to be treated as equals in the ordinary operations of society'. His emphasis on dignity allows him to differentiate between the idea of protecting from offence and the contention that the circulation of hate speech undermines dignity 'both in their own eyes and in the eyes of other members of society'. By forcing Muslim and 'Muslim-looking' people to reckon with stereotypes, smears, threats and accusations that they cannot avoid, these messages have a collectivizing logic and drive, 'associating ascriptive characteristics like ethnicity, or race, or religion with conduct or attributes that should disqualify someone from being treated as a member of society in good standing' (ibid: 5).

Liberal responses to Waldron's emphases are likely to be mixed, for as Eric Barendt notes, given constitutional guarantees of human dignity, 'the argument from human dignity is a strong one', and where the question of restricting what he terms 'extreme hate speech' is in play, it is difficult to see how a commitment to 'human dignity and rationality' can be marshalled in defence of material that 'demeans humanity itself' (2005: 33–4). Yet the advertisement in question is chosen for this scenario because it is not only demeaning but also, given the ubiquity of anti-Muslim prejudice, not *extreme*. Not only does it fall short of a threshold of incitement as 'hate speech', but the depth of the postracial denial of racism has also created a political space where public racist expression has become more generally vicious precisely because it allows for racial characterization and 'racial animations' to be invoked 'while denying that they add up to racism' (Goldberg, 2015: 87). Therefore, a liberal response may recognize the affront to dignity while regarding this freedom of political speech as more integral to the public good. Herein lies the fragility of Waldron's linking of individual dignity to the public good, as a contrasting theory of (communicative) consequentiality holds that this common goal is bolstered, not corroded, by offensive speech. That is, fundamental liberty of expression fosters pluralism, which provides the most sustained defence against prejudice by valorizing public criticism over 'driving attitudes underground'.

This requires tolerance for those opinions one may find objectionable – even if this results in *subjective* feelings of offence and hurt – as living with offensive speech requires the practice of self-restraint as a civic virtue, or what Lee Bollinger, in *The Tolerant Society* (1986), celebrates as an opportunity for personal and civic growth, using the exposure to hate speech as the chance to develop an active practice of tolerance. This self-formation is required by a 'marketplace of ideas', which, while ideally governed by norms of public conduct, is also a space of robust exchange, up to and including offence and ridicule. This may be unsettling, but there is no right not to be offended, and this is ultimately a price worth paying for maximizing liberty of conscience and expression, and for the belief that the best ideas, and more and better speech, garner the most persuasive influence.

A critical race theory response to Waldron might first question his straightforward, 'colourblind' acceptance of notions of dignity and equality. Race, as Charles W. Mills argues, 'is in no way an "after-thought", a "deviation" from ostensibly raceless Western ideals, but rather a central shaping constituent of those ideals' (1997: 14). The history of liberal ideas of political life is also a history of racialized exclusion from the ideal humanity judged capable of rationality, dignity and equality (Losurdo, 2011). Waldron's turn to dignity is a way of inscribing the social relationality of injury and working towards achieving equality. In the US, formal equality co-exists with institutional racism and the 'muted racism' of privatized, neoliberal inequality (Davis, 2007). A constitutional commitment to human dignity accompanies structural white supremacy that 'marks certain people as full humans and full citizens, while rendering others undeserving of legal protection, of "inalienable" rights, and thus killable' (Ciccariello-Maher, 2016).

However, Waldron's focus on dynamics of (self) recognition is critical in unsettling the reductive liberal tendency to gather all forms of personal, embodied and affective responses to racism under the banner of *offence*. The liberal insistence that the threshold for 'hate speech' can only be when it poses the risk of violence is to refuse how historical repertoires of signs are indexed to structures of racist violence and to the legitimation of that violence. As Martin Lawrence argues, when the Ku Klux Klan burn a cross on the lawn of a black person, or black church, 'the effect of this speech does not result from the persuasive power of an idea operating freely in the market. It is a threat; a threat … (that) does not need to be explicit because racially motivated violence is a well-known historical and contemporary reality' (1993: 53, in West, 2012: 234). The idea of 'offence' restricts the message to the utterance, and the consequence to the cognitive response of the *offended*, a double movement that closes off the insistence on systemic violence and contextual power relations that informs race critical responses:

Being made to fear for your life is not the same as feeling hurt by speech. Losing your job as a result of stereotypes or harassment contained in speech is not the same as feeling personally offended by that speech ... being outed against your will is not the same as having your feelings hurt by it. It is the deeds that flow from words which concern us, and which cannot be contained by the concept of offensiveness. (Cross, 2015)

## The subject

In scholarly and political arguments about the legitimacy of 'hate speech' as a concept, empirical data on the 'deeds that flow from words' are rarely featured, with the result that there are 'relatively few works on what ... hate speech feels and looks like, and what the ramifications for individuals targeted by hate speech might be' (Bangstad, 2015). As a consequence, different approaches appeal to divergently imagined subjects to ground their assessment of what hate speech is, and what it potentially does. Waldron's conceptualization of consequentiality depends on composing a subject that is at once normative (the subject of dignity) and socially situated (in relations of recognition and ascription). Race critical theory also insists on socially situated subjects, but less as normative figurations than subjects of embodied experiences. Mari Matsuda, for example, reflects Waldron's dual interpellation by insisting that the 'envisaged hearers' of 'messages of racial inferiority' are always also members of the 'historically oppressed group', and that living with this can cause physical and psychological harms (1993: 24–37). From this perspective, recognition of the experience of *being hated* cannot be excluded from how hate speech is understood; it is a key dimension of how the experience of racism generates a critical source of knowledge on the functioning of racism (Essed, 1991). Writing about covering the US presidential election and the 'destructive vitriol (Donald Trump) reserved for Muslims', and its enthusiastic networked amplification, the journalist Bim Adewunmi (2016) wrote:

It has an almost tangible weight, like a cloak – or more honestly and uncomfortably two large rocks, tethered to a stick across my shoulders – and it follows me around, invading every cranny of personal space. It crowds out my brain and steals my emotional bandwidth, broadcasting on a frequency it has no permission to access.

However, the liberal emphasis on what Craig Calhoun summarizes as 'an effective rational-critical discourse aimed at the resolution of political disputes' in the public sphere (1993: 269) remains intensely hostile to the contention that experience can produce 'legitimate' knowledge. This is not just because of a significantly different valence of dignity, insisting that 'it is an infringement of someone's autonomy or dignity – either as a speaker or a listener or both – to have speech curtailed' (Warburton, 2009: 16). It is because the vision of a political subject that transcends 'private' experience has, as Randi Gressgård outlines, deep roots in liberal and republican thought. Freedom and equality are intrinsic to the promise of humanity, but this promise, in republican terms, involves a struggle to guarantee ourselves mutually equal rights, and thus depends on the subject committing to a civic political culture and a universal, civic identity. Thus, republicanism emphasizes the educational and disciplinary role of institutions, and citizenship as a process of formation (2012). Liberalism imagines a similar universal subject, but its insistence on the individual capacity for reason and autonomy emphasizes public norms of behaviour over institutional formation. This accounts, as Risto Kunelius argues, for two closely related valuations of free speech in the public sphere: a republican emphasis on *argumentation* as the participative mode through which the public can 'reach at least temporarily a shared sense of justice through public reasoning and dialogue', and a liberal investment in attention, the capacity to hold power to account (2013: 31–2). To appeal to the 'subjectivity' of experience, therefore, is to attempt to bypass the necessarily disinterested work of trying to 'reasonably sort out hateful speech from legitimate discussion' (Slagle, 2009: 248).

While decades of feminist, poststructuralist and postcolonial critique have chipped away at the historical exclusions enacted by a 'liberal individualistic view of the subject, which defines perfectability in terms of autonomy and self-determination' (Braidotti, 2013: 20), in the 'free speech versus hate speech' debate this restricted notion of the admissible political subject is consistently reanimated and asserted. This, as Linda Martín Alcoff argues, is as a result of connecting experiential knowledge to an inability or unwillingness to transcend the 'constraints' of identity and submit claims to the test of rationality. This represents a chain of assumptions, she argues, that 'are hardwired into Western Anglo traditions of thought; by that I mean that they are rarely argued for or even made explicit' (2006: 37). (Though sometimes they are made very explicit: when France's Minister for Women's Rights and a founding member of SOS Racisme, Laurence Rossignol, contributed to France's endless 'hijab debate' in March 2016 by arguing that 'there are women that have chosen [to wear headscarves], there were also American *nègres* who were for slavery', her doubly racialized analogy assumed that publicly identifying through the visual marker of a headscarf constituted a renunciation of 'autonomy and self-determination' – the willful refusal of values discussed in Chapter 3.)

## Free speech and debatability

The assumption that the experience of being a target of racist communications has no weight in debates about 'hate speech' shades rapidly into the forms of dismissal that characterize postraciality. For that reason, in this brief section conclusion I want to offer an interim critique of dominant liberal free speech positions in terms of the dynamics of debatability (this is not to let 'hate speech' off the hook, conceptually or politically – it is further evaluated in relation to online and social media dynamics in the last section).

The first observation is that particular invocations of free speech often pay insufficient attention to actual speech, as communication. This is in part because the liberal formulation of free speech is defined by a historically justified horizon of resistance to censorship, and the potential arbitrariness and injustice of regulation through state authority. However, in resisting 'hate speech' as a category turned towards legal intervention, many free speech advocates consequently refuse *any* substantive engagement with actual speech and the social and contextual significance of communication. As John Durham Peters notes, 'refusing to make laws prohibiting speech and expression does not mean that speech and expression are necessarily free of ill effects. One can oppose censorship while maintaining a capacity for judgements about the value and quality of cultural forms' (2005: 9). That so many advocates of maximal free speech renege on this capacity for judgement suggests a detached idealism or proceduralism that, in its determination to avoid descending down a 'slippery slope', is happy to stand at the top of the hill, reminding society below of the rules of the game. As we shall see in the next section, this studied detachment has become profoundly vulnerable to ideological capture in a context where the production of 'free speech events' has become a generative mode of capturing public and media space for racist agitation.

Secondly, while it is far from inevitable that a defence of free speech leads to such thin understandings of speech, this thinness is sustained through the translucence of the imagined individual that speaks and listens in liberal argumentation. The problem with a certain genre of free speech claims, as Davina Cooper (2013) contends, is that they reduce speech to the laudable goal of 'getting closer to the truth' while excluding all other potential speech effects. This is made possible, she argues, because 'advocates of "robust debate" tend to treat speech akin to a missile system, where discrete units of meaning pass back and forth between fully intentional, fixed subjects (whose interests, concerns and agenda are clear and prior to any engagement)'. In societies marked by racial formation and socio-political inequality the problem with this vision of the public sphere is a familiar one, for as Wendy Brown argues, it 'always already eschews power and history in its articulation and comprehension of the social and the subject' (2006: 18). As the previous chapter suggested, this vision of debate is difficult to sustain in a context of communicative abundance and racial debris, where racist 'speech' is often not just anonymous but also digitally distributed, semi-automated, ubiquitous, ambient and ritualized.

Thirdly, the contention that the answer to 'hate speech' is more and better speech blithely assumes not only the absence of power and inequality in communicative relations, but also that the subjects interpellated by racialized discourse must invest of themselves in specific kinds of affective and political labour in response to what could be termed *deliberative distortion*. This is the idea that even if racist hate speech – or the less overt dog-whistling mythologies and cut-and-paste 'talking points' that proliferate in public culture – has no 'truth-seeking' dimension, it should be responded to as if it has. That is, the targets of racializing discourse are in effect appointed the custodians of public discourse ethics, compelled to observe rules that it is acknowledged their harassers disdain, and thus required to respond to messages that undermine their humanity *as if* these are contentions worthy of debate, and *as if* the ritual and performative racist contentions derived from the repertoires examined previously are open to engagement and refutation.

In this schema of deliberative inequality, the appropriate response to Waldron's sign is for 'Muslims' to argue that yes, you should serve us, speak to us, and let us in, and here are the reasons why. In this intensification of debatability, the targets of racist expression are expected to amplify and extend discourses inured to deliberative engagement, in the name of dialogue. This form of bracingly disembodied rationalism is echoed in the public culture cliché that 'there is no right not to be offended', and it is here that this vision of public participation most keenly intersects with postraciality. It individuates responsibility for racially ordered power, rendering invisible the plurality of ways in which people continuously deal with and confront mediated racist speech. It suggests that affective and political responses that do not resemble the rational fortitude of a projected liberal subject, historically and resiliently imagined as white, male and European, represent a failure of capacity or will.

# Free speech events: from *Charlie Hebdo* to 'Charlie Hebdo'

## Symbolic weight

Reviewing normative arguments on free speech and its limits, the philosopher Alan Haworth refuses a conclusive summary; ' … if I have a "lesson" for the reader at all, it is only to say this: here on the one hand are the arguments, here, on the other, is the world. I leave it to you to judge how closely they match' (1998: 50). Haworth, of course, is not juxtaposing philosophy with that rhetoric of the 'real world' so often used to suggest that academic knowledge is too abstract and rarefied to be useful. Much like Klug's thought experiment, Haworth's coupling of 'arguments' and 'world' underlines that ideas do not walk in straight lines; arguments as to how the world *ought to be* are shaped by investments and positions, striated with desires and projections, contingent on contexts and relations, and performative of actions and responses. This is all the more pronounced if, as the conclusion to the previous section suggests, an attention to the structures of race, and the dynamics of racism, are consistently layered back into normative assumptions and imaginaries.

If the purpose of the last section was to critically rehearse arguments *about* the world, the aim of this section is to examine arguments *in* the world, shifting from Waldron's abstracted scenario to a real event – the intensive communicative focus on the question of free speech and the meaning of racism that took shape in the aftermath of the attacks on the office of *Charlie Hebdo* and on a kosher supermarket in the east of Paris in January 2015. Marked by a constant recursivity that framed the attacks as primarily an assault on free speech, and the dominant response as primarily an affirmation of the foundational value of free speech, this section examines how divergent conflicts as to what constitutes free speech, and how free speech is constituted, overlapped in the charged and fractious aftermath.

The immediate aftermath was a moment of intense public emotion and anger in France, of mourning for the slaughter of well-known figures and ordinary workers. Solidarity was expressed on the day of the attacks in spontaneous gatherings in places such as the Place de la République – which became a 'living memorial' over the course of 2015, particularly after the November 22nd attacks – and expanded into the charged spectacle of the enormous *marches républicaines* of January 10th and 11th. The aftermath was a also moment of relentless communicative output, rapidly framed as a transformative political moment that generated, in the following days, weeks and months, an explosion of commentary and interpretation (for example, 4.6 books a month addressing the attacks were published in France between January 2015 and July 2016; see Amiraux and Fetiu, 2017). Condensed by the hashtag *#JeSuisCharlie,* the urgent and ambivalent invitation to symbolically *be Charlie* was accepted, modified, questioned and resisted in torrents of tweets, cartoons, memes, blogs and social media threads. As the story and the hashtag circulated transnationally, it took on divergent significance in different political and interpretative contexts and was appropriated to a wide variety of established agendas and antagonisms.

Speaking in advance of the publication of the 'Survivor's Issue' a week after the attack, the cartoonist Rénald Luzier – 'Luz' – alluded directly to this communicative spectacle: 'This current symbolic weight is everything Charlie has always worked against: destroying symbols, knocking down taboos, setting fantasies straight.' This burden of symbolic weight indexed *Charlie Hebdo* to what is better understood as 'Charlie Hebdo' – a dense field of meaning-making and affective investment, and an intensive spectacle of political identification and dis-identification (Titley, 2017). The question of free speech and its limits, particularly in relation to racism, was prominent in this symbolic freighting. However, to examine the intersection of arguments and world, it is not enough to rehearse them normatively, in the manner of the previous section. Prior to examining the different kinds of debates about free speech and racism which erupted, a framework for examining 'Charlie Hebdo' as a *media event* is required.

## 'Charlie Hebdo' as a 'media event'

The dominant response of Media and Communication Studies in the aftermath of the attacks was to investigate this spectacular if globally uneven concentration of communicative power and networked participation as a 'media event'. Media events bring publics into being in a variety of ways, and at varying scales and intensities; however, *media event theory* is informed by particular ways of imagining the media public. For much of the twentieth century, James Carey argues in *Communication as Culture*, studies of communication pivoted between an emphasis on 'communication as the transmission of signals or messages over distance for the purpose of control' or a ritual understanding of communication 'directed not towards the extension of messages in space but towards the maintenance of society in time, not the act of imparting information but the representation of shared beliefs' (1992: 5). In this latter tradition, Daniel Dayan and Elihu Katz conceptualized the 'media event' as extending the integrative drive of ritual through the phenomenology of the shared experience of *liveness*. Media events of the broadcast era summoned a national audience to a shared experience of occasion; they were the 'high holidays of mass communication', a break from routine viewing as either exceptional occurrences, or more generally 'ritual celebrations' that had the power to integrate otherwise spatially dispersed and socially diverse national societies through mass communication (1992: 1–16).

If this emphasis on the integrative dimension was always open to sociological and political question, the gradual development of a globalizing architecture of communications further complicated this function while amplifying the frequency and scope of unevenly if intensively shared media experiences. In an era of digital media connectivity, shared experience is often still hailed through projections of integrated community, but the distributed agency of networked communications, according to Hepp and Couldry, creates a space for different and often antagonistic constructions of the apparently unifying public 'We' to be articulated. Media events in the global age, they argue, are 'certain situated, thickened, centring performances of mediated communication that are focused on a specific thematic core, cross different media products and reach a wide and diverse multiplicity of audiences and participants' (2010: 13). 'Charlie Hebdo' was certainly 'thickened' by the focus on free speech, and quickened by its antagonistic generativity across multiple platforms and contexts. Yet as Annabelle Sreberny (2016) argued in a critique of this post-attacks turn to media event theory, the problem with the approach is that the necessary focus on concentrated communicative power also works to artificially isolate a singular happening as an event, rather than 'seeing such an event as lying within one or more historical narratives that helped produce its eventness in the first place'. Events are produced by the force of rival articulations working to establish their historicity, their causes and their significance. They become *events* through narrativization, and the struggle to substantiate these narratives is part of the *eventfulness* of the media event.

Each 'event', she argues, is in itself part of an immediate event-chain and inducted to a 'longer event-chain, where historical narratives compete for explanation, motivation, rationalization, and justification' (a process immediately apparent in *Le Monde*'s iconic front page of January 8th, declaring 'France's 9/11'). Understanding event-chains means accounting for how occurrences are invested with meaning through being linked to other events in time and space, and how what Sreberny terms the 'deterritorialized assemblage of contemporary event chains' is comprised of competing historical narratives and conflicting causal accounts circulating in an expansive media space. Thus, while what the French media dubbed 'the Charlie effect' was widely associated with the value of free speech (Marlière, 2017), adopting Sreberny's approach allows us to pay attention to the complex variety of ways in which 'Charlie Hebdo' became a site for often highly divergent investments in the value – or not – of free speech. The 'free speech' in question during 'Charlie Hebdo', therefore, involves not just different arguments and reference points, but also shaping contexts and structuring relations, as the following three dimensions illustrate.

## 'Charlie Hebdo' and media solidarity

The media event of 'Charlie Hebdo' was also configured as a media event about the media. Given the nature of the primary attack, the response of many journalists was personal and invested, with newsrooms gathering to tweet collective pictures of their journalists holding Joachim Roncin's original black and grey *'Je Suis Charlie'* sign. The media industry quickly demonstrated material solidarity with *Charlie Hebdo*'s determination to keep publishing: the newspaper *Libération* hosted the survivors; the Guardian Media Group, among other supporters, donated £100,000; and individual and institutional subscriptions soared. However; the question of symbolic solidarity prompted reaction – the venerable Istanbul newspaper *Cumhuriyet* ('The Republic') included images from *Charlie Hebdo* in a statement of solidarity on January 14th, which resulted in government attacks on the newspaper, and a charge of 'inciting public hatred' against the journalists Hikmet Cetinkaya and Ceyda Karan. It also sparked significant disagreement, with the question of whether to reproduce the magazine's previous cartoons of the Prophet Mohammed, and subsequently the cover of the *Survivor's Issue*, prompting very different editorial rationales as to the relationship of press freedom to free speech, and not just between those who did and did not republish.

In a context of digital proliferation, the decision to publish or not publish particular images had little to do with the 'media scarcity' era notion of gatekeeping, as the images, after all, could easily be retrieved from multiple sources. It was rather a deeply reflexive decision as to what the decision represented about the values of the media institution, and its relations to its audience. It was also one that took place in a context of extensive social media-generated pressure, demanding of newspaper editors in particular that they interpret freedom of expression as involving a non-negotiable reproduction of any cartoon or cover image deemed 'controversial' or 'blasphemous'. For the journalist and Free Speech Debate project founder Timothy Garton Ash (2015), the demand 'to be Charlie' for other media actors was clear:

> All the media of Europe should respond to the Islamist terrorist assassinations in Paris by coordinated publication next week of selected cartoons from Charlie Hebdo, and a commentary explaining why they are doing this. A week of solidarity, and of liberty. One in which all Europeans, including Muslims, reaffirm the commitment to free speech which alone enables us to combine diversity with freedom.

Ultimately, however, very few major newspapers responded to this call (Glatte, 2015). What followed instead was a charged yet reflexive public exchange between editors keen to explain or justify their decisions to their publics as to the relationship between editorial responsibility – which inevitably involves gatekeeping – and press freedom. In some instances, newspaper editors cited the fear of reprisals and therefore responsibility to their staff for non-publication. In this context, attempting to maintain a differentiation between reproducing the cartoons as 'solidaristic defiance' and as a 'normal news service to readers' is difficult (Wilby, 2015). Other public justifications explicitly differentiated solidarity with the messenger and the message, insisting that editorial responsibility is the exercise of freedom of expression, and thus also includes the right to discriminate as to what should be published on the basis of normative or political assessment. Roy Greenslade (2015), in the *Guardian*'s media blog, pointed to an obvious dimension often overlooked in invocations of the public, which is that people of Muslim faith who find the cartoons deliberately offensive are fully part of a newspaper's readership, and thus editors 'had to ask themselves if they should gratuitously insult a religion and its adherents, because a very small group of fanatics have misused its teachings'.

This sense that freedom of speech involves and also requires restraint and discrimination clashed profoundly with an 'activist' sense of freedom of speech pronounced among some European newspapers, particularly in the aftermath of the *Jyllands Posten* controversy – or 'Danish cartoon crisis' – in 2005–6 (Hervik et al., 2008). Sindre Bangstad, in analyzing the self-declared 'free speech fundamentalism' of influential Norwegian media editors in the period between the cartoon crisis and Anders Behring Breivik's murderous attacks in Oslo and Utøya in 2011, captures a wider dynamic in describing how Muslims came to be framed in journalistic discourse as the main threat to freedom of expression, a threat which required them to be 'educated', often through offence and mockery, in the values which define the open society (2014: 184–207). Similarly, Carolina Sanchez Boe has tracked how many French newspapers reprinted the *Jyllands Posten* Mohammed cartoons in 2006 as a gesture of editorial solidarity, generating a 'field of opinions' that was 'dominated by a discourse that focused on *defending freedom of speech and protecting our civilization*' (2017, original emphasis).

The hegemonic articulation of this understanding of free speech in the aftermath among French newspapers, Simon Dawes argues, frequently involved projecting an image of 'Anglophone cowardice' that elided the systemic differences in how press freedom is understood and institutionalized in France and the UK. His analysis draws on Hallin and Mancini's widely cited (2004) comparative model of media and political systems to argue that 'while both media systems can claim to have a free press ... press freedom is perhaps better understood as a spectrum (of extents of freedom) and as a very subjective term' (Dawes, 2015). In the 'negative freedom' emphasis of the 'Anglo-Saxon model', press freedom is primarily regarded as freedom from state interference, and the significant power of private ownership and the frequently overtly political designs of press owners are practically ignored. Conversely, the relationship between the state and media in France is 'historically close' and 'French journalists have tended to be more concerned with defending their unfettered right to free expression than with issues of political influence'. Consequently this sense of press freedom, 'stripped of its watchdog pretensions', has proven to be conducive to these more recent 'culture war' understandings of press freedom as a 'right to offend without recourse to any notion of the public interest'. In sum, in the aftermath of the attacks freedom of speech became a prism through which often strikingly divergent understandings of the role of the press in society were publicly negotiated.

## 'Charlie Hebdo' and free speech hypocrisy

Political violence is never informed or shaped by just one logic; however, it is plausible that the attack on *Charlie Hebdo* sought the communicative impact associated with the idea of *propagande par le fait* – propaganda of the deed, an act that inflicts symbolic as well as material or human damage. As well as seeking to intensify 'clash of civilization' style reactions by targeting a publication that had published caricatures of the Prophet Mohammed, it broadened the scope of jihadi terrorism from attacks on political and economic interests to carriers of cultural and symbolic power. Even within the logic of the killers' framework, therefore, a lethal attack on journalists is an assault on free expression. (According to Reporters without Borders [2016], 101 journalists were killed in 2015, with much of the violence against journalists constituting deliberate, silencing attacks on journalism). However, claims not just to defend freedom of speech, but also to embody it in civilizational terms, defined the immediate political response of the deeply unpopular Socialist Party government. 'France', Prime Minister Valls declared after the attacks, 'carries free speech everywhere'. 'The Republic', in the response of the President François Hollande, 'equals freedom of expression; the Republic equals culture, creation, it equals pluralism and democracy. This is what the assassins were targeting'.

Laurie Boussaguet and Florence Faucher's (2016) research on official communication strategy after the January and also November 2015 attacks details a keen awareness in government that they had a key role in shaping the construction of the event, and in providing a 'manichean and simple' message as to its meaning. The idea that the attack targeted eternal French values provided such a narrative hook, linking the attacks to 9/11 and other 'unprecedented' events in an event-chain designed to shut down discussion of the possible domestic and international causes of terrorism (Plenel, 2016). The force of this articulation provoked a critical public focus on apparently hypocritical actions by the state, with, for example, the attacks on journalists and press freedom, perpetrated by some of the world leaders invited to the march for national unity on January 11th, documented in real-time coverage on social media. However, the idea of hypocrisy or double standards, while important, does not capture something more fundamental about speech regimes, which is that the affirmation of free speech's foundational nature is often concurrent with the proscription of certain forms of political speech.

As Didier Fassin documents, a series of laws in France heavily circumscribe the legitimacy of political speech, including the so-called 2003 Sarkozy Law, 'establishing a punishment of up to six months in prison for insulting the national flag or anthem' (2015: 4). In the immediate aftermath of the attacks, the provision of the 2014 Cazeneuve Law, which created the crime of 'apology for terrorism', was used to arrest dozens of people – including children and people with learning difficulties – who were investigated often for little more than isolated comments or jokes in school, workplaces or public settings (Hajjat, 2017). The various forms of refusal of mainly racialized young people to 'respect' the minute's silence in schools were not regarded as free political expression, but as evidence of a potential threat, and disdain for the values of the secular Republic. As Minister of National Education Najat Vallaud-Belkacem stated in the National Assembly on January 14th, questions raised in high schools about the minute's silence by *those who are not Charlie* are 'above all intolerable to us, when we hear them at school, which has the duty to teach our values'.

In the name of valorizing free speech, therefore, certain forms of speech were ruled as punishable under legal frameworks that produce forms of political speech as free and unfree. And, in the context of what Jim Wolfreys (2015) has termed an 'Islamophobic spiral' in France, these forms of unfree speech were deterministically associated with 'Muslims' as a problem population. As the subject of legal surveillance and relentless cultural suspicion, the attacks intensified the political demand to continually *désolidariser* themselves and 'their community' from extremists, and to prove their loyalty to and compatibility with 'French values' (Hajjat, 2017). Consequently, the 'iconoclastic' approach of *Charlie Hebdo*'s satire was elevated beyond the status of expression that should unquestionably enjoy free speech to an iconic status as an expression of Republican virtue and national unity, and thus formed the basis for a further demand – display the correct subject position, prove that you are not offended, or face the consequences. In this demand, Philippe Marlière (2017) has argued, the 'neutrality' demanded by the state is revealed as a form of 'majoritarian assimilationism'. Republicanism, for all its fidelity to the idea of a general universal will, is a nationalism that has declared itself universal, and in so doing creates a double bind for those 'Muslims' obsessively fixed as its definitional Other. The demand for Muslims *to be Charlie* as a public act of 'desolidarisation' is inseparable from the demand to not appear, or identify, as a Muslim in public. As Mayanthi L. Fernando summarizes, 'As in colonial Algeria, Muslims in France are consistently tethered to their embodied, communal, racial and religious difference' (2015: 29).

## Charlie Hebdo and far-right scavenging

If the previous two realms of conflict over free speech involved attempts to link 'Charlie Hebdo' in an event-chain narrative to previous historical events, the final example involves a performative effort by the far-right to create and provoke future events in the event-chain. The most obvious attempt to extend the event-chain beyond 'Charlie Hebdo' involved staging public acts of apparent solidarity with the magazine, including trans-nationally memetic attempts to stage 'draw the Prophet' competitions. That several of these events were arranged quickly and independently of each other in the aftermath of the attacks is probably because this tactic first emerged after the *Jyllands Posten* cartoon conflict, and there was also a well-known attempt to establish an 'Everybody Draw Mohammed Day' in 2010 after online threats were made to the creators of the animated series *South Park*.

The first, unsuccessful, attempt to organize a 'Mohammed cartoon competition' was by the youth party of the *Perussuomalaiset* (True Finns), who had announced a competition and subsequent exhibition online on 14 February because the attacks 'once again show us the true nature of Islam' and 'the defence of freedom of speech concerns us all'. In April 2015, the small extreme-right Pro-NRW party in North Rhein-Westphalia successfully organized a competition entitled 'Freedom instead of Islam', with the winning entries posted on the 'free speech website' *Politically Incorrect*, a hugely successful 'counter-jihad' blog that was established in response to the *Jyllands Posten* cartoon controversy, and thus one of an important network of sites that have shaped a space for overt anti-Muslim racism by framing its 'honesty' as a refusal to surrender any more territory on freedom of speech.

However, by far the most significant attempt to further the event-chain through imitation garnered global headlines when two people were shot dead at a 'Muhammad Art Exhibit and Cartoon Contest' hosted at the Curtis Culwell Centre in Garland, Texas, in May 2015. The event was sponsored by Robert Spencer's website *Jihad Watch* and organized by the front group American Freedom Defense Initiative, established by Spencer and Pamela Geller and previously best known for the series of anti-Muslim subway ads in US cities which formed the basis for the initial discussion in this chapter. After the attack in Texas, other smaller tribute events were staged in Arizona, but this particular event also had transnational responses. Sharia Watch UK, fronted by the former UKIP candidate Anne Marie Waters, attempted to host a UK Draw Mohammed Competition and Exhibition in August 2015. The event was to be co-hosted with *Vive Charlie*, an 'online satirical magazine' established in April 2015 to 'exercise our rights to freedom of expression and freedom of speech', and which in practice acts as an online clearing house for material from the wider network of 'counter-jihad' and anti-Islam blogosphere.

A more successful event adaptation was staged by Geert Wilders and his Party for Freedom (PVV) in the Netherlands. Wilders had been a speaker at the event in Texas a day before the attack on the exhibition centre, and used this connection to demand of the Board of the Dutch Parliament that the winning cartoons from the Texas exhibition be displayed in the Parliament. This request was refused, but Wilders used the broadcast time allocated to the PVV by the Dutch Public Service Broadcaster to exhibit the winning cartoons on live television, on June 24th 2015, with the message that 'I do not broadcast the cartoons to provoke; I do it because we have to show that we stand for freedom of speech and that we will never surrender to violence. Freedom is our birthright. Freedom of speech must always prevail over terror and violence'.

Wilders was attempting to replicate the successful strategy of his 2008 film *Fitna*, a short, YouTube response-style video that expressly positioned itself in an event-chain narrative, as its opening shots reference Theo Van Gogh and Ayaan Hirsi Ali's (2003) film *Submission*, and the 'turban-shaped bomb' cartoon by Kurt Westergaard, which were included in the *Jyllands Posten* culture supplement cover from 2005. No Dutch broadcaster would accept *Fitna*, and it was broadcast online in April 2008, and subsequently became the subject of a freedom of speech roadshow, with Wilders, for example, being refused entry to the UK for a screening of his film in the House of Lords in February 2009. These attempts to claim a similar legitimacy by suturing 'Charlie Hebdo' to an event-chain narrative through such performative events were, with the exception of Wilders, mainly unsuccessful small-scale events organized by dispersed counter-jihad networks at their intersection with small far-right parties and movements. However, what is of interest in this event-chain is the structure of the event.

In *Courting the Abyss*, John Durham Peters (2005) argued that stand-offs over the remit of free expression depend on a 'threefold cast of characters'. There is firstly the protagonist who breaks a taboo in search of freedom. This act then seeks support from 'principled defenders of the open society', who may not agree or may disapprove of the message, but who will defend it not just on principle but instrumentally, as indicative of democratic health. Thirdly, there is the subject of the taboo, 'who takes offence?'. The historic template here is the march of the Nationalist Socialist Party of America through the Chicago suburb of Skokie (1977–78), an area populated by many elderly Holocaust survivors, and a march defended on First Amendment grounds by the American Council for Civil Liberties.

The dynamic of this triangulation, Durham Peters argues, is not just to open a space for racism through a recursive debate about the principle of freedom of speech, but also to position those who take offence as *the main problem*, as insufficiently integrated to the prevailing liberal-democratic norms. The attempt to integrate 'Charlie Hebdo' into an event-chain narrative of previous controversies seeks a shared threat to defining and non-negotiable European/Western values. The importance of a 'freedom of speech' frame to these spectacles is critical, even if it is as transparently opportunistic and strategic as the far-right turn to sexual freedom and gender equality as essential national characteristics. As such, these provocative media events work to inscribe racial logics – *what is the response of those incapable, or unwilling, of integration?* – for supposedly post-racial times.

# Hate speech and digital media platforms

To return in conclusion to the concept of hate speech, it is not difficult to find it similarly subject to complexity and distortion 'in the world'. Its usage is anyway often informed by a kind of exasperated worldliness, an insistence that communication does something and has effects, even if 'hate speech' as an action cannot be tracked and validated in determining terms of causality and consequence. As David Boromisza-Habashi argues, 'those who allege hate speech strive to achieve two social ends: to sustain a political and moral order in which hate speech is not tolerated, and to challenge other speakers who violate that political and moral order' (2013: 716). As such the basic idea of hate speech demands that hateful, racializing, scapegoating and humiliating communication be taken seriously, socially and politically, and that those who are subject to it have a right to contest it in terms that do not give precedence to speech as an abstract value. For all this worldly weight, nonetheless, the concept of hate speech is limiting as a framework for thinking about public communication, and this is particularly pronounced in relation to the domain of communication that it is now most firmly associated with – connective media platforms and the contemporary circulation of racist discourse.

The scale and speed of abusive communications facilitated and shaped by the networked interactivity of social media has come to be regarded as one of the most dominant aspects of platform media. It circulates both as ambient practice and spectacular outbreak (Sharma and Brucker, 2016). It is frequently a coordinated activity of the kinds of groups encountered in the previous chapter, and also a consequence of the networked opportunism provided by relative anonymity, immediate action-at-a-distance, and the generative dynamics of the social media 'pile-ons' which drive the 'increased visibility of social media activity directly attacking individuals and perpetuating everyday sexism and racism' (Highfield, 2016: loc 3394). Given the scale of abusive communications which connective media platforms can facilitate, there is a tendency in some popular commentary to regard it as somehow intrinsic to the form, or as a perversion of the participatory promise of interactive media. As Des Freedman (2014) argues, it should not come as a surprise that social media reflects 'the serious problems of the world in which it is located', and the tendency to regard 'hate speech' on social media as a consequence of mass access to a limited means of communication effects an unconvincing separation between what happens in and through social media from the broader socio-political processes that shape and frequently license it.

That said, it is also the case that the business model and affordances of social media platforms accelerate and amplify circulation in ways that have transformed the extent and reach of abusive communications. The idea of hate speech has become the main framework for understanding its dimensions and consequences, and for attempting to hold social media companies to account as content publishers and purveyors (Pohjonen, 2018). The real-time networking of social media communication sharpens the vexed question of incitement and causality, and there is certainly some evidence that under specific conditions social media dynamics act as an accelerant and opportunity structure for hate crime. A study by Müller and Schwarz, for example, examined an enormous corpus of anti-refugee posts on the Facebook pages of the far-right

*Alternative für Deutschland* party and demonstrated how 'anti-refugee hate crimes increase in areas with higher Facebook usage during periods of high anti-refugee salience' (2018: 3). However, as Pohjonen summarizes, much of the study of online hate speech is less concerned with thresholds of incitement than with insisting on two characteristics – that 'hate speech dehumanizes its victims according to their group identity, but it also amplifies the group identity of the perpetrator by attempting to create an antagonistic relationship between "us" and "them"' (2018: 6).

The problem with working definitions of online hate speech, however, is that the composite ideas of 'hate' and 'speech' are somewhat restrictive when it comes to understanding the discursive modalities and multi-media forms of digital racist expression. As Siapera and colleagues (2018) discuss, definitions of hate speech that converge on digital media inform divergent interventions in forms and processes of communication. While monitoring projects require precision in relation to the idea of 'imminent threat' to 'define the remit for judicial intervention', and social media companies require definitive approaches to content that demonstrably transgresses 'community standards', their research with civil society activists emphasized the need for 'more dynamic and nuanced definitions of racist speech' that allow for an understanding of how 'various expressions of hate speech, from illegal hate speech to thoughtless "banal racist" comments, tend to exist on a continuum of discursive online toxicity and reinforce one another' (2018: 34). Based on their research with activists involved in tracking or dealing with hate speech directed at minorities in Ireland, they propose a notion of 'racially loaded toxic speech' that 'conveys messages that entrench polarization; reinforce stereotypes; spread myths and disinformation; justify the exclusion, stigmatization, and inferiorization of particular groups; and reinforce exclusivist notions of national belonging and identity' (ibid: 38).

An expansive definition of this kind addresses the obvious tension between the desire for an actionable concept and the realization that 'hate' is only one modality of racist expression. The discussion of scavenging, fluency, debris and bricolage in previous chapters illustrated how these processes depend far less on overt hatefulness than on various forms of legitimation and reasonable aversion (and in fact, this gap between 'cold racism' and the connotations of hate speech has informed a predictable form of appropriation; the accusation that 'hate speech' is being used to shut down unpopular ideas and uncomfortable truths). This is not to underplay the exclusionary impacts of overt racist hate speech, but rather to emphasize the expansive repertoire of racializing discourses and practices which the concept of hate speech can neither encompass nor explain.

To this it could be added that the close association between 'hate speech' and individual agency further obscures the formative significance of platform affordances and dynamics to the articulation and circulation of 'racially loaded toxic speech'. Ariadna Matamoros-Fernández has suggested the term 'platformed racism' to capture the co-productivity of practice and platform, and the term has two senses, both of which are important for evaluating the explanatory and political salience of hate speech to digital media dynamics. The first 'evokes platforms as tools for amplifying and manufacturing racist discourse both by means of users' appropriations of their affordances and through their design and algorithmic shaping of sociability' (2017: 931). Platforms are not, despite their presentation by social media companies, neutral enablers of connection, but through their socio-technical design and economic prerogatives actively shape what it is that users do and are prompted to do. Zeynep Tufekci (2018), for example, has argued that YouTube's video-recommender system seems to promote and suggest videos that present ever more extreme and 'hardcore' content, linking, for example, videos of Donald Trump rallies to autoplaying 'white supremacist rants, Holocaust denials, and other disturbing content'. While these videos are likely to feature instances of overt hate speech, the public form this speech takes cannot be understood without incorporating the platform features and affordances that intensify its circulation.

The second aspect of 'platformed racism' more directly challenges the self-declared neutrality of social media companies by focusing on the 'mode of governance that might be harmful for some communities, embodied in platforms' vague policies, their moderation of content and their often arbitrary enforcement of rules' (Matamoros-Fernández, 2017: 931). Both Facebook and Twitter have been mired in controversy regarding both glaring inconsistencies in content moderation practices, and the lack of transparency as to content moderation policies and approaches. A 2017 study by ProPublica, for example, showed clear inconsistencies in whether or not anti-Muslim hate speech (involving calls for violence) was found to contravene 'community standards'. The study drew attention to the narrow, literal moderation remit which is inadequate for content that deploys sarcasm or ridicule, never minds the ways in which the intertextuality of memes can protect demeaning content against the threat of moderation. The lack of clarity in policies, unresponsiveness of moderation beyond automated processes, and delegated responsibility placed on those targeted by forms of 'racially loaded toxic speech' to drive the usually unsatisfactory process of moderation serve to reproduce wider racialized inequalities in terms of who can occupy and 'belong' in digital media space. The ambivalence this produces for people who also draw on connective media platforms for anti-racist aims and practices is the starting point for the next chapter.

# 6

## Anti-racism
## and digital media
## culture

# Introduction: the contradictions of the internet

From the insistence of anti-Black Face activism on the relation between the symbolic and material oppression, to the spontaneous expressions of anger and sorrow channelled into organizing to seek *#Justice4Trayvon*, to reporting fake 'Islamist' pages on Facebook, anti-racist actions and perspectives have featured consistently in the preceding analysis. The aim of this chapter is to provide an analytical framework for thinking about the significant range of anti-racisms that take shape through and in relation to digital media culture. It seeks to draw out different understandings of anti-racism at work in and across contexts, the forms of media work they engage in, and the public horizons that drive their interventions. Prior to that, however, a tension that has shadowed these previous discussions, and that loomed large in the analysis of connective media-enabled 'hate speech', needs to be addressed.

As Veronica Barassi (2015) notes, 'the development of mobile technologies and web 2.0 platforms has marked a new and complex transformation of repertoires of mediated political action'. These emergent possibilities for communicative participation and cooperation were rapidly invested with democratic promise, a promise distorted in the clumsy combination of technological determinism and Eurocentrism that marked discourses about 'Twitter Revolutions', and which paid insufficient attention to the dependence on infrastructures and platforms under corporate control and organized as commercial enterprises. As a consequence, a significant body of academic work has been divided between those that 'argued that the new web, for its interactive features, was offering unprecedented possibilities for user engagement, creativity and cooperation ... and those that have instead highlighted the fact that far from being democratic, web 2.0 technologies were in fact strengthening new forms of capitalist exploitation and corporate surveillance' (2015: 7). This contradiction needs to be addressed initially to situate mediated anti-racist action, and a useful starting point can be found in our global font of modern knowledge.

The online encyclopedia *Wikipedia* is now so ubiquitous that *Wikipedia* entries on aspects of *Wikipedia* constitute a distinctive genre on the site. The entry 'Racial bias on Wikipedia' focuses on collating criticism of its often scant and patchy entries on 'Black history', and racial bias in the framing and exposition of particular entries.

The banner message at the top of the article warns that 'the examples and the perspective in this article deal primarily with the U.S. and do not represent a worldwide view of the subject' (a qualification sometimes lacking in academic discussions of racism). Famous for its presumed fidelity to a 'wisdom of crowds' logic, the 'racial bias' entry links to a *Huffington Post* article which argues that the preponderance of 'technically inclined, English-speaking white-collar men' within the site's user hierarchy accounts for 'Wikipedia's gender and racial bias problem' (Boboltz, 2015). The *HuffPo* article takes this one-line demographic summary from, in turn, a hyperlinked Wikipedia entry, this time concerning 'The average Wikipedian'.

The entry goes on to highlight efforts to address the problem, pointing to several 'edit-a-thon' initiatives, including one involving Wikimedia D.C. and Howard University – a historically African American institution – during Black History Month in 2015, which brought together staff and students to coordinate a list of entries that needed to be expanded, and to identify potential entries that were completely absent, often centring on African American achievements neglected or marginalized in the existing database (Smith, 2015). While, as *Wired* reported in the same year, the Wikipedia Foundation has demonstrated a commitment to enhancing 'the coverage of women, minorities, the LGBTQ community and other under-represented groups on Wikipedia' (Lapowsky, 2015), not all such initiatives are conducted as cooperative ventures, nor focused on a representational logic. The #whitecurriculum campaign in the UK, for example, which seeks to challenge the often taken-for-granted whiteness, Eurocentrism and elided coloniality of modern social science and humanities curricula, chose the same period to seek to organize a 'decolonise Wikipedia' editing event (WMCW collective, UCL 2015). Here, the aim was not just to augment the site with new or expanded entries, but also to unpick the practice of knowledge production through a critique of what Barnor Hesse (2007) terms the 'white analytics' which 'routinely ignore colonial and racial formations' in established thought and institutionalized knowledge.

There is no contradiction between Wikipedia's institutional commitment to diversity and the resilient pervasiveness of 'white analytics' in its mode of knowledge construction. As José Van Dijck documents, central to Wikipedia's operation are its 'five pillars' or principles, including the 'core content policy' of striving for a 'neutral point of view' (NPoV). The NPoV rule, she argues, is 'a guiding principle for building a functional apparatus, but that apparatus simultaneously shapes the meaning of neutrality as the "average opinion" or "shared interpretation'" (2013: 142). Van Dijck quotes the historian Daniel O'Sullivan, who criticizes this view-from-nowhere proceduralism as a 'bureaucratic policing' that stunts the project's 'potential to proliferate voices and dissent', meaning that 'it is in danger of merely mirroring the typical knowledge economies of the West' (2011: 48, in 2013: 141–2). Neutrality imagined in such terms intimately overlaps with the #whitecurriculum's pithy notion of the racialized-as-white subject as the 'Greenwich Mean Time of identity' (op.cit.). It also feeds smoothly into the drive of debatability, where the salience and status of racism as a topic, causal factor or 'accusation' is a recurrent focus of Wikipedia's 'edit wars'.

In a large-scale data study in ten different language versions, Yasseri et al. (2014) ranked the topics that produce edit wars according to the occurrence of 'mutual reverts', that is, where one editor substantially undoes the work of another, restoring a previous version, and vice versa. Topics such as 'Muhammad' 'Race and intelligence', 'circumcision' and 'Christianity' featured in the English language top ten, whereas 'Israel, Adolf Hitler, The Holocaust and God' were the most contested-in-common across language groups. Robert S. Wolff's (2013) study of the 'Origins of the American Civil War' entry examines one such revert conflict by focusing on the 'crowd-sourced' crafting of the entry, drawing on the changes to the entry over time and the discussions archived on the entry's discussion page. Noting how historical entries become sites where the ways 'the past possesses different meanings' are articulated, Wolff documents an editing conflict over the inclusion of the term racism, prompted by its deletion by a contributor from descriptions of 'non-slaveowning whites in the South' on the grounds that 'The term is a modern one and not neutral for a historical article' (2013: 68).

Given Wikipedia's privileged position in Google's search rankings, it is frequently a site not just for debatability's circuitries but also for racist trolling and information laundering. In particular, articles on 'race and intelligence'-related topics are prime sites of sustained activity for the far-right.[1] In a report for the Southern Poverty Law Centre, Justin Ward (2018) notes how the organizational assumption that editing is undertaken in good faith to improve the quality of an article means that while anonymous vandalism is easy to detect, adept contributors associated with 'scientific racism' and 'human biodiversity' journals and blogs 'tend to maintain a moderate, non-confrontational tone and adopt a posture of academic neutrality, so they are less likely to run afoul of site-wide rules and more likely to make edits that stand'.

These glimpses of racist and anti-racist struggle over publicized meaning on Wikipedia work with, against and around what Van Dijck terms the site's 'consensual apparatus', not only comprised of the principles and community orientations mentioned, but also managed through a 'sociotechnical system of sophisticated protocols distributing permission levels' to different contributors within a hierarchy of user categories (op. cit.: 136). This user hierarchy involves the integration of human and non-human agents, as the use of 'bots' – scripts for auto-mated editing – are critical to dealing with the sheer scale of content produced through site activity. Wikipedia's 'engineered social order', as Van Dijck describes it, 'is an integral system of human–bot interaction that helps produce and maintain a kind of modulated sociality which is unprecedented in scale' (ibid: 138). These various forms of racist antagonism, and varied trajectories of anti-racist action, are facilitated and shaped by the form, structures and processes of *Wikipedia* as a sociotechnical system.

That these opposing political tendencies take shape in and through *Wikipedia* indicates that the internet, as Whitney Philips and Ryan Milner point out, is *ambivalent,* that is, the already-existing ambiv-alence of 'basic behavioural and aesthetic dimensions of everyday expression' are 'thrown into hyperdrive ... by the tools of digital mediation' (2017: 15). The idea of ambivalence recalls how previ-ous, critical histories of media technologies and forms have underlined the need to avoid 'asserting that everything has gotten worse, or ... assuming that there has been a continuous improvement' (Briggs and Burke, 2005: 4). That this pattern of assertion has renewed the temptation of pendular swings of optimism and pessimism may be frustrating, but it can be comprehended in relation to what 'new media' seemed to offer: the redistribution of communicative resources and possibilities beyond the 'few-to-many' power relations of the mass media era. In Des Freedman's (2014) evaluation:

> Going back to the 'sterile debate' between digital optimists and pessimists about the extent to which digital platforms facilitate opacity *or* transparency, scarcity *or* abundance and indeed dis-tributed *or* concentrated power, the point is that an emphasis on contradiction allows us to understand that it is not a question of choosing one or the other but of appreciating the tensions and constraints that shape the dynamics of the digital world. Indeed it is entirely possible that social media can be tools of empowerment

*and* control, that the internet is subject to centrifugal *and* centripetal pressures and that the web both encourages new voices *and* consolidates existing ones. By accentuating a materialist approach that acknowledges the contradictions of capitalist development ... we can avoid the pitfalls of a binary approach and reject the determinism of those who fetishize technology above all else. (2014: loc 2079)

Freedman's insistence on capitalist contradiction has particular resonances on the terrain of race. The paradox of corporate social media is that while it now presents a significant infrastructure for public discourse, it is privately owned, and attuned to 'deriving profits from all communicative aspects of life' (Langlois, 2014: 170). *If the service is free, you are the product*; as is by now well-known, social media corporations accumulate immense stocks of data, not just informing targeted consumer and behavioural profiling but also facilitating forms of surveillance predicated on accruing patterned knowledge about the practices, habits and lives of their users. Profiling and surveillance are historically racialized practices, and therefore the 'racial structure' of the internet has emerged as a key site of Internet Studies' otherwise relatively limited engagement with race and racism (see Daniels, 2012). The presumed neutrality of technology has been critiqued by examining how a 'racial ideology *about* technology' associates 'whiteness with "progress", "technology", and "civilization", while situating blackness within a discourse of "nature", "primitivism" and pre-modernity' (Hobson, 2008: 114). Research on structuration goes past such cultural narratives and the everyday racism amplified in online spaces to ask, as Charlton McIlwain questions, 'what significance and use-value does race have in the political economy of the web, and how does racial meaning and value get systematically produced and circulated throughout the web?' (2017: 1077).

Research on Google's search engine, for example, has demonstrated how racial logics become embedded in code and informational architecture. Safiya Noble's work on how 'privately managed, black-boxed information-sorting tools have become essential to many data-driven decisions' (2018: 2) offers the idea of 'algorithmic oppression' to describe how, for example, the commercially oriented curatorial work of algorithmic sifting proliferates racialized and sexualized imagery of women of colour. The technical features and affordances of social media platforms are similarly implicated. The photo-sharing platform

Flickr's 'auto-tagging' feature generated headlines for adding the labels 'ape' and 'animal' to photos of black people (Hern, 2015). A study by the independent investigative journalism newsroom *ProPublica* in 2016 demonstrated how Facebook's advertising micro-targeting allowed advertisers to exclude target audiences by 'ethnic affinity' – a category Facebook assigns to users on the basis of online behaviour rather than opt-in identification – raising the possibility of automated discrimination in ads for rental housing or services (Angwin and Parris Jr, 2016; for further methodological discussion, see Neel, 2016). The US-based Data for Black Lives Movement (2018) has subsequently called on Facebook to commit anonymized data to a public data trust which would be available to black researchers and community-led organizations to 'fill the gaps in publicly available data that is outdated, full of errors, and often collected as a tactic of law enforcement, with the intent of criminalization and surveillance'.

Contradiction entails, however, that at the same time as historically entrenched forms of racist profiling and stereotyping may be extended and amplified through corporate digital structures, the same structures facilitate their public contestation. It is not just the case that connective media provide a contingent but important site for racialized subjects to confront their elision or misrepresentation, or, indeed, the limits of always having to respond to racism. Digital media platforms have been formative in the flourishing of anti-racist media projects, actors historically marginalized from or forced to struggle for inclusion in a mediated public sphere dependent on capital-intensive print technologies and broadcast infrastructure. Consequently, a prominent genre of projects focuses on increasing the presence and diversity of 'voices' from communities or backgrounds consistently excluded from the national public sphere, or granted access under particular conditions and through limiting frames.

Sustained media practices have also developed from responses to crises where media misrepresentation has played an acute role. *Megafonen* (Megaphone), the 'new popular movement' that first took shape in the Stockholm suburb of Husby in 2008, was founded after the murder of a local football player, Ahmed Ibrahim Ali: ' ... it was out of frustration over what was perceived in Husby youth community as a discriminatory representation of the murder ... that the Megaphone took off as the voice of Husby, challenging the dominant media's stigmatising stereotypes of suburbia – a new "megaphone" for voices seldom heard' (Schierup et al., 2014: 14). As a social justice, housing and popular education movement, *Megafonen*'s media work has been shaped by '(understanding) … the need to create our own platforms, structures and activities which allowed us to develop intellectually, socially, mentally as equal citizens' (quoted in Schierup et al., 2018: 11). This embedded media capacity proved critical during the Stockholm urban uprising in 2013, where *Megafonen* was able to document police violence and 'stubbornly (work) to make the public and politicians look beyond the burning cars to see the reality of unequal citizenship and the structural issues to explain what was taking place' (ibid: 15). Similarly, *Trappy Blog* is one of several websites to be developed in the deprived and socially segregated *quartiers populaires* of Paris – in this instance in Trappes in the Saint-Quentin-en-Yvelines area – with the intention of providing young people with a platform to not only respond to sensationalist reporting, but also to develop local journalism for and about their neighbourhoods. While using social media in conventional ways, *Trappy Blog* has disseminated its journalism by reaching agreements with *France Info* and *Alternatives Économique*s to feature its articles on their sites.

As with the far-right networks discussed previously, cross-platform media logics have ensured that in each of these cases, projects that have been initiated on one platform have been able to 'scale up' their operations and extend their remits and forms across sites of media work, expanding from the desire to 'give voice' to developing journalism practices, forms of community media, and funding strategies. The reality of contradiction is not just that the expanded media space allows for the circulation of more 'racist and anti-racist content', but also that its political economy, architecture and platform affordances simultaneously extend racializing processes while expanding the space for anti-racist action. Capturing the reality of contradiction, therefore, requires far more than lists and counter-lists, sobering or inspiring though these examples of racializing extension and anti-racist amplification may be. To understand, as Barassi (2015) argues, how the internet and connective media are impacting on political participation and democratic processes, 'we should not focus on disruption and continuity, but we should instead explore the complex dialectics between transformation and continuity; between the technical and the social; between the political economy of the web and its lived critique'. The next section lays out the dimensions of an analytical framework for anti-racism in digital media culture, before proceeding to examine domains of anti-racist action with a mediated dimension.

# Anti-racism and digital media: an analytical framework

## Anti-racism: plurality and divergence

The first dimension is the particularity of forms of anti-racism. In an essay assessing the critical relevance of contemporary practices, Ghassan Hage (2015) identifies six key functions evident in histories of anti-racism: *reducing the incidence of racist practices* ('making it difficult for racists to externalise their racism whether in society at large [everyday racism] or within institutions [structural racism]'); *fostering a non-racist culture* (challenging stereotypes, educating people about the 'consequences of their views', working to demonstrate how racism works with and intersects with other processes and structures); *supporting the victims of racism* (from emergency material, physical and emotional support to insisting on the 'social and historical nature of the psychological fault lines that make racialized subjects particularly vulnerable to racist injury'); *empowering racialized subjects* (avoiding creating heroic relations of dependency and supporting and being led by the struggle of those racialized in society); *transforming racist relations into better relations* (by approaching racism as a set of 'bad relations' that require challenge and transformation into better modes of co-existence); and *fostering an a-racist culture* (to work from transforming relations to a 'state of affairs in which racial identification is no longer a relevant or salient mode of identification') (2015: loc 2995–3091).

While these aspects recur in the media actions discussed subsequently, to take them directly as a framework *for* anti-racism is complicated by the fact that anti-racism, as Alastair Bonnett notes, 'cannot be adequately understood as the inverse of racism' (2000: 2). Varying traditions of anti-racism operate with different understandings of racism, its relations to 'race', its intersection with class and gender and what is required to confront it. This divergence is often shaped not only by the contextuality of movements, but also by differences over tactics that recur across contexts, such as whether and how to confront far-right street movements (see Bray, 2018, for a discussion). It is also the case that anti-racist mobilizations, particularly involving larger left movements and/or professional non-governmental organizations, differ hugely on the question of 'empowering racialized subjects' and trusting in the leadership of those who experience racism in society (Lentin, 2004: 237–304).

Further, as Hage argues, 'anti-racism needs to always remain in touch with the alter-racial, those imaginings of an non- or a-racial society with which it needs to be continuously injected at every stage of the anti-racist struggle' (2015: loc 3205). As Chapter 1's discussion of varying interpretations of postracialism indicated, these alter-racial visions can differ profoundly. And, as the subsequent discussion of anti-racist universalism and decolonial anti-racism in interpretations of Riss's Alan Kurdi cartoon demonstrated, they can be openly antagonistic to each other. In some assessments, this poses a political problem. According to Michel Wievorka, 'scavenging' has an accretive power for racist discourse, but works to weaken anti-racism, for

> ... racists are not troubled by possible internal contradictions ... but anti-racism cannot function this way; it does not stand in a perfectly symmetrical relationship to the evil that it opposes. It becomes ineffectual and even counterproductive the more it appears to be incoherent and, worse still, incapable of overcoming its contradictions, whereas racism draws its strength from amalgamating the processes it effects. (2015: 147)

Do the complex cultural space of digital media production, and the often intensive generativity of social media dynamics, exacerbate this? This chapter emphasizes the need to avoid totalizing assessments, and to focus on the contingency of media dynamics and the contextual shape of political action. However, it does argue that given the temporal-spatial shifts in how racism produces racialized populations as a problem, and how it integrates a shifting corpus of rationales, discourses and associations, the networked and transnational space of exchange structured by digital media provides significant opportunities not just for anti-racist connection, but also for imagination. When viewed transnationally, Alana Lentin argues in her study of European anti-racist movements,

> The temporal differences between anti-racisms in different settings, their varying speeds, the diversified conceptualisations of 'race' and racism and the radically different standpoints of activists, both across countries and between organisations in a single society, contribute to ensuring that something is always 'going on'. (2004: 305)

It is the wager of this chapter that, while the individualizing drive and subjectification of social media remains to be reckoned with, digital media space intensifies this sense of 'something always going on' in multiple ways: the transnational sharing of resources and sources of inspiration; the mediated commemoration of events and well-known and unjustly obscured anti-racist activists; digital storytelling about past and current struggles and the repertoires of action and thought they mobilize; rolling interactive critiques of media texts, and challenges to dominant news framings; visual archives and meme circulation that provide access to what could be termed an 'anti-racist debris'. A proper survey of different traditions of anti-racism is beyond the scope of this chapter, but as an observation, it is often the case that histories and iconographies of resistance from the US dominate the anti-racist imagination. Digital media culture provides transnational access to important historical resources and contemporary connections from multiple contexts.[2] The challenge, under these conditions, involves not only the dynamics of contradiction, but also translation and relational work.

## Anti-racist action: agency and public political culture

If anti-racism is a heterogeneous site of political traditions, understandings and strategies, what does anti-racism in and through digital media seek to achieve, and on what basis? Here, once again, it is worth adapting from research on anti-racist politics to think about media practices. In her study of political movements, Lentin maps anti-racist practices 'along a continuum of proximity-to-distance from the public political culture of the nation-state' (2004: 36). The concept of 'public political culture' is drawn from John Rawls' understanding of it as a widely shared and thus legitimating ensemble of ideas associated with 'democracy as a principle ordering of the modern, western state' (ibid: 2). Lentin's continuum, while acknowledging that these positions are very often blended in practice, places forms of anti-racism in relation to these hegemonic ideas. At one end, proximity involves combating racism through discourses of human rights, meritocracy or fairness, values assumed to be upheld by the state, and 'inscribed in national political culture'. At the other, distance is marked by a focus on the state as an ambivalent institutionalization and nexus of power, hence 'anti-racism in this view necessarily contains a critique of modern nation-state histories, which are as much narratives of colonialism, fascism, and the suppression of immigrants' rights as they are those of universal suffrage, the defence of human rights and the suppression of totalitarianism' (ibid: 3).

This provides a basis for analyzing the divergent ways in which anti-racists understand and relate to the nation-state as *both* a racist and anti-racist configuration, and therefore whether and to what extent they look to the institutions of state, and the norms of public political culture, for the 'solutions' to racism (ibid: 39–44). Proximity-to-distance, in terms of mediated anti-racism, has two intertwined dimensions. The first is discursive, focusing on what values and vocabulary an action lays claim to, the extent to which these draw on the presumed norms of the public sphere *as anti-racist norms*. The second is practice-based, involving the degree to which the action intervenes in the logic and dynamics of the platform/medium, or depends on intervention in the medium by a regulatory or disciplinary agency to confront racism.

Practices may simultaneously mark their distance from and draw on the presumed norms of public political culture. For example, Van Zoonen et al.'s (2010) study of response videos on YouTube to Geert Wilder's propaganda video *Fitna* demonstrates how one cluster of videos sought 'dialogue', patiently 'explaining Islam' and engaging in comment thread discussion, whereas another cluster was aimed at 'culture-jamming' by uploading hundreds of very short videos tagged as 'Fitna' or 'Geert Wilders', thus 'exploiting the typical internet features of information abundance and burying the movie under other ones with a contrasting message' (2010: 1289). This simultaneity illustrates that the continuum is intended as a heuristic device, an analytical orientation to examining actions, not a drive to categorize them or rank them for 'purity'. For example, the direct action of tearing down the anti-Muslim subway posters, and going to court to have them legally removed – as discussed in Chapter 5 – are separated from each other on this continuum by the question of legality. Yet in practice, direct action and legal remedy are not always in tension, with both deployed within large movement strategies. On the other hand, there is ostensibly less of a gap between the Black History Month edit-a-thon and the #CurriculumSoWhite intervention, in that both are intervening in the consequences of neutrality-as-colourblindness. However, given the former was conducted in public cooperation with Wikipedia, and the latter autonomously, their orientation to the consensual values of 'public political culture' is quite different.

## Anti-racist media: genres, practices, publics

This analytical framework requires paying attention to the multiplicity of media practices, and the varying publics that they seek to address and potentially mobilize into some form of action. This applies to social media practices, for as Tim Highfield notes, 'To understand everyday politics *on* social media, we also need to understand the practices, logics and vernacular of everyday social media' (2016: loc 1348, original emphasis). It also needs to be considered how these practices are appropriated, scaled and adapted for political interventions. Anti-racist media practices draw on the resources and repertoires of action developed through broader oppositional media work. Leah Lievrouw (2011) provides a useful typology of 'genres of alternative and activist new media', focusing on *culture jamming, alternative computing* (such as antifa hackers 'doxxing' far-right activists by accessing their identities and personal details on far-right sites and making them publicly available) *participatory journalism* (as with *Megafonen* and *Trappy Blog*'s work), and *commons knowledge* (central to the edit-a-thon strategies of mobilizing 'outsider' knowledge) (2011: 19–26). Social media use is most closely associated with the final genre, of 'mediated mobilization', where users 'cultivate interpersonal networks online and … mobilise those networks to engage in live and mediated collective action' (ibid: 25).

As activist media genres assume some form of collective action, it is important to broaden the conceptual framework to include media interactions that are less coordinated and more ambient. Of relevance to anti-racist practice is the literature on 'citizen media', defined by Clemencia Rodriguez as 'communication spaces where citizens can learn to manipulate their own languages, codes, signs and symbols empowering them to name the world in their own terms' (2011: 24). In Baker and Blaagaard's (2016) formulation, the category of 'citizen media' holds open a space for 'unaffiliated' action in relation to the collective orientation of 'activist' media, despite the evident overlaps in practices and genres. While their conceptualization of citizen media as 'the physical artefacts, digital content, practices, performative interventions and discursive formations of affective sociality produced by unaffiliated citizens as they act in public space' (ibid: 16) usefully broadens the scope for thinking about anti-racist media practices, the concept of 'citizen media' arguably does not. It is the intention, in conceptualizations of citizen media, to reclaim the idea of 'citizen' to a sense of participation beyond a formalist understanding of the political status conferred within the system of nation-state sovereignty. Yet if, as Chapter 3 argued, it is the very system of stratified rights that produces migrant 'illegality', then it is difficult to anchor the category of 'citizen media' in relation to anti-racist politics that, inter alia, contests how race is renewed in and through the distribution of citizenship.

Finally, it is necessary to think about the publics addressed, shaped and called into being by these media practices. While this analysis has been consistently critical of ideas of the 'public sphere' conceived of as unitary and given political coherence by processes of public deliberation, it must also be noted that the desire to address, intervene in, or influence *the* public remains a critical threshold for many – though by no means all – forms and traditions of anti-racist activism. It is important to be careful as to what this threshold does and does not involve. Imagining 'the public' as a space of political action does not mean orienting action towards the insidious banality of 'public opinion', blunting critique and interventions so as not to alienate a mythic 'middle ground', reproducing the policing of public/private distinctions in the service of 'acceptable politics', or conceding legitimacy to dominant constructions of whiteness. Rather, it is the recognition that, in the context of the nation-state, where struggle is focused on building consciousness of racist structures and practices, forging alliances, and forcing change within institutions, state practices and the distribution of socio-cultural power, 'the public' retains this unitary, rather than unified, charge.

Of course, this charge co-exists with a keen awareness that the conditions and processes of public discourse have become hugely complex, and that the proliferation of technologies that shift the conditions for participation in public communication also transforms the contours and textures of publics. While decades of media and communication research have cumulatively examined the (uneven and unequal yet powerful) globalization of communications, it is certainly the case, as Ingrid Volkmer argues, that there is a residual 'dominance of the paradigm of territorial boundedness of publics in the debate of public communication' (2014: 13). However, a more subtle yet equally pressing limitation is the difficulty of conceptualizing the scale, multiplicity and subjectivity of communicative terrains:

Whereas decades ago, trans-border communication was understood as being either 'international' (i.e. connecting nations), 'trans-national' (reaching sections of several nations simultaneously) or 'spatial' (a secluded sphere of digital flow), today's globalized communications across advanced micro-networks of subjective platforms are no longer 'trans-border' but rather discursively interrelated. In this sense, the communication sphere within a globalized scope is no longer an extension but is situated in interrelated subjective micro-networks. In other words, the global and the national and even the local are no longer distinct spheres but merge in particular in contexts of communicative spheres across diverse sites of subjective micro-networks. (ibid: 2–3)

These conditions transform understandings and practices of public engagement, and exist in tension with the critical threshold of 'the public' enfolded to the still-resilient political formation of the nation-state. Further, they proliferate, as Chapter 1 discussed, what Volkmer calls 'public horizons'. The 'horizon' is infused with a sense of possibility, not only of the 'reflexive interdependence' and potential relations that develop between actors, but also of limit, as these dynamic and shifting densities of communicative action are 'scattered across different discursive sites within globalized communicative horizons' (ibid: 8). This adds a further layer of ambivalence, and informs, as the next section examines, the concerted theoretical attention to frequently significant, yet transient and contingent, mediated publics.

# Mobilizing oppositional and resistant publics

## Counter-publics and public formulations

Arguably there is a pronounced inattention[3] in Media and Communication Studies to histories of independent media-making informed by anti-racist aims and sensibilities, beyond struggles to transform dominant modes of representation (Chapter 2), or to challenge structural inequalities in access to media institutions. This empirical inattention is most pronounced when contrasted with the degree of critical theoretical engagement invested in questions of representation and recognition, particularly in relation to conceptualizing the 'public sphere'. One of the most influential interventions on these lines has been Nancy Fraser's (1990) notion[4] of the 'subaltern counter-public'. Fraser takes aim at the ideological presumption of open access to the political life of the 'bourgeois public sphere', and the attendant understanding of the democratic role of deliberative engagement. In her analysis, this idealization is ahistorical, predicated on eliding how 'Women of all classes were excluded from official political participation precisely on the basis of ascribed gender status, while plebeian men were formally excluded by property qualifications. Moreover, in many cases, women and men of racialized ethnicities of all classes were excluded on racial grounds' (1990: 63).

When these historical elisions are addressed, Fraser argues, it becomes clear that the public was never unitary, but composed of multiple, competing and frequently silenced, antagonistic publics. While these legally forced exclusions have been democratically resisted and transformed over time, a latent idealization of the public as a space of interaction between equal interlocutors endures. This promotes magical thinking; the durability of structured and informal inequalities vanish from idealized sight, and the multiplicity and antagonisms of intersecting publics are elided in favour of the insistent unity invoked in 'the public'. The idea of subaltern counter-publics disrupts this imaginary, conceptualizing them as spaces 'where members of subordinated social groups invent and circulate counter discourses to formulate oppositional interpretations of their identities, interests and needs' (ibid). These spaces have a dialectical character, in that they are often maintained as 'spaces of withdrawal and regroupment' while also functioning 'as bases and training grounds for agitational activities directed towards wide publics' (ibid: 68).

In a reflection on Fraser's argument in her essay on the historical emergence of 'the Black Public Sphere' in the US, Catherine R. Squires (2002) accepts this dialectical dimension while questioning the suppositions that the counter-public as *concept* can too easily reproduce. The 'counter' dimension has, in much usage, been given coherence through either a presumption of 'shared marginal identity', or the expression of relatively coherent counter-ideologies. This tendency to fix resistant and mobilizing practices within 'counter-public' collectives often fails to reflect either the intersectional 'heterogeneity of marginalized groups' or the diversity of public-making practices. Publics are not straightforward expressions of group identity, rather

> ... a Black public is an emergent collective composed of people who (a) engage in common discourses and negotiations of what it means to be Black, and (b) pursue particularly defined Black interests. This definition, although still wedded to the idea that there is a Black social group, does allow for heterogenous Black publics to emerge, and also for people who do not identify as Black, but are concerned with similar issues, to be involved in a coalition with Black people. (2002: 454).

This emphasis on the coalitional practices and tensions at play in a given formation stresses that resistant publics do not solely take shape as a reaction to oppression, but also as a consequence of 'internal politics' and contingent access to material and symbolic resources. Based on a reading of African American liberation struggles during the nineteenth and twentieth centuries, Squires integrates the idea of a 'counter-public' into a more relational, heuristic model. A public can *enclave* itself, focusing on internal debate and collective intellect, while avoiding repressive and derogatory treatment in the wider public sphere, or respond as a *counter-public*, engaging in wider debate and movement-building, or act as a *satellite*, deliberately building shared interests and capacities on its own terms (to the extent possible) while strategically engaging in periodic wider public engagement (ibid: 457–63).

The counter-public encompasses media activism, but as a dimension of broader collective and communicative mobilization. Nevertheless, discussions of resistant and alternative media action have, in recent decades, been oriented to this concept, and it is important to situate it in the digital media era by carrying forward the careful differentiation that emerges in historicized accounts such as Squires'. Éric Fassin (2018), for example, draws substantially on Fraser's account to argue that social media has become a space where that which normally remained inaudible in 'dominant public space' in France can now be heard. The 'counter-publics' forcing anti-racist, feminist and queer perspectives into the 'national conversation' demonstrate that their marginality is not, as is so often suggested in dismissive account of 'identity politics', a consequence of 'separatism', but a product of exclusion. Racialized people in France, he argues, seized on social media as a 'subaltern counter-space' in a context where there was no room in dominant public space for the anger that had gathered in protests against state racism and racism in public culture, and where social media was an obvious alternative to a mainstream media that simply 'never gives them the chance to speak'.

In his assessment, this powered a particular dialectic between movement retrenchment and public agitation, as a powerful political vocabulary derived from the decolonial movement, Afrofeminism and other anti-racist and intersectionalist political currents became more pronounced in an 'expanded discursive space'. Fassin's use of the idea captures the force of certain political relations in contemporary France, namely that the public organizing of decolonial and autonomous anti-racist movements has been treated, by politicians on the left as well as the right, as an unacceptable expression of 'communitarianism' that violates the 'neutrality' of the Republican public sphere. That is, counter-public activity is framed as *contrary to the public*, a charge which leaves the racialized construction of the public outside of the discussion.[5]

Yet while the idea of counter-publics remains relevant as a starting point for capturing relations of exclusion and antagonism in public culture, and the contextual specificity of his discussion is a useful reminder that transnational platforms also facilitate intensely localized dynamics, the counter-public idea does not fully capture the ways in which coalitional anti-racisms are networked and mediated.

In the febrile atmosphere following the January 2015 Paris attacks, a mesh of political opinions and identifications was mediated through the deceptively dialectical hashtags *#JeSuisCharlie* and *#JeNeSuisPasCharlie*. In Simon Dawes' analysis, the speed with which these hashtags circulated underscored the slowness of 'traditional French media to even acknowledge the polysemy … of discordant voices (that) sought to make themselves heard to say that, although they also condemned the attacks, they were not Charlie' (2017: 180). When it did become a focus of mainstream media discussion, little attempt was made to distinguish the very different critiques mediated by the negation of 'I am Charlie', framing instead the hashtag as evidence of a division between 'the reasoned political subjectivity of the French state and media, and the discredited moral subjectivity of those who "do not accept or understand republican values"' (Dawes, 2015: 4).

As Romain Badouard's (2016) study of the *#JeNeSuisPasCharlie* hashtag demonstrates, the assumption that these two opposing hashtags mapped onto any such substantive polarization of public debate was not borne out in the data. At most, the polyphony could be organized into three broad, equally distributed tendencies: a rejection of *Charlie Hebdo* as an incarnation of the 'spirit of 1968' reviled by ultra-Catholic, traditionalist and identitarian tendencies on the capacious French political right-wing; a widespread critical position best described as 'I am Charlie, but', which sought to condemn the attacks while marking a distance from the politics of the publication, or from the coerciveness of 'national unity'; and a concentrated focus by French Muslims on the effects of the celebration of a 'right to offend' in a public context where Muslim identities are consistently held up for scrutiny and adjudication.

To capture this mediated multiplicity, Dawes turns to one of several concepts formed to capture the transience of digitally mediated formations. Drawing on Axel Bruns and Jean E. Burgess's (2011) idea of 'ad hoc publics' that are mobilized through and shape intensive media events begins to mark out certain limits to the analytical value of the 'counter-public' for media analysis. While the ad hoc public of *#JeNeSuisPasCharlie* was formed in opposition to the dominant media and political establishment framing of the attacks, and 'in part gave expression to a sense of voiceless-ness for the Muslim community in the French public sphere', the hashtag was not a straightforward mechanism for mobilizing counter-publics. It acted as a discursive device for the 'heterogenous construction' of a collective identity given transitory coherence through how oppositional expression is materialized by and through Twitter (Dawes, 2017: 185–8). Consequently, Salovaara argues that the dominant focus on *what people were trying to say* through the hashtag ignores the 'spatiality of events, their networked structure, and the role of human and non-human actors in re-assembling complex political subjectivities' (2015: 103).

The interplay of these dimensions indicates why Twitter's 'near instantaneous, multiplex, globalized, socially networked and public' character has prompted considerable theorization as to how it facili-tates and shapes public formations (Murthy, 2013: 100). Co-joining an analysis of the 'techno-sociality' of connective media to Squires' anti-essentialist analysis, Sanjay Sharma's (2013) study of 'Black Twitter' emphasizes the problem of reducing Twitter's 'digital-race assemblage' to the expression of '*a priori* identitarian categories'. The idea of 'Black Twitter' – a shorthand encompassing significant African American Twitter usage, the circulation of memes and hashtags, and the prevalence of 'Black cultural trending topics' – gained general attention initially as a way of countering perceptions of the internet as a white space, while also, inevitably, being fetishized as a cultural novelty (Brock, 2012). Sharma argues that the significance of Black Twitter 'does not hinge on claiming a "hashtag community" as a radical online anti-racist practice' (2013: 48), recalling Paul Gilroy's criticism of anti-racisms that misrep-resent 'the rich complexity of black life by reducing it to nothing more than a response to racism' (1990: 208).

It also draws attention to the limits of focusing on user identity and behaviour to the exclusion of the technocultural operations of digital media, leading to 'inadequately perceiving the production of new forms of racial coding, interaction and emergence' (ibid: 64). Analyzing the mobilization of (anti-racist) publics does not require jettisoning a focus on political agency and the discursivity of interventions, but requires attending also to their *materialization*, and thus their contingency. 'Networked publics', as boyd has suggested, must be understood in rela-tion to '(1) the space constructed through networked technologies and (2) the imagined collective that emerges as a result of the intersection of people, technology and practice' (2010: 39). By focusing on Twitter as a platform, and conceptual understandings of the public formations it connects and structures, the remainder of this section sets out some ways in which anti-racist politics has taken public shape through the micro-blogging site.

## Hashtag publics

In the previous chapters, the discussion of Twitter has focused on its role as a platform for news dissemination, processes of disinformation, and expansive participation in heightened and intensive 'public horizons'. In a discussion of social media, politics and 'affective publics', Zizi Papacharissi (2014) captures these aspects in her description of it as a 'social awareness system', built on its 'always on' and 'real time' properties, acting as a conduit for information flows between different networked publics. The generativity of Twitter stems from its particular communicative affordances, as 'addressivity and conversational markers are essential to the formation and direction of information flows via Twitter. Networked publics are further textually rendered through the use of hashtags that define a topic of a direction for information sharing' (2014: 33).

Hashtags, as *#JeSuisCharlie* attests, do not just organize content and connect dispersed users. They also act as discursive devices, intensifying and diversifying engagements, amplifying certain themes, and shaping evanescent sociality. Papacharissi distinguishes between 'endogenous tags', which are generated by Twitter-specific activities, and 'exogenous tags', which relate to an event outside of the Twitter system, such as breaking news or response to a political situation (ibid: 33–4).

This communicative architecture and the practices that have developed through it accentuate Twitter as a 'contemporary medium for storytelling, enabling co-creating and collaborative filtering that sustains ambient and affective engagement for the publics it interconnects' (ibid, 2014: 27). Taking these dimensions and practices onto the terrain of anti-racism, one way of understanding anti-racisms mediated by Twitter is as interventions in dominant modes of story-telling; disrupting some, augmenting others, and collectively narrating still more. Perhaps the most evident of these is confronting racist expression and racializing logics, in everyday encounters in the informational flow or through the intensive and accelerated dynamics that take shape around breaking news or spectacular events. Elizabeth Poole et al.'s (2018) study of the hashtag *#StopIslam* examines how an anti-Muslim hashtag was disrupted by being flooded with counter-narratives. While this hashtag is regularly attached to a steady stream of tweets about different events or news stories, and is regularly used in multi-hashtagged posts, it received heightened use after a terrorist attack in Brussels in March 2016, and it is this immediate aftermath their study covers.

It demonstrates how an 'ad hoc public' took shape around jamming and redirecting the hashtag through messages of solidarity and contesting the racializing connection made between non-state violence and 'Muslim culture'. While the message 'Stop Islam' seems unambiguous, #StopIslam as a form of metadata and a rhetorical device is more contingent. Hashtags, James McVey and Heather Woods point out, 'rely on semantic abstraction in order to open up conversation to the public world of strangers. The discursive flexibility of the hashtag allows it to bound the scope of digital discourse while simultaneously opening up the discourse to widespread viral circulation' (2016: 2). Viral circulation in turn opens it up to counter-narrative dilution and contest, so much so, in this instance, that it garnered significant media coverage (*The Washington Post*'s story, '#StopIslam Twitter-trended for all the right reasons', also draws attention, of course, to the fact that the hashtag was *able* to trend; Dewey, 2016).

Poole et al.'s account is careful to push past the headline celebration to draw out some other aspects: participating in the hashtag exposed some users to trolling, and once the viral event dissipated, the hashtag reverted to its ambient use as a rhetorical organizing device for anti-Muslim racism. This is hardly surprising, as the hashtag is deployed as a quotidian gesture by small yet dense far-right constellations that have greater network longevity than intensive 'ad hoc' formations. As a semiotic marker and algorithmic construction, a hashtag cannot definitively be 'reclaimed'. It is also undoubtedly the case that such forms of engagement produce amplification. Increased participation in public discourse, Philips and Milner argue in their treatment of ambivalence, is subject to the 'double-edged sword of affective attunement', where participation involves 'unprecedented immediacy, public visibility and at times outright ferocity' (2017: 191). Yet for all the risks posed by the ambivalence of amplification, the underlying problem is that social media *anyway* amplifies the public visibility and circulation of racialized discourse, and as such, anti-racist activism cannot leave it to be propagated unchallenged. Interventions should be reflective and strategic, certainly, but if engagement amplifies what is already circulating, it is still better that racist content proliferates with opposition coagulating in the flow.

Teasing out the precise dimensions of contradiction and ambivalence activated by and within specific public formations guards against a tendency to regard ephemerality and ambient connection as evidence of the political weakness of 'hashtag politics', without sufficient consideration of the public horizon of such actions. A critical distinction made by Squires (2002) in her discussion of the Black Public Sphere is that to judge communicative action solely according to its productive relation to other forms of political action is to confuse the 'discursive actions of a public sphere, and the political success of that sphere. Political strategies and activities emerge from exchanges of ideas and inspiration, and the primary function of a public sphere is to support such discourse. Whether or not these ideas foment successful political campaigns is another matter, albeit an important one' (2002: 452).

This distinction is not made in the service of a banal distinction between theory and practice, or between a realm of rarified contemplation and the world of pragmatic action. Rather, it resists reducing the development of shared understanding, argument elaboration, collective identification and 'internal' critique to teleological assumptions about political mobilization. It is not incidental, therefore, that recent research examining anti-racist engagement on Twitter hones in on how hashtags have been mobilized to disrupt postracial story telling, not only to insert the salience of race to 'social conversations' but also to insist on its complexity and intersectional force. Hashtags work to drive discourse in particular directions, providing openings for stories, experiences and critique. In her study of 'racial justice activist hashtags', Rachel Kuo understands this as central to building sustained networks, as 'their primary value may be in elevating and circulating discourse, but these hashtags can help establish grounds for participation, build individual and collective identity, and organize for collective action' (2016: 496).

The study examines hashtags that circulated and garnered attention transnationally, but which were initiated and achieved resonance and intensity in a particular context, in this instance 'racialized and feminist online publics' predominantly located in the US. Racial justice activist hashtags are circulated to call attention to injustice, by highlighting neglected issues or to reframe discourse by drawing out aspects elided in dominant narratives. Kuo draws on Squires' heuristic model of publics to argue that hashtags, even in the volatile space of Twitter, can support 'enclave' practices, shaping 'internal' discourse production and shared understandings – 'hashtags offer discursive frame processes in articulating and circulating observed events and experiences' (ibid). Enclavic formations on Twitter can never be hermetic; the idea of 'context collapse' has migrated from academic discourse to wider usage precisely because it captures the widely-shared experience of navigating the relationship between an 'imagined audience' and the overlapping publics of connective media platforms (Marwick and boyd, 2011). However, these hashtags also have a counterpublic valence, as 'members of a racialized digital counterpublic who have been perceived as "invisible" within the public at large utilize hashtags to make their presence and message more visible to publics dominated by whiteness' (Kuo, op.cit.).

Given the lingering polarization of perspectives on social media and politics, the idea of 'hashtag politics' is unlikely to lose a resonance of misplaced gravity, or of a misguided turn to the symbolic at a moment when social movements appear fragmented and politically weakened. However, empirical studies have drawn much of the heat from this polarization by examining the public horizons articulated around these kinds of hashtags, and examining their networked formation and modes of expression. They are aware of the tensions between the utility of connective media and how the 'architectures of digital media networks can reproduce the emphasis on the individual that is at the core of neoliberal racial ideologies, creating the potential for dominant racial logics to map easily onto digital networks' (Florini, 2015: 441).

Theresa L. Petray and Rowan Collin (2017), drawing on the feminist anthropologist Sherry Ortner, draw attention to the 'serious games' of playful, ironic or memetic communications within hashtag publics. Their study of the hashtag #whiteproverbs examines the satirical recasting of common forms of racism denial, stereotyping and 'justifying non-White disadvantage' as folk sayings – proverbs tell stories, but mediated by this hashtag, they disrupt a practised story of innocence and denial. The hashtag foregrounds the importance of humorous reversal, sarcasm and pointed exaggeration to Twitter's 'platform vernacular', opening a space where civility and 'respectability' cannot be easily pressed as putative requirements for public dialogue. While this study analyzed a large corpus of tweets, it paid qualitative attention to the engagement of participants 'involved in movements for Aboriginal and Torre Strait Islander equality, refugee rights, and anti-racism more generally' (2017: 7). For these participants, the hashtag was not a surrogate form of activism, but a discursive exercise in building shared understandings, highlighting 'the rules of whiteness and race as currently played out in Australia' (ibid: 8). While hashtag publics are characterized by significant divergences in network power (Papacharissi, 2014), this corpus of research suggests that in particular contexts and contingent constellations they provide a meaningful space of expression for those who experience racism and intersecting oppressions to examine them, and to negotiate positions, develop analyse and establish connections.

It is a somewhat different issue if 'hashtag activism' that confronts racist expression and racializing logics claims a more substantive or direct relation to social change and political mobilization. Here there is certainly a risk, as Natalie Fenton argues, that 'collective solidarity is replaced by a politics of visibility that relies on hashtags, "Likes" and compulsive posting of updates that hinge upon self-presentation as proof of individual activism' (2016: 44). There is no ideology without desire, and the individualizing drive of social media is in constant tension with the negotiation of 'reflexive interdependence' in mutable public formations. In relation to anti-racism, the temptation of self-presentation as proof of individual activism acquires a particular inflection. Sara Ahmed (2004a) has argued that white declarations of anti-racism risk failing 'to examine how sayings are not always doings, or to put it more strongly, to show how the investment in saying as if saying was doing can actually extend rather than challenge racism'. This tendency is what Ahmed terms 'the non-performativity of anti-racism', where performative speech, in John L. Austin's sense, means that 'the issuing of the utterance is the performing of an action' (1975: 6).

The gesture of recognizing whiteness, and testifying as to confronting one's own racism, is often presented as 'evidence' of anti-racist commitment and as a form of political action. However, 'anti-racist speech in a racist world is an unhappy performative': the conditions are not in place that would allow such 'saying' to 'do' what it 'says'. Instead, such 'non-performative' declarations recentre whiteness that has 'happily' demonstrated that it is not racist, and thus 'allows racism to remain the burden of non-white others' (ibid). This non-performativity is invited by social media, heightened both by the corporate imperative of discourse production, and the cultural presumption that connective media platforms are racially neutral, and thus coded as 'white' (Brock, 2012). And while non-performative, it involves performance; declarations and 'call outs' that constitute what Tim Engles calls a 'white antiracist slacktivism' that 'carries a sense of responsibility only as far as self-aggrandizing *expressions* of solidarity' (2017: 104, original emphasis).

While the individualizing drive and subjectification of social media are constantly to be negotiated as structural aspects of these platforms, destructive behaviours can be and are reckoned with within movements and networks. The potential of counter-public formations to generate a mobilizing sense of 'something always going on' is important for anti-racist imaginings, for building shared understandings, and generating ideas and affinities. The value of this, particularly given the communicative and political-conceptual challenges of postracial debatability, does not depend on ignoring the ways in which Twitter is also a space of ambiguous and destructive drives, and modulated and managed participation.

# Acting on, acting through media

## Social media and media criticism

In myriad ways, social media platforms are used to engage, critique and even attempt to hold media representations and reporting to some form of account. As Chapter 2 suggested, this ceaseless circulation articulates a quotidian politics of representation and offers the possibility of more sustained interventions in media practices. It does so ambivalently, in an environment where it inevitably contributes to the production of an extraordinary scale of commodified discourse. Critical treatments of the boosterish notion the 'attention economy' emphasize how the corporate capture of attention has become a means of producing value, or attempting to (Fuchs, 2014). The generalized struggle for attention in heavily mediated contexts has consequences for forms of political action that must generate means of 'attention acquisition' (Tufekci, 2013). The expanded capacity to comment on media work, and in some instances to impact on it, proposes another vector of ambivalence: how can those engaged in media critique *draw attention* by participating in the flows and through the platforms that constantly 'solicit us as subjects of attention' (Read, 2014)?

Recent research on media audiences suggests that digital participation encompasses shifting modes of *paying* attention. The 'hybrid media practice' of combining watching a live broadcast or stream with simultaneous engagement through social media platforms has been described as 'back channelling' (Finger and De Souza, 2012), 'co-connected viewing' (Pittman and Tefertiller, 2015) 'second screening' (Laursen and Sandvik, 2014), or the actions of an emerging 'viewertariat' (Anstead and O'Loughlin, 2011). For Vaccari et al. (2015), the process of switching between live broadcast and Facebook and Twitter in particular is best described as dual screening, a 'complex bundle of practices' more mixed than the 'TV first, social media second' implication of 'second screening'. The preponderance of research on dual screening is focused on news consumption, particularly in relation to the immediacy of intensive media events, and oriented towards testing the relation between these practices and forms of political participation (de Zúñiga et al., 2015). Accelerated news cycles and 'totemic political events' such as elections provide 'greater opportunities for active and strategic intervention, framing and reframing by a wide array of actors' (Vaccari et al., 2015: 1042).

Apryl Williams and Vanessa Gonlin (2017) investigate 'second screening' within Black Twitter's milieu, but their focus is on commentary practices around the television show *How to Get Away with Murder* (for which Viola Davis was the first black woman to win Lead Actress in a Drama at the Emmy Awards). They are dismissive of the idea that these practices are inherently 'dialogue-enabling', given inequalities in technology and social platform capital. Rather, second-screening practices are used to reflect on what 'fuller representations of Black women that challenge the typical media portrayals of women of color' could look like, and how the question of authenticity is to be navigated and negotiated. Such practices are closely related to the community-building orientation of counter-publics, shaped not so much towards an intervention in media practices as discursivity refracted through a shared textual focus.

The surveillance orientation and addressivity of social media extend established forms of critical engagement with media representation which presuppose the social significance of media and its role in circulating racist discourse. Media monitoring – a 'series of observational, analytical, evaluative and critical activities by independent (non-media) organizations focusing on the practices and the products of mass media and mass media workers' (Van Dijck, 1995) – is arguably the most prevalent of these.[6] The immediacy of social media allows for media monitoring to be folded into the news story or media event. The *Collectif Contre l'Islamophobie en France* (CCIF), which is relentlessly targeted by right-wing and also ultra-laïc media, uses its blog to fact-check and analyze hostile media coverage, and often to directly respond to the sources, integrating its media monitoring into its broader surveillance of incidents of anti-Muslim racism. Beyond organized groups, a vast range of actors use dedicated Twitter accounts and Storify blogs to monitor and critique media output in often very specific ways. The now-defunct Tumblr 'Réflexe Niqab' documented a journalistic 'niqab reflex', using images of women in niqab to anchor stories that had some general or marginal reference to Islam or immigration, and also using photos of veiled women from other contexts and times to illustrate stories about contemporary France (for example, in a story about a survey of how

'French people do not want religious signs visible in businesses', a photo of a veiled woman sorting pomegranates in Afghanistan was used).[7]

Given the popularity of the business model of tapping out racism as a way of generating online 'outrage', strategies have developed which seek to minimize the value of racist clickbait, from circulating versions of deliberately provocative articles on text storage sites so that they can be read without directing traffic to the host site, to more sustained strategies. The campaign Stop Funding Hate was established in the UK in the summer of 2016 in response to sustained anti-migrant headlines in the British right-wing press, particularly *The Daily Mail*. It set out to reduce the profitability of sensationalist headlines by targeting companies with published ethical guidelines who were advertising in these newspapers, and used Twitter to publicly draw attention to the incongruity.[8]

The capacity of networked publics to hold racializing reportage or representations to some form of account is not insignificant. At the same time, it is shot through with ambivalence. Sara Ahmed has written of the 'defensive fantasy' of the 'angry person of color', which functions to position racism as an excess of emotion: 'It is as if we talk about racism because we are angry, rather than being angry because of racism' (2012: 159). In the context of the churn of social media, and its association with immediate and unruly affect and response, there is a risk that anti-racist expression is folded dismissively into assumptions about the 'angry internet' – *Slate's* 'Year of Outrage' project in 2014 was introduced by noting that 'People were upset about TV Stars and wheelchairs and lattes and racism and war' (Turner, 2014). Knowing when and how to navigate the noise is an increasingly important strategic question.

In some assessments, noise is a structural feature of the communicative environment. In *Now*, French anarchist collective The Invisible Committee states that 'This world no longer needs explaining, critiquing, denouncing. We live in a fog of commentaries and commentaries on commentaries, of critiques and critiques of critiques of critiques, of revelations that don't trigger anything, other than revelations about the revelations' (2017: 6). Acting politically in this noise, they argue, is not to give up on speech, but to commit to speech that commits one: 'one can talk about conflicts, and one can talk *from the midst of conflict*' (ibid: 7). In the same vein, Macgilchrist and Böhmig (2012) make a case for media critique amidst media saturation as a minimal practice of 'tiny rips'. Their study of blog responses to the launch – and saturation media coverage – of Thilo Sarrazin's generic anti-immigrant narrative of national decline *Deutschland schafft sich ab* ('Germany Abolishes Itself', 2010) regards this writing as provoking the need to constantly restabilize hegemonic meanings, where 'the blogs written about the Sarrazin case have torn tiny fissures in the mediascape, contesting the view circulating broadly in the news media that Muslim immigrants are the cause of Germany's current social and economic problems' (2012: 97). The minimal task of anti-racist media critique and action on social media may be one, to mix these metaphors, of finding the tiny fissures in the fog.

## Witnessing, mediating

They turn up with seemingly ever-increasing frequency in timelines: recorded in supermarkets and garage forecourts, cafes and street corners, videos of racist abuse are uploaded or livestreamed and rapidly accumulate shares and commentary. They are picked up by news aggregator and content-hungry news sites and often, depending on a combination of their egregiousness and virality, become mainstream news stories, receiving editorial framing and soliciting official comment. As a media form and practice, the proliferation of videos of racist abuse constitutes a loose sub-set of the mass proliferation of mediated witness accounts shaped by the ubiquity of smartphones and networked mobile media, which are in turn a dimension of the 'visual sociality' that the proliferation of online video instantiates (Lindgren, 2017: 123–4). The experience of social time and interaction is increasingly also the experience of potential moments or objects for mediation.

In its legal or moral sense, to witness is a form of mediation, a critical yet imperfect transformation from seeing to saying, from the happenstance of witnessing to the imperative of bearing witness (see Peters, 2001). The idea of witnessing also has a pre-digital sense in communication studies, integral to phenomenological considerations of the liveness of broadcasting, which produces a sense of audience co-presence in the media event while making 'the act of witness into an intimate and domestic act' (Ellis, 2000: 32). Thinking about mediated witnessing requires negotiating these jarring senses, as the everyday media spectator is also a subject sporadically hailed to some relation to those 'distant others' whose conflict, suffering or conditions are witnessed through representations. The moral ambivalence of mediated proximity is acute, as, in Susan Sontag's (2003) formulation, we may 'regard the pain of others' while not being able to act on it, and can routinely access images of atrocity while not being accountable to them.

The immediacy of live-streaming and the presumed veracity of video-recording shifts the relation between 'seeing' and 'saying' as modalities of witnessing, while also implicating the witnessing subject as a performative actor in the media event that unfolds through and around the content they circulate. 'Connective witnessing' has emerged as a contingent and strategic practice available to movements and individuals (Mortensen, 2015). In a short space of time bystander videos have transcended their status as 'user-generated content' in news packages to being easily loaded or streamed through digital media across platforms, and thus becoming an 'integral part of civic action, which has a bearing on the orchestration, communication, media coverage and political handling of events' (2015: 1395). The reference to civic action underlines the relation of mediated witnessing research to forms of collective action, in particular protest, which is discussed subsequently. At the same time, there is a lack of specific consideration in this literature of forms of interventionist witnessing in racialized interactions: the ways in which racialized social relations impact on who can act as what kind of witness, and how witnessing videos with an apparent anti-racist intent are circulated, framed and received in the wider media ecosystem.

Videos of racist incidents are interventions in the dynamics of an abusive situation enacted by the presence of the witness – who may be the person under attack, or a bystander – and the phone as witnessing technology. They are often circulated as an act seeking some form of justice, from specific redress such as an apology, to the assumption that public exposure exacts a social cost. They are at once a document of the everyday and of the spectacular, of the persistence of racism but also of its putatively unexpected public irruption. Consequently, one approach to the circulation of these videos has been to read them symptomatically, as instantiations of deeper racial articulation. 'My Britain is fuck all' – Paul Gilroy (2012) hones in on this line from a rant on a crowded tram between Croydon and Wimbledon in London by 36-year-old Emma West in late 2011. West's riff – 'What's this country coming to? A load of black people and a load of fucking Polish?' – has been viewed millions of times online, and this viral circulation led to her facing charges for racially aggravated disorder, and defending herself by explaining that she had been taking anti-depressants and drinking alcohol earlier that day. This explanation is a widespread one in relation to such celebrity or 'everyday' outbursts, and it begs a question not of mitigation but of symptomatic implication: why is racism the mode through which illness or unhappiness seems to be inevitably expressed?

That her manifest bitterness and resentment 'could be articulated spontaneously as a heartfelt commentary on race, nationality and belonging',

Gilroy argues, is a question of what was discussed in Chapter 1 as *fluency*, 'not the spontaneous outpouring of an injured white working class that the uncomprehending or ignorant commentariat would have you believe. It is the effect of an accumulated racism and misoxeny which has been significant in fluctuating its presence in the British political life since the end of World War Two' (2012: 394). Gilroy's attentiveness to the affective grammar of racialized explanation and complaint, to this scripted spontaneity, cautions against constructing a genre of 'anti-racist witnessing' that neglects the situatedness of interactions and the repertoires they take shape through. Concomitantly, this kind of socio-textual reading also requires thinking about the video as a media artefact in circulation.

Shakuntala Banaji (2013) has examined the huge range of YouTube response videos tagged to the original video of West, mainly confessional-to-camera vlogs proposing a 'take' on what the incident says about racism, but also overlaying dialogue on the footage or splicing it with other visual material. As a subject of commentary, the video invites diagnosis more than symptomatic reading, with responses linking West's outburst to putative mental illness or class position, thus enacting resilient modes of exceptionalization. Alana Lentin (2015) tracks a similar process in relation to a 'bus racism' video in Australia, where the intervention of other passengers was parlayed, in media coverage, into evidence of a 'stereotype of Australian national character, as easy-going and "intolerant of intolerance", while any connection between the passenger's racist outburst and the politico-historical context in which it is couched fades into the background'. The question raised by this is not a mechanistic one of individualized versus structural analyses of racism, as the accumulated circulation of these videos has consequences across different domains of action.

In the absence of research, there is only speculation. As well as being of some sort of restitutive or testimonial value to those subject to abuse, videos may work performatively, disturbing, as Laila Lalami (2018) has argued, the enactment of the 'belief that public space belongs exclusively to white people', thus posting an incremental warning that 'the assertion of private authority now comes with a social cost'. To enter into circulation is also to activate circuits of debatability, to signify relationally with related videos to constitute a mediated ritual of making racist speech public, which may support narrow postracial modes of recognition of what racism is, and how it is being *exposed*. However, there is much research to be done on the media and social life of this accumulation of videos: how they accrete generic elements, the differential impacts of live-streamed and recorded documents, the tendency of recording witnesses to supply a running commentary (thus aware, in the moment of witnessing, of potential and desired audiences, and securing narrative meaning) and the ways they are remediated and framed by news outlets.

It is a different story in relation to the sousveillance of racist police violence in the US where video witnessing is centrally considered in the rich body of work on the communicative life of the protest networks organized around #BlackLivesMatter. Although the hashtag #BlackLivesMatter is used to stand in for – and creates a narrative of – linear political action commencing in the aftermath of the killing of Trayvon Martin in 2012 and intensifying after the police murder of Michael Brown in Ferguson, Missouri, in August 2014, the hashtag itself did not come to signify a movement until after the Ferguson protests (Freelon et al., 2016). The extraordinary police repression meted out to protestors was intensively mediated, and the impact of the proximity of professional journalists with a diverse milieu of activists and protestors has been the focus of several studies. For Barnard (2018), a significant result of Twitter's temporal role as a 'hybrid journo-activist space' during the protests was that 'networked publics' succeeded not only in drawing attention to police brutality, but also in documenting and amplifying and thus linking together individual cases of violence against People of Colour into an 'undeniable pattern explained only by structural racism' (2017: 5).

In a sharp intervention, Allissa V. Richardson argues that witnessing as a theoretical framework breaks down in relation to these particular forms of racialized violence, as it cannot explain 'what makes a poor person of color more likely to bear witness to … police brutality, than perhaps a middle-class black or white person living in America's affluent suburbs?' (2017: 675–6). The question is blunt, but the answer is far from reductive, proposing a theory of 'mobile-mediated black witnessing'. As a practice, it emerges from a collective sense of a history of witnessing, of 'participating in a long line of storytellers' who have documented lynching, Klan violence and previous experiences of police brutality. In media terms, witness videos are circulated through 'Black Twitter' as an 'ad hoc news outlet' operating in the real time of an event or its immediate aftermath, with the effect that 'the speed with which black subgroups within the general black population communicate, internally and externally, has reshaped the imagined publics and counterpublics of raced spaces, both in the real world and online' (ibid: 691).

In a complementary analysis, Nicholas Mirzoeff's study of Black Lives Matter integrates the ubiquity of mediated witnessing into a theory of the 'space of appearance'. The public occupation of space by racialized people and their allies creates the condition 'where you and I can appear to each other and create a politics', an exchange that produces shared affect and 'no surplus for expropriation, but by our consent it is possible to mediate that dialogic space into materially shareable and distributable forms' (2017: 32). Thus secured, the space of appearance is instantiated through 'three streams of visibility': witnessing in person and through machine-generated imagery, protest as rendering injustice visible, and through mediatization that ensures a 'co-presence between physical and digital spaces' (ibid: 90). Physically, mediatically and politically, the 'space of appearance' refutes the police injunction that 'there is nothing to see here'.

The aim of this chapter has been to assess, on the basis of the evident ambivalence of digital networks, the ways in which connective media practices are integrated to and extend anti-racist actions, practices directed both at the conviviality of online spaces, and as a dimension of multi-faceted socio-political mobilizations. While not downplaying the unsettling and often destructive aspects of this ambivalence, and the kinds of primarily performative online politics it can engender, what is striking in much of the research discussed is the extent to which activists reflexively integrate an awareness of these systemic limitations and interpersonal distortions to their political expectations and communicative practices. Political action is not driven or determined by ideas alone, but in the contemporary violently racist 'postracial' moment, the circulation of anti-racist ideas, arguments, resources and inspiration matters. The potential for transnational points of connection, translation and recognition matters also, as the affective and political awareness that something is 'always going on' provides joy without comfort in the otherwise exhausting eddies, currents and traps in the circuitries of debatability.

# Endnotes

1   There is also the Swedish far-right 'alternative encyclopedia' *Metapedia*, originally established by the now-defunct Nazi *Nordiska förbundet* (Nordic Union) in 2006, which has grown into an 'ambitious pan-European project' providing entries in 18 languages (Arnstad, 2015: 106–7).

2   On, for example, the ways in which Ferguson protests were linked to Gaza solidarity protests, but also a refusal of this transnational solidarity, see Annie Olaluku-Teriba, 'Afro-Pessimism and the (Un)Logic of Anti-Blackness', *Historical Materialism*, www.historicalmaterialism.org/articles/afro-pessimism-and-unlogic-anti-blackness#_ftn12

3  Note here areas that are not covered in this book; Indigenous media, multicultural 'migrant' media, etc. See Tanja Dreher, 2010, on community media.

4  The idea of 'counter-public' in this discussion is somewhat distinct from Michael Warner's influential discussion in *Publics and Counterpublics* (2005).

5  Consequently, relatively small-scale autonomous events are amplified by hostile media coverage and social media campaigns into problems that require political responses. In 2017, the Mayor of Paris, Anne Hidalgo, announced that she was seeking to ban the Nyansapo Afro-Feminist festival, as it was 'banning whites from attending'. This repeated the deliberate mischaracterization prepared through hostile media coverage; the festival proposed a range of discussion spaces, some open to all, and some organized as 'enclaves' in the service of self-emancipation, as the aim of the festival made clear: 'In our communities and in a society which is western, capitalist and patriarchal, we want to struggle against all the oppressions which relate to our position as black women … (and to) make African and African-descendent voices heard in their diversity, as our Afro-Feminism is not a monolithic whole. Finally, it is to reclaim our identities and our image as black women (and people assigned identities as women)'.
   See the website of the Mwasi Collectif Afrofeministe: https://mwasicollectif.com

6  Organized approaches to media monitoring are distinctly under-researched, despite the significant investment in the practice by international bodies that tend to monitor compliance with professional codes of conduct, and also by 'minority' groups and anti-racist campaigns. Downing and Husband, in one of the few treatments of the practice, question the public impact of large-scale monitoring exercises, for 'as activists know, a single example, forthrightly exploited and vigorously defended, may have a greater impact than an extensive body of data subject to sophisticated factor analysis and theorised with elegant erudition' (2005: 157).

7  https://reflexeniqab.tumblr.com/post/101490948266/20-minutes

8  https://stopfundinghate.org.uk/

# References

Abdel-Fadil, Mona (2016) 'The "Rape Game": Framing the Cologne and Stockholm Events', *Religion Going Public* [online] 7 March. Available at http://religiongoingpublic.com/archive/2016/the-rape-game-framing-the-cologne-and-stockholm-events (accessed 24 November 2018).

Ackermann, Seth (2016) 'An Open Letter to Riss, Care of the Internet (by Daniel Scheidermann)', *Too Hot for Jacobin blog* [online] 14 January. Available at http://toohotforjacobin.blogspot.com/2016/01/an-open-letter-to-riss-care-of-internet.html (accessed 8 November 2018).

Addley, Esther (2016) 'Six in Ten British Films Have No Named Black Characters – Study', *The Guardian* [online] 6 October. Available at www.theguardian.com/film/2016/oct/06/six-in-10-british-films-have-no-named-black-characters-bfi

Adewunmi, Bim (2016) 'For Muslims Like Me, Trump's Words Are A Daily Nightmare', *BuzzFeedNews* [online] 17 June. Available at www.buzzfeed-news.com/article/bimadewunmi/living-with-anti-muslim-rhetoric (accessed 25 November 2018).

Ahmed, Sara (2004a) 'Declarations of Whiteness: The Non-Performativity of Anti-Racism', *Borderlands* [online] *3*(2). Available at www.borderlands.net.au/vol3no2_2004/ahmed_declarations.htm (accessed 25 November 2018).

Ahmed, Sara (2004b) *The Cultural Politics of Emotions*. Edinburgh: Edinburgh University Press.

Ahmed, Sara (2010) 'Feminist Killjoys (and Other Willful Subjects)', *The Scholar and Feminist Online* [online] *8*(3). Available at http://sfonline.barnard.edu/polyphonic/ahmed_01.htm (accessed 18 November 2018).

Ahmed, Sara (2012) *On Being Included: Racism and Diversity in Institutional Life*. Durham, NC and London: Duke University Press.

Alam, Yunis and Husband, Charles (2013) Islamophobia, community cohesion and counter-terrorism policies in Britain, *Patterns of Prejudice*, *47*(3): 235–52.

Alcoff, Linda M. (2006) *Visible Identities: Race, Gender and the Self*. Oxford: Oxford University Press.

Aleem, Zeeshan (2016) 'Why Germany's Famously Tolerant Chancellor Just Proposed a Burqa Ban', *Vox* [online] 6 December. Available at www.vox.com/world/2016/12/6/13854214/germany-angela-merkel-burqa-ban (accessed 19 November 2018).

Alexander, Claire (2017) 'Racing Islamophobia', in F. Elahi and O. Khan (eds), *Islamophobia: Still A Challenge For Us All*. London: Runnymede Trust. pp. 13–15.

Allen, Chris (2012) *A review of the evidence relating to the representation of Muslims and Islam in the British media* [online], University of Birmingham, Institute of Applied Social Studies, School of Social Policy. Available at www.birmingham.ac.uk/Documents/college-social-sciences/social-policy/

IASS/news-events/MEDIA-ChrisAllen-APPGEvidence-Oct2012.pdf (accessed 25 November 2018).

Alsultany, Evelyn (2012) *Arabs and Muslims in the Media Race and Representation after 9/11*. New York and London: New York University Press.

Amin, Ash (2010) The remainders of race, *Theory, Culture & Society*, *27*(1): 1–23.

Amiraux, Valérie and Fetiu, Arber (2017) 'After the Drama: The Institutionalisation of Gossiping About Muslims', in G. Titley, D. Freedman, G. Khiabany and A. Mondon (eds), *After Charlie Hebdo: Terror, Racism and Free Speech*. London: Zed.

Andrejevic, Mark (2013) *Infoglut: How Too Much Information Is Changing the Way We Think and Know*. New York and London: Routledge.

Angwin, Julia and Parris Jr, Terry (2016) 'Facebook Lets Advertisers Exclude Users by Race', *Propublica* [online] 28 October. Available at www. propublica.org/article/facebook-lets-advertisers-exclude-users-by-race (accessed 25 November 2018).

Anstead, Nick and O'Loughlin, Ben (2011) The emerging viewertariat and BBC Question Time: television debate and real-time commenting online, *International Journal of Press/Politics*, *16*(4): 440–62.

Appadurai, Arjun (2006) *Fear of Small Numbers: An Essay on the Geography of Anger*. Durham, NC and London: Duke University Press.

Arnstad, Henrik (2015) Ikea fascism: metapedia and the internationalization of Swedish generic Fascism, *Fascism: Journal of Comparative Fascist Studies*, *4*: 103–17.

Athique, Adrian (2013) *Digital Media and Society: An Introduction*. Cambridge: Polity.

Austin, John L. (1975) *How to Do Things with Words*, 2nd edn. Edited by J.O. Urmson and M. Sbisà. Cambridge, MA: Harvard University Press (1st edn, 1962).

Back, Les (2002) Aryans reading Adorno: cyber-culture and twenty-first-century racism, *Ethnic and Racial Studies*, *25*(4): 628–51.

Badouard, Romain (2016) 'Je ne suis pas Charlie: pluralité des prises de parole sur le web et les réseaux sociaux', Lefébure P. & Sécail C. (dir.), *Le défi Charlie. Les médias à l'épreuve des attentats*, Lemieux Editeur, collection Mundo médias.

Baker, Mona and Blaagaard, Bolette B. (eds) (2016) *Citizen Media and Public Spaces: Diverse Expressions of Citizenship and Dissent*. London and New York: Routledge.

Balibar, Etienne and Wallerstein, Immanuel (1991) *Race, Nation, Class: Ambiguous Identities*. London: Verso.

Balkenhol, Markus, Mepschen, Paul and Duyvendak, Jan W. (2016) 'The Nativist Triangle: Sexuality, Race and Religion in the Netherlands', in J.W. Duyvendak, P. Geschiere and E. Tonkens (eds), *The Culturalization of Citizenship: Belonging and Polarization in a Globalizing World*. Basingstoke: Palgrave Macmillan. pp. 97–112.

Banaji, Shakuntala (2013) Everyday racism and 'my tram experience': emotion, civic performance and learning on YouTube, *Comunicar*, *20*(40): 69–78.

Bangstad, Sindre (2011) 'Fighting Words That Are Not Fought', *The Immanent Frame: Secularism, Religion and Public Sphere* [online] 14 June. Available at https://tif.ssrc.org/2011/06/14/fighting-words/ (accessed 25 November 2018).

Bangstad, Sindre (2013) Inclusion and exclusion in the mediated public sphere: the case of Norway and its Muslims, *Social Anthropology/Anthropologie Sociale, 21*(3): 356–70.

Bangstad, Sindre (2014) *Anders Breivik and the Rise of Islamophobia.* London: Zed.

Bangstad, Sindre (2015) 'Hate Speech: The Dark Twin of Free Speech', *Sindre Bangstad* [online]. Available at www.sindrebangstad.com/hate-speech-the-dark-twin-of-free-speech/ (accessed 25 November 2018).

Barassi, Veronica (2015) *Activism on the Web: Everyday Struggles against Digital Capitalism.* New York and London: Routledge.

Barendt, Eric (2005) *Freedom of Speech*, 2nd edn. Oxford: Oxford University Press.

Barnard, Stephen R. (2018) Tweeting #Ferguson: mediatized fields and the new activist journalist, *New Media & Society, 20*(7): 2252–71.

Barot, Rohit and Bird, John (2001) Racialization: the genealogy and critique of a concept, *Ethnic and Racial Studies, 24*(4): 601–18.

Bartlett, Jamie (2014) *The Dark Net Inside the Digital Underworld.* London: Heinemann.

Bauman, Zygmunt (2003) *Wasted Lives: Modernity and its Outcasts.* Cambridge: Polity.

Bawer, Bruce (2011) *The New Quislings: How the International Left Used the Oslo Massacre to Silence Debate About Islam.* New York: Broadside.

Bawer, Bruce (2013) 'Sweden's March into Oblivion: The Fruits of Denial', *Frontpage Magazine* [online] 19 December. Available at www.frontpage-mag.com/fpm/213603/swedens-march-oblivion-bruce-bawer (accessed 25 November 2018).

Bayoumi, Moustafa (2015) *This Muslim American Life: Dispatches from the War on Terror.* New York and London: New York University Press.

Beaumont-Thomas, Ben (2018) 'This Is America: Theories Behind Childish Gambino's Satirical Masterpiece', *Guardian* [online] 9 May. Available at www.theguardian.com/music/2018/may/07/this-is-america-theories-donald-glover-satirical-video-childish-gambino (accessed 19 November 2018).

Benkler, Yochai, Faris, Robert, Roberts, Hal and Zuckerman, Ethan (2017) 'Study: Breitbart-led Right-wing Media Ecosystem Altered Broader Media Agenda', *Columbia Journalism Review* [online] 3 March. Available at www.cjr.org/analysis/breitbart-media-trump-harvard-study.php (accessed 25 November 2018).

Bennett, Samuel, ter Wal, Jessika, Lipiński, Artur, Fabiszak, Małgorzata and Krzyżanowski, Michał (2013) 'The representation of third-country nationals in European news discourse', *Journalism Practice, 7*(3): 248–65.

Berlet, Chip and Carol Mason (2015) 'Swastikas in Cyberspace: How Hate Went Online', in P. A. Simpson and H. Druxes (eds), *Digital Media Strategies of the Far-Right Online.* Lanham, MD: Lexington Books.

Bethencourt, Francisco (2013) *Racisms: From the Crusades to the Twentieth Century.* Princeton, NJ: Princeton/Oxford University Press.

Bhattacharyya, Gargi and Murji, Karim (2013) 'Introduction: race critical public scholarship', *Ethnic and Racial Studies*, *36*(9): 1359–73.

Bigo, Didier (2002) Security and immigration: toward a critique of the governmentality of unease, *Alternatives*, *27*: 63–92.

Bleich, Eric (2011) *The Freedom to be Racist?* New York: Oxford University Press.

Boboltz, Sara (2015) 'Editors Are Trying To Fix Wikipedia's Gender And Racial Bias Problem', *Huffington Post* [online] 15 April. Available at www.huffingtonpost.com/2015/04/15/wikipedia-gender-racial-bias_n_7054550.html (accessed 25 November 2018).

Bollinger, Lee (1986) *The Tolerant Society*. New York: Oxford University Press.

Bonilla-Silva, Eduardo (2015) *Racism without Racists: Color-Blind Racism and the Persistence of Racial Inequality in America*, 5th edn. New York: Rowman & Littlefield (1st edn, 2003).

Bonnett, Alastair (2000) *Anti-Racism*. London: Routledge.

Boromisza-Habashi, David (2013) 'Hate Speech', in K. Tracy (ed.), *The International Encyclopedia of Language and Social Interaction*, 3 vols. Hoboken, NJ: Wiley-Blackwell. pp. 715–25.

Boulila, Stefanie C. and Carri, Christiane (2017) On Cologne: gender, migration and unacknowledged racisms in Germany, *European Journal of Women's Studies*, *24*(3): 286–93.

Boussaguet, Laurie and Faucher, Florence (2016) The politics of symbols: reflections on the French Government's framing of the 2015 terrorist attacks, *Parliamentary Affairs*, *71*(1): 169–95.

Bowling, Benjamin (1998) *Violent Racism: Victimization, Policing and Social Context*. New York: Oxford University Press.

Bowman-Grieve, Lorraine (2009) Exploring 'stormfront': a virtual community of the radical right, *Studies in Conflict & Terrorism*, *32*(11): 989–1007.

boyd, danah (2010) 'Social Network Sites as Networked Publics: Affordances, Dynamics, and Implications', in Z. Papacharissi (ed.), *Networked Self: Identity, Community, and Culture on Social Network Sites*. New York and London: Routledge. pp. 39–58.

Bozic, Martha, Barr, Caelainn, McIntyre, Niamh and Noor, Poppy (2018) 'Revealed: Immigration Rules in UK More Than Double in Length', *The Guardian* [online] 27 August. Available at www.theguardian.com/uk-news/2018/aug/27/revealed-immigration-rules-have-more-than-doubled-in-length-since-2010

Braidotti, Rosi (2013) *The Posthuman*. Cambridge: Polity.

Bray, Mark (2018) *AntiFa: The Anti-Fascist Handbook*. London: Melville House.

Brienen, Rebecca P. (2018) 'Types and Stereotypes: Zwarte Piet and his Early Modern Sources', in P. Essed and I. Hoving (eds), *Dutch Racism*. Leiden: Brill.

Briggs, Asa and Burke, Peter (2005) *A Social History of the Media: From Gutenberg to the Internet*. Cambridge: Polity.

Brock, André (2012) From the blackhand side: Twitter as a cultural conversation, *Journal of Broadcasting & Electronic Media*, *56*(4): 529–49.

Brown, Andrew (2011) 'Anders Breivik's Spider Web of Hate', *The Guardian Comment is Free*, [online] 7 September. Available at www.guardian.co.uk/commentisfree/2011/sep/07/anders-breivik-hate-manifesto (accessed 5 January 2019).

Brown, Wendy (2006) *Regulating Aversion: Tolerance in the Age of Identity and Empire*. Princeton, NJ: Princeton University Press.

Brüggeman, Michael (2014) Between frame setting and frame sending: how journalists contribute to news frames, *Communication Theory*, 24(1): 61–82.

Bruns, Axel and Burgess, Jean E. (2011) 'The Use of Twitter Hashtags in the Formation of Ad Hoc Publics', *Proceedings of the 6th European Consortium for Political Research (ECPR) General Conference 2011*, University of Iceland, Reykjavik.

Burris, Val, Smith, Emery and Strahm, Ann (2000) White supremacist networks on the internet, *Sociological Focus*, 33(2): 215–35.

Butler, Judith (2009) *Frames of War: When is Life Grievable?* London: Verso.

Caiani, Manuela and Kröll, Patricia (2015) The transnationalization of the extreme right and the use of the Internet, *International Journal of Comparative and Applied Criminal Justice*, 39(4): 331–51.

Caiani, Manuela and Parenti, Linda (2013) *European and American Extreme Right Groups and the Internet*. Burlington, VT: Ashgate.

Calhoun, Craig (1993) Civil society and the public sphere, *Public Culture*, 5(2): 267–80.

Calhoun, Craig J. (2002) The class consciousness of frequent travelers: toward a critique of actually existing cosmopolitanism, *The South Atlantic Quarterly*, 101(4): 869–97.

Camus, Jean-Yves and Lebourg, Nicolas (2017) *Far-Right Politics in Europe* Translated by J.M. Todd. Cambridge, MA: Belknap.

Carey, James (1992) *Communication as Culture: Essays on Media and Society*. New York and London: Routledge.

Castelli Gattinara, Pietro (2018) 'Europeans, Shut the Borders: Anti-Refugee Mobilisation in Italy and France', in D. della Porta (ed.), *Solidarity Mobilizations in the 'Refugee Crisis': Contentious Moves*. Cham: Palgrave Macmillan. pp. 271–98.

Chadwick, Andrew (2013) *The Hybrid Media System: Politics and Power*. Oxford: Oxford University Press.

Chamayou, Grégoire (2015) *Drone Theory*, London: Penguin.

Chauvin, Sébastien, Coenders, Yannick and Koren, Timo (2018) Never having been racist: explaining the Blackness of Blackface in the Netherlands, *Public Culture*, 30(3): 509–26.

Chouliaraki, Lilie and Stolic, Tijana (2017) Rethinking media responsibility in the refugee 'crisis': a visual typology of European news, *Media, Culture & Society*, 39(8): 1162–77.

Christensen, Miyase and Christensen, Christian (2013) The Arab Spring as meta-event and communicative spaces, *Television & New Media*, 14(4): 351–64.

Ciccariello-Maher, George (2016) 'Yes, Philando Castile was Killed for the Color of his Skin', *Jacobin* [online] 19 July. Available at www.jacobinmag.com/2016/07/philando-castile-police-brutality-fields-white-supremacy

Clifton, Eli (2011) 'Oslo Terrorist's Manifesto Cited Many Islamophobic Bloggers and Pundits', *Think Progress* [online] 25 July. Available at https://thinkprogress.org/chart-oslo-terrorists-manifesto-cited-many-islamophobic-bloggers-and-pundits-e10907ffa87/ (accessed 19 November 2018).

Cobb, Jasmine N. (2011) 'No we can't!': postracialism and the popular appearance of a rhetorical fiction', *Communication Studies*, *62*(4): 406–21.

Coenders, Yannick and Chauvin, Sébastien (2017) Race and the pitfalls of emotional democracy: primary schools and the critique of Black Pete in the Netherlands, *Antipode: A Radical Journal of Democracy*, *49*(5): 1244–62.

Cohen, Phil and Gardner, Carl (1982) *It Ain't Half Racist, Mum: Fighting Racism in the Media*. London: Comedia.

Cohen, Stanley (2001) *States of Denial: Knowing About Atrocities and Suffering*. Cambridge: Polity.

Cole, David (2012) 'More Speech is Better', *New York Review of Books* [online] 16 October. Available at www.nybooks.com/daily/2012/10/16/more-speech-better/ (accessed 5 January 2019).

Cooper, Davina (2013) 'Question Everything? Rape Law/Free Seech', *Critical Legal Thinking* [online] 28 November. Available at http://criticallegal thinking.com/2013/11/28/question-everything-rape-law-free-speech/ (accessed 25 November 2018).

Cottle, Simon (ed.) (2000) *Ethnic Minorities and the Media: Changing Cultural Boundaries*. Buckingham: Open University Press.

Couldry, Nick (2010) *Why Voice Matters: Culture and Politics after Neoliberalism*. London: Sage.

Couldry, Nick (2012) *Media, Society, World: Social Theory and Digital Media Practice*. Cambridge: Polity.

Cowell, Alan (1995) 'Teaching Nazi Past to German Youth', *New York Times*. Available at https://www.nytimes.com/1995/06/09/world/teaching-nazi-past-to-german-youth.html (accessed 5 January 2019).

Cross, Katherine (2015) '"I Find This Offensive": How "Offense" Discourse Traps Us Into Inaction', *Feministing*. Available at http://feministing.com/2015/02/12/i-find-this-offensive-how-offense-discourse-traps-us-into-inaction/#.VNz_aqXkRH8.twitter

Crouch, Colin (2004) *Post-Democracy*. Cambridge: Polity.

Curran, James (2002) *Media and Power*. London: Routledge.

Daniels, Jessie (2009) Cloaked websites: propaganda, cyber-racism and epistemology in the digital era, *New Media & Society*, *11*(5): 659–83.

Daniels, Jessie (2012) Race and racism in Internet Studies: a review and critique, *New Media & Society*, *15*(5): 695–719.

Davis, Angela Y. (2008) 'Recognizing Racism in the Era of Meoliberalism', in *Vice Chancellor's Oration on the Elimination of Racial Discrimination*. Perth, Western Australia. Available at www.omi.wa.gov.au/Resources/Publications/Documents/orations/Recognizing_Racism_in_the_Era_of_Neoliberalism_davis.pdf (last accessed 25 November 2018).

Davis, Dana-Ain (2007) Narrating the mute: racializing and racism in a neoliberal moment, *Souls: A Critical Journal of Black Politics, Culture and Society*, *9*(4): 346–60.

Dawes, Simon (2015) 'Charlie Hebdo, Free Speech and Counter-Speech', *Sociological Research Online* [online] *20*(3): 3. Available at http://www. socresonline.org.uk/20/3/3.html (last accessed 25 November 2018).

Dawes, Simon (2017) '#JeSuisCharlie, #JeNeSuisPasCharlie and ad hoc publics', in G. Titley et al. (eds), *After Charlie Hebdo: Terror, Racism, Free Speech*. London: Zed.

Dayan, Daniel and Katz, Elihu (1992) *Media Events: The Live Broadcasting of History*. Cambridge, MA: Harvard University Press.

De Genova, Nicholas (2013) Spectacles of migrant 'illegality': the scene of exclusion, the obscene of inclusion, *Ethnic and Racial Studies, 36*(7): 1180–98.

De Genova, Nicholas (2017) The 'European' question: migration, race and postcoloniality in 'Europe', *Social Text, 34*(3): 75–102.

De Jong, Anne (2019) 'Gaza, Black Face and Islamophobia: Intersectionality of Race and Gender in (Counter-)Discourse in the Netherlands', in P. Edded, K. Farquharson, K. Pillay and E.J. White (ed.), *Relating Worlds of Racism: Dehumanisation, Belonging and the Normativity of European Whiteness*. Basingstoke: Palgrave Macmillan.

De Koning, Anouk (2016) Tracing anxious politics in Amsterdam, *Patterns of Prejudice, 50*(2): 109–28.

De Koster, Willem and Houtman, Dick (2008) Stormfront is like a second home to me, *Information, Communication & Society, 11*(8): 1155–76.

De Leeuw, M. and van Wichelen, Sonja (2016) 'Institutionalizing the Muslims Other: *Naar Nederland* and the Violence of Culturalism', in P. Essed and I. Hoving (eds), *Dutch Racism*. Leiden: Brill.

De Nie, Michael (2004) *The Eternal Paddy: Irish Identity and the British Press 1798-1882*. Madison, WI: University of Wisconsin Press.

De Zúñiga, Homero Gil, Garcia-Perdomo, Victor and McGregor, Shannon C. (2015) What is second screening? Exploring motivations of second screen use and its effect on online political participation, *Journal of Communication, 65*(5): 793–815.

Dean, Jodi (2009) *Democracy and Other Neoliberal Fantasies*. Durham, NC: Duke University Press.

Debord, Guy (1967) *The Society of the Spectacle*. Detroit, MI: Black & Red.

Delphy, Christine (2015) *Separate and Dominate: Feminism and Racism After the War on Terror*. London: Verso.

Demmers, Jolle and Mehendale, Sameer S. (2010) 'Neoliberal xenophobia: The Dutch case', *Alternatives: Global, Local, Political 35*(1): 53–71.

Deuze, Mark (2006) Participation, remediation, bricolage: considering principal components of a digital culture, *The Information Society, 22*(2): 63–75.

Dewey, Caitlin (2016) '#StopIslam Trended For All the Right Reasons', *Washington Post* [online] 22 March. Available at www.washingtonpost. com/news/the-intersect/wp/2016/03/22/stopislam-twitter-trended-for-all-the-right-reasons/?noredirect=on&utm_term=.dec4df21fb55

Dovey, Jon (2000) *Freakshow: First Person Media and Factual Television*. London: Pluto.

Downing, John D.H. (1999) 'Hate Speech' and 'First Amendment Absolutism' discourses in the US, *Discourse & Society*, *10*(2):175–89.

Downing, John D.H. (n.d.) 'Racism, Ethnicity and Television', *The Encyclopedia of Television* [online]. Available at http://www.museum.tv/eotv/racismethni. htm

Downing, John D.H. and Husband, Charles (2005) *Representing 'Race': Racisms, Ethnicities and Media*. London: Sage.

Dreher, Tanja (2010) Speaking up or being heard? Community media interventions and the politics of listening, *Media, Culture & Society*, *32*(1): 85–103.

du Boucheron, Alexandra (2018) '"Noire N'est Pas Mon Metier": 16 Actrices Signent un Livre-Manifeste Pour une Representation Plus Juste au Cinéma', *France Info* [online] 3 May. Available at www.francetvinfo. fr/societe/droits-des-femmes/noire-n-est-pas-mon-metier-16actrices-signent-un-livre-manifeste-pour-une-representation-plus-juste-au-cinema_ 2735277.html

Eckert, Lynn M. (2011) A critique of the content and viewpoint neutrality principle in modern free speech doctrine, *Law, Culture and the Humanities*, *7*(2): 264–88.

Eco, Umberto (1995) 'Ur-Fascism', *New York Review of Books* [online] 22 June. Available at www.nybooks.com/articles/1995/06/22/ur-fascism/ (last accessed 25 November 2018).

Ekman, Mattias (2014) The dark side of online activism: Swedish right-wing extremist video activism on YouTube, *MedieKultur*, *56*: 79–99.

Ekman, Mattias (2015) Online Islamophobia and the politics of fear: manufacturing the green scare, *Ethnic & Racial Studies*, *38*(11): 1986–2002.

Ekman, Mattias (2018) Anti-refugee mobilization in social media: the case of soldiers of Odin, *Social Media + Society*, *January–March*: 1–11.

Ellis, John (2000) *Seeing Things: Television in an Age of Uncertainty*. London: IB Tauris.

Ellison, Nicole B. and boyd, danah (2013) 'Sociality Through Social Network Sites', in W.H. Dutton (ed.), *The Oxford Handbook of Internet Studies*. Oxford: Oxford University Press. pp. 151–72.

Engles, Tim (2017) 'Racialized Slacktivism: Social Media Performances of White Antiracism', in T.M. Kennedy, J.I. Middleton and K. Ratcliffe (eds), *Rhetorics of Whiteness: Postracial Hauntings in Popular Culture, Social Media and Education*. Carbondale, IL: Southern Illinois University Press. pp. 92–111.

Entman, Robert M. (1993) Framing: toward clarification of a fractured paradigm, *Journal of Communication*, *43*(4): 51–8.

Esajas, Mitchell (2016) 'Lessons from the Civil Rights Movement: Reflections on the Long Movement for Black Liberation from Atlanta to Amsterdam', *Humanity in Action* [online]. Available at www.human ityinaction.org/knowledgebase/730-lessons-from-the-civil-rights-move ment-reflections-on-the-long-movement-for-black-liberation-from- atlanta-to-amsterdam

Essed, Philomena (1991) *Understanding Everyday Racism*. London: Sage.

Essed, Philomena and Muhr, Sarah Louise (2018) 'Entitlement Racism and its Intersections: An Interview with Philomena Essed, Social Justice Scholar', *Ephemera: Theory & Politics in Organization.* Available at www.ephem erajournal.org/contribution/entitlement-racism-and-its-intersections-inter view-philomena-essed-social-justice

Eyerman, Ron (2008) *The Assassination of Theo Van Gogh: From Social Drama to Cultural Trauma.* Durham, NC: Duke University Press.

Fadil, Nadia (2016) Are we all secular/ized yet? Reflections on David Goldberg's *Are We All Postracial Yet, Ethnic and Racial Studies 39*(13): 2261–8.

Fanon, Frantz (1952[1986]) *Black Skins, White Masks.* London: Pluto.

Farkas, Johan, Schou, Jannick and Neumayer, Christina (2018) Cloaked Facebook pages: exploring fake Islamist propaganda in social media, *New Media & Society, 20*(5): 1850–67.

Fassin, Didier (2015) In the name of the Republic: untimely meditations on the aftermath of the Charlie Hebdo attack, *Anthropology Today, 31*(2): 3–7.

Fassin, Éric (2012) Sexual democracy and the new racialization of Europe, *Journal of Civil Society, 8*(3): 285–88.

Fassin, Éric (2018) 'L'irruption des Contre-Publics', *Analyse, Opinion, Critique* [online] 14 February. Available at https://aoc.media/opinion/2018/02/13/ lirruption-contre-publics/ (accessed 5 January 2019).

Fekete, Liz (2008) *Integration, Islamophobia and Civil Rights in Europe.* London: Institute of Race Relations.

Fekete, Liz (2009) *A Suitable Enemy: Racism, Migration and Islamophobia in Europe.* London: Pluto.

Fekete, Liz (2012) The Muslim conspiracy theory and the Oslo massacre, *Race & Class, 53*(30): 30–47.

Fekete, Liz (2016) 'Flying the Nativist Flag', *Open Democracy* [online] 10 June. Available at www.opendemocracy.net/uk/austerity-media/liz-fekete/ flying-nativist-flag (accessed 25 November 2018).

Fekete, Liz (2018) *Europe's Fault Lines: Racism and the Rise of the Right.* London: Verso.

Fell, Alison S. (2011) 'Beyond the Bonhemme Banania: Lucie Cousturier's Encounters with West African Soldiers During the First World War', in J. Kitchen, A. Miller and L. Rowe (eds), *Other Combatants, Other Fronts: Competing Histories of the First World War.* Newcastle: Cambridge Scholars Publishing. pp. 225–54.

Fenton, Natalie (2008) 'Bridging the Mythical Divide: Political Economy and Cultural Studies Approaches to the Analysis of the Media', in E. Devereux (ed.), *Media Studies: Key Issues and Debates.* London: Sage.

Fenton, Natalie (ed.) (2010) *New Media, Old News: Journalism & Democracy in the Digital Age.* London: Sage.

Fenton, Natalie (2016) *Digital, Political, Radical.* Cambridge: Polity.

Fernando, Mayanthi L. (2015) 'France after Charlie Hebdo: Forum Response', *Boston Review* [online] 24 February. Available at http:// bostonreview.net/forum/france-after-charlie-hebdo/mayanthi-l-fernando- response-france-after-charlie-hebdo-fernando

Finger, C. and De Souza, F.C. (2012) A new way of watching TV on the couch or anywhere, *Revista FAMECOS, 19*(2): 373–89.

Fish, Stanley (2012) 'The Harm in Free Speech', *The New York Times Opinionator Blog* [online] 4 June. Available at https://opinionator.blogs.nytimes.com/2012/06/04/the-harm-in-free-speech/ (accessed 5 January 2019).

Florini, Sarah (2015) This week in Blackness, the George Zimmerman acquittal, and the production of a networked collective identity, *New Media & Society, 19*(3): 439–54.

Foley, Gary (1997) 'Native Title is not Land Rights', *The Koori History Website* [online] September. Available at www.kooriweb.org/foley/essays/pdf_essays/native%20title%20is%20not%20land%20rights.pdf (accessed 5 January 2019).

Fox, Andrew (2016) 'The Media Event as Enhanced News Story: How User-Generated Content Determines the News Agenda', in A. (ed.), *Global Perspectives on Media Events in Contemporary Society*. Hershey, PA: IGI Global. pp. 17–27.

Foxman, Abraham H. and Wolf, Christopher (2013) *Viral Hate: Containing Its Spread on the Internet*. New York: St. Martin's Press.

Frank, Chandra (2014) 'Using Blackface to Make a Point', *Africa is a Country* [online] 19 November. Available at www.africasacountry.com/2014/11/using-blackface-to-make-a-point (accessed 19 November 2018).

Fraser, Nancy (1990) Rethinking the public sphere: a contribution to the critique of actually existing democracy, *Social Text, 25/26*: 56–80.

Fredrickson, George M. (2002) *Racism: A Short History*. Princeton, NJ: Princeton University Press.

Freedman, Des (2014) *The Contradictions of Media Power*. London: Bloomsbury Academic.

Freelon, Deen, Mcilwaine, Charlton D. and Clarke, Meredith D. (2016) *Beyond the Hashtags: #Ferguson, #Blacklivesmatter, and the Online Struggle for Offline Justice*. Washington, DC: The Center for Media & Social Impact.

Froio, Caterina and Ganesh, Bharath (2018) 'The Transnationalisation of Far Right Discourse on Twitter', *European Societies*, 20 July. Available at www.tandfonline.com/doi/full/10.1080/14616696.2018.1494295 (accessed 5 January 2019).

Fuchs, Christian (2014) *Social Media: A Critical Introduction*. London: Sage.

Garner, Steve (2010) *Racisms: An Introduction*. London: Sage.

Garner, Steve and Selod, Saher (2015) The racialization of Muslims: empirical studies of Islamophobia, *Critical Sociology, 41*(1): 9–19.

Garton Ash, Timothy (2015) 'Europe's media must unite and stand against the assassin's veto', *The Globe and Mail*, January 8th. Available at: https://www.theglobeandmail.com/opinion/europes-media-must-unite-and-stand-again-the-assassins-veto/article22360163/ (last accessed 23 January 2019)

Georgiou, Myria and Zaborowski, Rafal (2017) *Media Coverage of the 'Refugee Crisis': A Cross-European Perspective*. Strasbourg: Council of Europe.

Gilbert, Jeremy (2013) *Common Ground: Democracy and Collectivity in an Age of Individualism*. London: Pluto.

Gilmartin, Mary, Burke Wood, Patricia, and O'Callaghan, Cian (2018) *Borders, Mobility and Belonging in the Era of Brexit and Trump*. Bristol: Policy.

Gilroy, Paul (1990) *There Ain't No Black on the Union Jack*. London: Routledge

Gilroy, Paul (2004) *After Empire: Melancholia or Convivial Culture?* London: Routledge.

Gilroy, Paul (2012) 'My Britain is fuck all': zombie multiculturalism and the race politics of citizenship, *Global Studies in Culture and Power, 19*(4): 380–97.

Gimenez, Elsa and Voirol, Olivier (2017) 'Les agitateurs de la toile: L'internet des droits extrêmes', *Réseaux, 2*: 9–37.

Giroux, Henry A. (2003) Spectacles of race and pedagogies of denial: anti-black racist pedagogy under the reign of neoliberalism, *Communication Education, 52*(3–4): 191–211.

Glatte, Sarah (2015) 'Charlie Hebdo Cartoons: To Republish or Not to Republish?', Free Speech Debate [online] 19 May. Available at https://free-speechdebate.com/discuss/charlie-hebdo-cartoons-to-republish-or-not-to-republish/ (accessed 5 January 2019).

Goldberg, David T. (2002) *The Racial State.* Hoboken, NJ: Wiley-Blackwell.

Goldberg, David T. (2015) *Are We All Postracial Yet?* Cambridge: Polity.

Göle, Nilüfer (2017) *Daily Lives of Muslims: Islam and Public Confrontation in Contemporary Europe.* London: Zed.

Goodman, David (2015) Before hate speech: Charles Coughlin, free speech and listeners' rights, *Patterns of Prejudice, 49*(3): 199–224.

Gordon, Lewis R. (2005) Through the zone of nonbeing: a reading of *Black Skin, White Masks* in celebration of Fanon's eightieth birthday, *The C.L.R. James Journal, 11*(1): 1–43.

Graeff, Erhardt, Stempeck, Matt and Zuckerman, Ethan (2014) 'The Battle for "Trayvon Martin": Mapping a Media Controversy Online and Off-line', *First Monday* [online] *19*(2–3). Available at https://firstmonday.org/article/view/4947/3821 (accessed 5 January 2019).

Gray, Herman (2013) Subject(ed) to recognition, *American Quarterly, 65*(4): 771–98.

Greene, Eric (1998) *Planet of the Apes as American Myth: Race, Politics, and Popular Culture.* Middletown, CT: Wesleyan University Press.

Greenslade, Roy (2015) Available at www.theguardian.com/media/2015/jan/11/charlie-hebdo-cartoons-uk-press-publish

Gregory, Derek (2004) *The Colonial Present.* Oxford: Blackwell.

Gressgård, Randi (2012) *Multicultural Dialogue: Dilemmas, Paradoxes, Conflicts.* Oxford and New York: Berghahn.

Groot, Nadja and de Kroon, Eefje (2013) '"Black Pete" and the Legacy of Racism in the Netherlands', *Open Society Foundations* [online] 14 November. Available at www.opensocietyfoundations.org/voices/black-pete-and-legacy-racism-netherlands (accessed 19 November 2018).

Guerrero, Lisa and Leonard, David J. (2012) 'Playing Dead: The Trayvoning Meme and the Mocking of Black Death', *New Black Man* [online] 29 May. Available at www.newblackmaninexile.net/2012/05/playing-dead-trayvoning-meme-mocking-of.html (accessed 18 November 2018).

Guild, Elspeth, Groenendijk, Kees and Carrera, Sergio (2009) 'Understanding the Contest of Community: Illiberal Practices in the EU?' In E. Guild, K. Groenendijk and S. Carrera (eds), *Illiberal States: Immigration, Citizenship and Integration in the EU.* Farnham: Ashgate.

Guillaumin, Colette (1995) *Racism, Sexism, Power and Ideology*. London: Routledge.

Hage, Ghassan (1998) *White Nation: Fantasies of White Supremacy in a Multicultural Society*. Annandale, VA: Pluto.

Hage, Ghassan (2015) *Alter-Politics: Critical Anthropology and the Radical Imagination*. Melbourne: Melbourne University Press.

Hage, Ghassan (2017) *Is Racism an Environmental Threat? Debating Race*. Cambridge: Polity.

Hajjat, Abdellali (2017) 'A Double-bind Situation? The Depoliticization of Violence and the Politics of Compensation', in G. Titley, D. Freedman, G. Khiabany and A. Mondon (eds), *After Charlie Hebdo: Terror, Racism, Free Speech*. London: Zed.

Hale, Chris W. (2012) Extremism on the World Wide Web: a research review, *Criminal Justice Studies: A Critical Journal of Crime, Law and Society*, 25(4): 343–56.

Halikiopoulou, Sofia and Vasilopoulou, Daphne (2015) *The Golden Dawn's Nationalist Solution: Explaining the Rise of the Far Right in Greece*. Basingstoke: Palgrave Macmillan.

Hall, Stuart (1980) 'Race, Articulation and Societies Structured in Dominance', in United Nations Educational Scientific and Cultural Organisation (ed.), *Sociological Theories: Race and Colonialism*, Paris: UNESCO. pp. 305–45.

Hall, Stuart (1981) 'The Whites of their Eyes: Racist Ideologies and the Media', in G. Bridges and R. Brunt (eds), *Silver Linings*. London: Lawrence & Wishart.

Hall, Stuart (2017) *The Fateful Triangle: Race, Ethnicity, Nation*. Edited by Kobena Mercer. Cambridge, MA: Harvard University Press.

Hall, Stuart (2017[1978]) 'Racism and Reaction' in *Selected Political Writings: The Great Moving Right Show*. Durham, NC: Duke University Press.

Hallin, Daniel C. and Mancini, Paolo (2004) *Comparing Media Systems: Three Models of Media and Politics*. Cambridge: Cambridge University Press.

Hannaford, Ivan (1996) *Race: the History of an Idea in the West*. Washington, DC: Woodrow Wilson Center.

Haraway, Donna (1989) *Primate Visions: Gender, Race and Nature in the World of Modern Science*. New York: Routledge.

Harries, Bethan (2014) 'We need to talk about race', *Sociology*, 48(6): 1107–22.

Hartigan, John Jr (2010) *What Can You Say? America's National Conversation on Race*. Stanford, CA: Stanford University Press.

Hawley, George (2017a) *Making Sense of the Alt-Right*. New York: Columbia University Press.

Hawley, George (2017b) 'The Long History of White Nationalism in America', *Literary Hub* [online] 16 August. Available at https://lithub.com/the-long-history-of-white-nationalism-in-america/ (last accessed 25 November 2018).

Haworth, Alan (1998) *Free Speech*. London and New York: Routledge.

Haworth, Alan (2015) *Free Speech (All that Matters)*. London: Hodder and Stoughton.

Heinze, Eric (2016) *Hate Speech and Democratic Citizenship*. Oxford: Oxford University Press.

Hepp, Andreas and Couldry, Nick (2010) 'Introduction: Media Events in Globalized Media Cultures', in N. Couldry, A. Hepp and F. Krotz (eds), *Media Events in a Global Age*. Abingdon: Routledge. pp. 1–20.

Hern, Alex (2015) 'Flickr Faces Complaints Over "Offensive" Auto-tagging for Photos', *The Guardian* [online] 20 May. Available at www.theguardian.com/technology/2015/may/20/flickr-complaints-offensive-auto-tagging-photos (accessed 5 January 2019).

Hervik, Peter, Eide, Elisabeth and Kunelius, Risto (2008) 'A Long and Messy Event', in A. Phillips, R. Kunelius and E. Eide (eds), *Transnational Media Events: The Mohammed Cartoons and the Imagined Clash of Civilizations*. Gothenburg: Nordicom.

Herz, Michael and Molnar, Peter (2012) *The Content and Context of Hate Speech: Rethinking Regulation and Responses*. Cambridge: Cambridge University Press.

Hesmondhalgh, David and Toynbee, Jason (eds) (2008) *The Media and Social Theory*. London and New York: Routledge.

Hesse, Barnor (2004) Im/plausible deniability: racism's conceptual double bind, *Social Identities*, *10*(1): 9–29.

Hesse, Barnor (2007) Racialized modernity: an analytics of white mythologies, *Ethnic and Racial Studies*, *30*(4): 643–63.

Highfield, Tim (2016) *Social Media and Every Day Politics*. Cambridge: Polity.

Hobeika, Alexandre and Villeneuve, Gaël (2016) Une communication par les marges du parti? Les groups Facebook proches du Front National, *Réseaux*, 2017/2–3(202–203): 213–40.

Hobson, Janelle (2008) Digital whiteness, primitive blackness: racializing the 'digital divide' in film and new media, *Feminist Media Studies*, 8(2): 111–26.

Hockenos, Paul (2012) 'He's Not Alone', *Foreign Policy* [online] 19 April. Available at https://foreignpolicy.com/2012/04/19/hes-not-alone/ (accessed 19 November 2018).

Holt , Jared (2018) 'White Supremacy Figured Out How to Become YouTube Famous', *Right Wing Watch* [online]. Available at www.rightwingwatch.org/report/white-supremacy-figured-out-how-to-become-youtube-famous/ (accessed 5 January 2019).

hooks, bell (1992) *Black Looks: Race and Representation*. Boston, MA: South End.

Horsti, Karina (2016) Digital Islamophobia: the Swedish woman as a figure of pure and dangerous whiteness, *New Media & Society*, *19*(9): 1440–57.

Hoskins, Andrew and O'Loughlin, Ben (2009) Media and the myth of radicalization, *Media, War & Conflict*, 2(2).

Ibrahim, Yasmin (2007) 9/11 as a new temporal phase for Islam: The narrative and temporal framing of Islam in crisis, *Contemporary Islam*, *1*: 37–51.

Jackson, John L. (2008) *Racial Paranoia: The Unintended Consequences of Political Correctness and the New Reality of Race in America*. New York: Basic Civitas.

Jacobs, Ronald N. (2014) 'Media Sociology and the Study of Race', in S. Waisbord (ed.), *Media Sociology: A Reappraisal*. Cambridge: Polity.

James, Malcom, Rashid, Naaz and Munawar, Nabila (2018) 'Stop Dehumanising Muslim Women for Political Gain', *Red Pepper* [online] 16 August. Available at www.redpepper.org.uk/stop-dehumanising-muslim-women-for-political-gain/ (accessed 18 November 2018).

Jarrett, Kylie and Naji, Jeneen (2016) What would media studies do? Social media Shakespeare as a technosocial process, *Borrowers and Lenders: The Journal of Shakespeare and Appropriation*, *10*(1).

Jensen, Klaus B. (2013) Definitive and sensitizing conceptualizations of mediatization, *Communication Theory*, *23*(3): 203–22.

Kallis, Aristotle (2015) 'A Thin Red Line? Far Right and Mainstream in a Relational Perspective', in G. Charalambous (ed.), *The European Far Right: Historical and Contemporary Perspectives*. Oslo: PRIO.

Kapoor, Nisha (2018) *Deport, Deprive, Extradite: 21st Century State Extremism*. London: Verso.

Kavan, Zdenek (2016) 'Racism in Post-Communist Central Europe', *Discover Society* [online] 1 June. Available at https://discoversociety.org/2016/06/01/racism-in-post-communist-central-europe/

Kearns, Erin, Betus, Allison and Lemieux, Anthony (2 April, 2018) Why do some terrorist attacks receive more media attention than others?, *Justice Quarterly*, forthcoming. Available at https://ssrn.com/abstract=2928138 or http://dx.doi.org/10.2139/ssrn.2928138

Kelley, Robin D.G. (2013) 'The US v. Trayvon Martin', *Counterpunch* [online] 15 July. Available at www.counterpunch.org/2013/07/15/the-us-v-trayvon-martin/ (last accessed 18 November 2018).

Kellner, Douglas (2015) 'Cultural Studies, Multiculturalism and Media Culture', in G. Dines, J. Gail, M. Humez, B. Yousman and L. Bindig Yousman (eds), *Gender, Race and Class in the Media*. London: Sage.

Keskinen, Suvi (2017) The 'crisis' of white hegemony, neonationalist feminities and antiracist feminism, *Women's Studies International Forum*, *68*: 157–63.

Klein, Adam (2012) Slipping racism into the mainstream: a theory of information laundering, *Communication Theory*, *22*: 427–48.

Klein, Adam (2017) *Fanaticism, Racism and Rage Online: Corrupting the Digital Sphere*. Basingstoke: Palgrave Macmillan.

Klug, Brian (2014) The limits of analogy: comparing Islamophobia and antisemitism, *Patterns of Prejudice*, *48*(5): 442–59.

Klug, Brian (2015) 'The Moral Hysteria of Je Suis Charlie', *Mondoweiss* [online] 11 January. Available at https://mondoweiss.net/2015/01/moral-hysteria-charlie/ (accessed 5 January 2019).

Kryżanowski, Mihail and Wodak, Ruth (2009) *The Politics of Exclusion: Debating Migration in Austria*. New Brunswick, NJ: Transaction.

Kumar, Deepa (2012) *Islamophobia and the Politics of Empire*. Chicago, IL: Haymarket.

Kundnani, Arun (2007) *The End of Tolerance: Racism in 21st Century Britain*. London: Pluto.

Kundnani, Arun (2012) Radicalization: the journey of a concept, *Race & Class*, *54*(2): 3–25.

Kundnani, Arun (2014) *The Muslims Are Coming! Islamophobia, Extremism and the Domestic War on Terror*. London: Verso.

Kunelius, Risto (2013) 'The Satanic Pendulum: Notes on Free Speech, the Public Sphere and Journalism in 2013', in U. Carlsson (ed.), *Freedom of Expression, Revisited Citizenship and Journalism in the Digital Era*. Göteborg: Nordicom. pp. 27–44.

Kuo, Rachel (2016) Racial justice activist hashtags: counterpublics and discourse circulation, *New Media & Society, 20*(2).

Kyriakides, Christopher (2017) Words don't come easy: Al Jazeera's migrant-refugee distinction and the European culture of (mis)-trust, *Current Sociology, 65*(7):933–52.

Lalami, Laila (2018) 'The Social Shaming of Racists is Working', *The Nation* [online] 24 May. Available at www.thenation.com/article/the-social-shaming-of-racists-is-working/ (accessed 5 January 2019).

Langlois, Ganaele (2014) *Meaning in the Age of Social Media.* Basingstoke: Palgrave Macmillan.

Lapowsky, Issie (2015) 'Meet the Editors Fighting Racism and Sexism on Wikipedia', *Wired* [online] 3 May. Available at www.wired.com/2015/03/wikipedia-sexism/ (accessed 5 January 2019).

Laursen, Ditte and Sandvik, Kjetil (2014) Talking with TV shows: simultaneous conversations between users and producers in the second-screen television production voice, *Northern Lights: Film & Media Studies Handbook, 12*(1):141–60.

Lawrence, Charles R. (1993) 'If He Hollers Let Him Go: Regulating Racist Speech on Campus', in M. Matsuda et al. (eds), *Words that Wound: Critical Race Theory, Assaultive Speech and the First Amendment.* Boulder, CO: Westview.

Lee, Benjamin (2015) A day in the "swamp": understanding discourse in the online counter-jihad nebula, *Democracy and Security, 11*(3): 248–74.

Lentin, Alana (2004) *Racism & Anti-Racism in Europe.* London: Pluto.

Lentin, Alana (2015) 'Racism in public or public racism: doing anti-racism in 'post-racial' times', *Ethnic and Racial Studies*, DOI: 10.1080/01419871.2016.109640.

Lentin, Alana (2016) 'The Lure of "Frozen" Racism', *Occupied Times* [online] 31 March. Available at https://theoccupiedtimes.org/?p=14225 (accessed 18 November 2018).

Lentin, Alana and Titley, Gavan (2011) *The Crises of Multiculturalism: Racism in a Neoliberal Age.* London: Zed.

Lievrouw, Leah A. (2011) *Alternative and Activist New Media.* Cambridge: Polity.

Lindgren, Simon (2017) *Digital Media and Society.* London: Sage.

Ling, Justin (2017) 'Follow the Money' *Vice News* [online] 22 August. Available at https://news.vice.com/en_ca/article/wjz73q/inside-rebel-medias-big-money-anti-islam-crusade (accessed 5 January 2018).

Lipsitz, George (2015) From Plessy to Ferguson, *Cultural Critique, 90*: 119–39.

Losurdo, Domenico (2011) *Liberalism: A Counter-History.* London: Verso.

Louw, Eric (2010) *The Media and Political Process.* London: Sage.

Lovink, Geert (2011) *Networks Without a Cause.* Cambridge: Polity.

Lowles, Nick (2017) *Breitbart: A Rightwing Plot to Shape Europe's Future.* London: Hope Not Hate.

Luibhéid, Eithne (2013) *Pregnant on Arrival: Making the Illegal Immigrant.* Minneapolis, MN: University of Minnesota Press.

Lunt, Peter and Livingstone, Sonia (2013) Media studies' fascination with the concept of the public sphere: critical reflections and emerging debates', *Media, Culture & Society, 35*(1): 87–96.

Macedo, Donaldo and Gounari, Panayota (eds) (2005) *The Globalization of Racism*. London: Routledge.

Macey, David (2000) *Frantz Fanon: A Biography*. London: Verso.

Macgilchrist, Felicitas and Böhmig, Inse (2012) Blogs, genes and immigration: online media and minimal politics, *Media, Culture & Society, 34*(1): 83–100.

Mackey, Robert (2014) 'Belgian Paper Apologizes Over Racist Images of Obama Used in Satire', *New York Times Lede blog* [online] 24 March. Available at https://thelede.blogs.nytimes.com/2014/03/24/belgian-paper-apologizes-over-racist-images-of-obama-used-in-satire/ (accessed 5 January 2019).

MacMaster, Neil (2001) *Racism in Europe 1870-2000*. Basingstoke: Palgrave.

Maïga *et collectif* (2018) *Noire n'est pas mon metier*. Paris: Le Seuil.

Mair, Peter (2013) *Ruling the Void: The Hollowing of Western Democracy*. London: Verso.

Maitra, Ishani and McGowan, Mary Kate (2012) *Speech & Harm: Controversies Over Free Speech*. Oxford: Oxford University Press.

Malik, Kenan (2012) 'Interview with Kenan Malik', in M. Herz and P. Molnar (eds), *The Content and Context of Hate Speech: Rethinking Regulation and Responses*. Cambridge: Cambridge University Press.

Malik, Sarita (2002) *Representing Black Britain: Black and Asian Images on Television*. London: Sage.

Mammone, Andrea, Godin, Emmanuel and Jenkins, Brian (eds) (2013) *Varieties of Right-Wing Extremism*. London: Routledge.

Mann, Michael (2004) *Fascists*. Cambridge: Cambridge University Press.

Margolis, Michael and Moreno-Riaño, Gerson (2016) *The Prospect of Internet Democracy*. London: Routledge.

Marlière, Philippe (2017) 'The Meaning of "Charlie": The Debate on the Troubled French Identity', in G. Titley, D. Freedman, G. Khiabany and A. Mondon (eds), *After Charlie Hebdo: Terror, Racism and Free Speech*. London: Zed.

Martina, Egbert A. (2013) 'The Delicious Pleasures of Racism', *Processed Lives* [online] 15 October 2013. Available at https://processedlives.word-press.com/2013/10/15/the-delicious-pleasures-of-racism/ (accessed 19 November 2018).

Marwick, Alice E. and boyd, danah (2011) 'I tweet honestly, I tweet passionately': Twitter users, context collapse, and the imagined audience, *New Media & Society, 13*(1): 114–33.

Mast, Nina (2018) 'Meet Peter Imanuelsen, aka Peter Sweden', *Media Matters for America* [online] 12 January. Available at www.mediamatters.org/blog/2018/01/12/meet-peter-imanuelsen-aka-peter-sweden-bigoted-conspiracy-theorist-who-frequent-source-american-alt/219064 (accessed 5 January 2019).

Matamoros-Fernández, Ariadna (2017) Platformed racism: the mediation and circulation of an Australian race-based controversy on Twitter, Facebook and YouTube, *Information, Communication & Society, 20*(6): 930–46.

Matsuda, Mari (1993) 'Public Responses to Racist Speech: Considering the Victim's Story', in M. Matsuda et al. (eds), *Words that Wound: Critical Race Theory, Assaultive Speech and the First Amendment*. Boulder, CO: Westview.

Matthes, Jörd and Kohring, Matthias (2008) The content analysis of media frames: toward improving reliability and validity, *Journal of Communication*, *58*(2): 258–79.

Maussen, Marcel and Grillo, Ralph (2013) Regulation of speech in multicultural societies: introduction, *Journal of Ethnic and Migration Studies*, *40*(2): 174–93.

Maza, Carlos (2017) 'Why White Supremacists Love Tucker Carlson', *Vox* [online] 21 July. Available at www.vox.com/videos/2017/7/21/16008190/strikethrough-white-supremacists-love-tucker-carlson (accessed 5 January 2019).

Mazower, Mark (1998) *Dark Continent: Europe's Twentieth Century*. London: Allen Lane/Penguin.

McIlwain, Charlton (2017) Racial formation, inequality and the political economy of web traffic, *Communication & Society*, *20*(7): 1073–89.

McNally, David (2011) *Global Slump: The Economic and Politics of Crisis and Resistance*. Oakland, CA: PM Press.

McVey, James A. and Woods, Heather S. (2016) Anti-racist activism and the transformational principles of hashtag publics: from #handsupdontshoot to #pantsupdontloot, *Present Tense: A Journal of Rhetoric in Society*, *5*(3).

Meer, Nasar (2013) Racialization and religion: race, culture and difference in the study of Antisemitism and Islamophobia, *Ethnic and Racial Studies*, *36*(3): 285–98.

Meer, Nasar, Dwyer, Claire and Modood, Tariq (2010) Beyond 'angry Muslims'? Reporting Muslim voices in the British press, *Journal of Media and Religion*, *9*: 216–31.

Meleagrou-Hitchens, Alexander and Brun, Hans (2013) *A Neo-Nationalist Network: The English Defence League and Europe's Counter-Jihad Movement*. London: ICSR.

Michel, Noémi (2016) Accounts of Inquiry as Misappropriations of Race: Towards a Critical Black Politics of Vulnerability, *Critical Horizons*, *17*(2): 240–59.

Miekle, Graham (2016) *Social Media: Communication, Sharing and Visibility*. London: Routledge.

Miller-Idris, Cynthia (2018) *The Extreme Gone Mainstream: Commercialization and Far Right Youth Culture in Germany*. Princeton, NJ: Princeton University Press.

Mills, Charles W. (1997) *The Racial Contract*. Ithaca, NY: Cornell University Press.

Minkenberg, Michael (2011) *The Radical Right in Europe: An Overview*. Bielefeld: Verlag Bertelsmann Stiftung.

Mirzoeff, Nicholas (2017) *The Appearance of Black Lives Matter*. Miami, FL: NAME Publications.

Modood, Tariq (2005) *Multicultural Politics: Racism, Ethnicity, and Muslims in Britain*. Minneapolis, MN: University of Minnesota Press.

Mondon, Aurélien and Winter, Aaron (2017) 'Republican Secularism and Islamophobia', in G. Titley, D. Freedman, G. Khiabany and A. Mondon (eds), *After Charlie Hebdo: Terror, Racism and Free Speech*. London: Zed.

Moore, Kerry (2013) 'Asylum shopping' in the neoliberal social imaginary, *Media, Culture & Society*, *35*(3): 348–65.

Moore, Kerry, Berry, Mike and Garcia-Blanco, Inaki (2018) Saving refugees or policing the seas? How the national press of five EU member states framed news coverage of the migration crisis, *Justice, Power and Resistance*, *2*(1): 66–95.

Moore, Kerry, Mason, Paul and Lewis, Justin (2008) *Images of Islam in the UK: the Representation of British Muslims in the National Print news Media 2000-2008*. Cardiff: Cardiff School of Journalism, Media and Cultural Studies. Available at www.channel4.com/news/media/pdfs/Cardiff%20 Final%20Report.pdf (accessed 5 January 2019).

Morsi, Yassir (2017) *Radical Skin, Moderate Masks*. London: Rowman & Littlefield.

Mortensen, Mette (2015) Connective witnessing: reconfiguring the relationship between the individual and the collective, *Information, Communication & Society*, *18*(11): 1393–406.

Mudde, Cas (2010) *The Ideology of the Extreme Right*. Manchester: Manchester University Press.

Mudde, Cas (2014) The far right and the European elections, *Current History*, *113*(761): 98–103.

Müller, Karsten and Schwarz, Carlo (2018) 'Fanning the Flames of Hate: Social Media and Hate Crime', *Semantic Scholar*. Available at https://pdfs. semanticscholar.org/b19c/8a6eb0a519749a724a34b677aa7d3cf24e74.pdf (accessed 5 January 2019).

Munnik, Michael B. (2017) From *voice* to *voices*: identifying a plurality of Muslim sources in the news media, *Media, Culture & Society*, *39*(2): 270–81.

Muraja, Tuomas (2015) 'Perussuomalaisten Huhtasaari kiistää liittyneensä itse Facebookin rasistiseen ryhmään', *Helsingin Sanomat* [online] 2 July. Available at www.hs.fi/politiikka/art-2000002835716.html (accessed 18 November 2018).

Murji, Karim and Solomos, John (eds) (2015) *Theories of Race and Ethnicity: Contemporary Debates and Perspectives*. Cambridge: Cambridge University Press.

Murray, Douglas (2017) *The Strange Death of Europe: Immigration, Identity, Islam*. London: Bloomsbury.

Murthy, Dhiraj (2013) *Twitter: Social Communication in the Twitter Age*. Cambridge: Polity.

Narkowicz, Kasia and Pędziwiatr, Konrad (2016) 'Why Are Polish People So Wrong about Muslims in Their Country?, *Open Democracy* [online] 13 January. Available at www.opendemocracy.net/can-europe-make-it/ kasia-narkowicz-konrad-pedziwiatr/why-are-polish-people-so-wrong-about-muslims-in (accessed 5 January 2019).

Neel, Seth (2016) 'Facebook's Race-targeted Ads Aren't As Racist As You Think', *Wired* [online], 9 November. Available at www.wired.com/2016/11/ facebooks-race-targeted-ads-arent-racist-think/ (accessed 5 January 2019).

Neiwert, David (2017) *Alt-America: The Rise of the Radical Right in the Age of Trump*. London: Verso.

Ngo, Madeleine (2018) '"No ghettos in 2030": Denmark's controversial plan to get rid of immigrant neighbourhoods', *Vox* [online] 3 July. Available at www.vox.com/world/2018/7/3/17525960/denmark-children-immigrant-muslim-danish-ghetto (accessed 7 January 2019).

Nielsen, Rasmus K., Cornia, Alessio and Kalogeropoulos, Antonis (2016) *Challenges and Opportunities for News Media and Journalism in an Increasingly Digital, Mobile, and Social Media Environment,* Council of Europe report DGI(2016) 18.

Noble, Safiya U. (2014) Teaching Trayvon: race, media and the politics of spectacle, *The Black Scholar, 44*(1): 12–29.

Noble, Safiya U. (2018) *Algorithms of Oppression: How Search Engines Reinforce Racism.* New York: New York University Press.

O'Sullivan, Daniel (2011) 'What is an Encyclopedia? From Pliny to Wikipedia', in G. Lovionk and N. Tkacz (eds), *Critical Points of View: A Wikipedia Reader.* Amsterdam: Institute for Network Cultures.

Ojala, Markus and Pöyhtäri, Reeta (2018) Watchdogs, advocates and adversaries: journalists' relational role conceptions in asylum reporting, *Media and Communication, 6*(2): 168–78.

Oltermann, Philip and Helmore, Edward (2017) 'Swedish Police Comments "Taken Out of Context" in Film Cited by Trump', *The Guardian* [online] 20 February. Available at www.theguardian.com/world/2017/feb/20/swedish-police-comments-taken-out-of-context-in-film-cited-by-trump (accessed 9 January 2019).

Omi, Michael and Winant, Howard (1995) *Racial Formation in the United States.* London: Routledge.

Orgad, Shani (2012) *Media Representation and the Global Imagination.* Cambridge: Polity.

Pai, Hsiao-Hung (2016) *Angry White People: Coming Face-to-Face with the British Far Right.* London: Zed.

Papacharissi, Zizi (2011) *A Private Sphere: Democracy in a Digital Age.* Cambridge: Polity.

Papacharissi, Zizi (2014) *Affective Publics: Sentiment, Technology, and Politics.* Oxford: Oxford University Press.

Paul, Joshua (2014) Post-racial futures: imagining post-racialist anti-racism(s), *Ethnic and Racial Studies, 37*(4): 702–18.

Paxton, Robert O. (2004) *The Anatomy of Fascism.* London: Penguin.

Peters, Chris and Witschge, Tamara (2014) From grand narratives of democracy to small expectations of participation, *Journalism Practice, 9*(1): 19–34.

Peters, John D. (2001) Witnessing, *Media, Culture & Society, 23*(6): 707–23.

Peters, John D. (2005) *Courting the Abyss: Free Speech and the Liberal Tradition.* Chicago, IL: University of Chicago Press.

Peters, John D. (2008) 'Afterword: In Quest of Even Better Heresies', in A. Phillips, R. Kunelius and E. Eide (eds), *Transnational Media Events: The Mohammed Cartoons and the Imagined Clash of Civilizations.* Gothenburg: Nordicom.

Petray, Theresa L. and Collin, Rowan (2017) 'Your privilege is trending': confronting whiteness on social media, *Social Media + Society.* Available at https://doi.org/10.1177%2F2056305117706783

Phelan, Sean (2017) 'Critical Discourse Analysis and Media Studies', in J. Flowerdue and J.E. Richardson (eds), *The Routledge Handbook of Critical Discourse Studies*, London: Routledge.

Philips, Whitney and Milner, Ryan (2017) *The Ambivalent Internet: Mischief, Oddity, and Antagonism Online*. Cambridge: Polity.

Philo, Greg, Briant, Emma and Donald, Pauline (2013) *Bad News for Refugees*. London: Pluto.

Pickering, Michael (2001) *Stereotyping: The Politics of Representation*. Basingstoke: Palgrave.

Pickering, Michael (2008) *Blackface Minstrelsy in Britain*. Burlington, VT: Ashgate.

Pitcher, Ben (2009) *The Politics of Multiculturalism: Race and Racism in Contemporary Britain*. Basingstoke: Palgrave Macmillan.

Pitcher, Ben (2014) *Consuming Race*. London: Routledge.

Pittman, Matthew and Tefertiller, Alec C. (2015) With or without you: connected viewing and co-viewing Twitter activity for traditional appointment and asynchronous broadcast television models, *First Monday*, *20*(7). Available at https://firstmonday.org/article/view/5935/4663

Plenel, Edwy (2016) *For the Muslims*. London: Verso.

Poell, Thomas and Van Dijck, José (2014) 'Social Media and Journalistic Independence', in J. Bennett and N. Strange (eds), *Media Independence: Working with Freedom or Working for Free?* New York: Routledge. pp. 182–201.

Pohjonen, Matti (2018) *Horizons of Hate: A Comparative Approach to Social Media Hate Speech, Vox-Pol Network of Excellence.*

Poole, Elizabeth, de Quincey, Ed and Giraud, Eva (2018) 'Contesting #stopislam: tensions around hate speech on social media', *British Academy Review*, *33* (summer). Available at www.thebritishacademy.ac.uk/sites/default/files/BAR33-06-Poole.pdf (accessed 7 January 2019).

Potok, Mark (2017) 'The Year in Hate and Extremism', *Intelligence Report* [online] 15 February, Southern Poverty Law Centre. Available at www.splcenter.org/fighting-hate/intelligence-report/2017/year-hate-and-extremism (accessed 7 January 2019).

Pred, Allan (2000) *Even in Sweden: Racisms, Racialized Spaces, and the Popular Geographical Imagination*. Oakland, CA: University of California Press.

Ramalingam, Vidhya and Frenett, Ross (2013) 'The Failed EDLK Rally Plot Shows How Much Extremists Need Each Other', *The Guardian* [online] 1 May. Available at www.theguardian.com/commentisfree/2013/may/01/failed-edl-rally-plot-extremists-need (accessed 7 January 2019).

Ramamurthy, Anandi (2013) *Black Star: Britain's Asian Youth Movements*. London: Pluto.

Rancière, Jacques (2010) 'Racism: A Passion From Above', *Monthly Review* [online] 23 September. Available at https://mronline.org/2010/09/23/racism-a-passion-from-above/ (accessed 7 January 2019).

Rane, Halim, Ewart, Jacqui and Martinkus, John (2014) *Media Framing of the Muslim World: Conflicts, Crises and Contexts*. Basingstoke: Palgrave Macmillan.

Read, Jason (2014) 'Distracted By Attention', *The New Inquiry* [online] 18 December. Available at https://thenewinquiry.com/distracted-by-attention/ (accessed 7 January 2019).

Reed Jr, Adolph (2013) 'Django Unchained, or, The Help: How "Cultural Politics" is Worse Than No Politics At All, and Why', *Nonsite* [online] 25 February. Available at https://nonsite.org/feature/django-unchained-or-the-help-how-cultural-politics-is-worse-than-no-politics-at-all-and-why# (accessed 18 November 2018).

Reed, Touré F. (2018) 'Between Obama and Coates', *Catalyst* [online] *1*(4): Winter. Available at https://catalyst-journal.com/vol1/no4/between-obama-and-coates (accessed 9 January 2019).

Renton, James and Gidley, Ben (eds) (2017) *Antisemitism and Islamophobia in Europe: A Shared Story*. London: Palgrave Macmillan.

Richardson, Allissa V. (2017) Bearing witness while Black, *Digital Journalism*, *5*(6): 673–98.

Richardson, John E. (2006) 'Who Gets to Speak? A Study of Sources in the Broadsheet Press', in E. Poole and J.E. Richardson (eds), *Muslims and the News Media*. London: I.B.Tauris.

Rodriguez, Clemencia (2011) *Citizens' Media against Armed Conflict: Disrupting Violence in Colombia*. Minneapolis, MN: University of Minnesota Press.

Roediger, David (2008) *How Race Survived U.S. History:From Settlement and Slavery to the Obama Phenomenon*. London: Verso.

Rowbotham, Sheila (2011) *Dreamers of a New Day: Women Who Invented the Twentieth Century*. London: Verso.

Rutazibwa, Olivia U. (2016) From the everyday to IR: in defence of the strategic use of the r-word, *Postcolonial Studies*, *19*(2): 191–200.

Saeed, Amir (2007) Media, racism and Islamophobia: the representation of Islam and Muslims in the media, *Sociology Compass*, *1*(2): 443–62.

Saha, Anamik (2018) *Race and the Cultural Industries*. Cambridge: Polity.

Said, Edward (1978) *Orientalism*. London: Pantheon.

Salem, Sara and Thompson, Vanessa (2016) Old racisms, new masks: on the continuing discontinuities of racism and the erasure of race in European contexts, *Nineteen Sixty Nine: An Ethnic Studies Journal*, *3*(1). Available at https://escholarship.org/uc/item/98p8q169

Salovaara, Inka (2015) #JeSuisCharlie: networks, affects and distributed agency of media assemblage, *Conjunctions: Transdisciplinary Journal of Cultural Participation*, *2*(1).

Sanchez Boe, Carolina (2017) 'From Jyllands Posten to Charlie Hebdo: Domesticating the Mohammed Cartoons', in G. Titley, D. Freedman, G. Khiabany and A. Mondon (eds), *After Charlie Hebdo: Terror, Racism and Free Speech*. London: Zed.

Saull, Richard, Anievas, Alexander, Davidson, Neil and Fabr, Adam (2015) *The Longue Durée of the Far-Right: An International Historical Sociology*. London: Routledge.

Schierup, Carl-Ulrik, Ålund, Aleksandra and Kings, Lisa (2014) Reading the Stockholm riots – a moment for social justice?, *Race & Class*, *55*(3): 1–21.

Schierup, Carl-Ulrik, Ålund, Aleksandra, and Neergard, Anders (2018) 'Race' and the upsurge of antagonistic popular movements in Sweden, *Ethnic and Racial Studies, 41*(10): 1837–54.

Shabi, Rachel (2013) 'The Reaction to the Woolwich Murder Denies British Muslims a Political Voice', *The Guardian* [online] 28 May. Available at www.theguardian.com/commentisfree/2013/may/28/woolwich-murder-british-muslims (accessed 7 January 2019).

Sharma, Sanjay (2013) Black Twitter? Racial hashtags, networks and contagion, *New Formations, 78*: 46–64.

Sharma, Sanjay and Brooker, Phillip (2016) '#notracist: Exploring Racism Denial Talk on Twitter', in J. Daniels, K. Gregory and T. McMillan Cottom (eds), *Digital Sociologies*. Bristol: Policy Press. pp. 463–85.

Sharma, Sanjay and Nijjar, Jasbinder (2018) The racialized surveillant assemblage: Islam and the fear of terrorism, *Popular Communication, 16*(1): 72–85.

Shifman, Limor (2014) *Memes in Digital Culture*. Boston, MA: MIT Press.

Shohat, Ella and Stam, Robert (1994) *Unthinking Eurocentrism: Multiculturalism and the Media*. London: Routledge.

Siapera, Eugenia, Moreo, Elena and Zhou, Jiang (2018) *Hate Track: Tracking and Monitoring Online Hate Speech*. Dublin: IHREC.

Siapera, Eugenia and Veikou, Mariangela (2016) 'The Digital Golden Dawn: Emergence of a Nationalist-Racist Digital Mainstream', in A. Karatzogianni, D. Nguyen and E. Scafinelli (eds), *The Digital Transformation of the Public Sphere*. Basingstoke: Palgrave.

Siegel, Jacob (2015) 'Dylann Roof, 4chan, and the New Online Racism', *Daily Beast* [online] 29 June. Available at www.thedailybeast.com/dylann-roof-4chan-and-the-new-online-racism (accessed 7 January 2019).

Silvennoinen, Oula (2016) 'But – Where Do These People Come From? The (Re)emergence of Radical Nationalism in Finland', *Sicherheits Politik-Blog* (online) 4 April. Available at www.sicherheitspolitik-blog.de/2016/04/04/but-where-do-these-people-come-from-the-reemergence-of-radical-nationalism-in-finland/ (accessed 7 January 2019).

Silverstone, Roger (2007) *Media and Morality: On the Rise of the Mediapolis*. Cambridge: Polity.

Sivanandan, Ambalavaner (1990) *Communities of Resistance: Writing on Black Struggles for Socialism*. London: Verso.

Sivanandan, Ambalavaner (2008) *Catching History on the Wing: Race, Culture and Globalisation*. London: Pluto.

Slagle, Mark (2009) An ethical exploration of free expression and the problem of hate speech, *Journal of Mass Media Ethics, 24*: 238–50.

Smith, Jada F. (2015) 'Howard University Fills in Wikipedia's Gaps in Black History', *New York Times* [online] 19 February. Available at www.nytimes.com/2015/02/20/us/at-howard-a-historically-black-university-filling-in-wikipedias-gaps-in-color.html (accessd 7 January 2019).

Solomos, John (2013) 'Contemporary Forms of Racist Movements and Mobilisation in Britain', in R. Wodak, M. Khosravinik and B. Mral (eds), *Right-Wing Populism in Europe: Politics and Discourse*. London: Bloomsbury Academic.

Solomos, John and Back, Les (1996) *Racism and Society*. Basingstoke: Palgrave Macmillan.

Song, Miri (2014) Challenging a culture of racial equivalence, *British Journal of Sociology* [online] *65*(1): 107–29. Available at https://doi.org/10.1111/1468-4446.12054 (last accessed 18 November 2018).

Sontag, Susan (2003) *Regarding the Pain of Others*. New York: Farrar, Straus and Giroux.

Squires, Catherine R. (2002) Rethinking the Black public sphere: an alternative vocabulary for multiple public spheres, *Communication Theory, 12*(4): 446–8.

Sreberny, Annabelle (2016) The 2015 Charlie Hebdo killings, media event chains, and global political responses, *International Journal of Communication, 10*: 3485–502.

St Louis, Brett (2015) 'Can Race be Eradicated? The Post-Racial Problematic', in K. Murji and J. Solomos (eds), *Theories of Race and Ethnicity: Contemporary Debates and Perspectives*. Cambridge: Cambridge University Press.

Stam, Robert and Shohat, Ella (2012) *Race in Translation: Culture Wars Around the Postcolonial Atlantic*. New York: New York University Press.

Sussman, Robert Wald (2014) *The Myth of Race: The Troubling Persistence of an Unscientific Idea*, Boston, MA: Harvard University Press.

Taylor, Keeanga-Yamahtta (2016) *From #BlackLivesMatter to Black Liberation*. Chicago, IL: Haymarket.

Tebble, Adam J. (2006) Exclusion for democracy, *Political Theory, 34*(4): 463–87.

Titley, Gavan (2017) 'Introduction: Becoming Symbolic – From *Charlie Hebdo* to "Charlie Hebdo"', in G. Titley, D. Freedman, G. Khiabany and A. Mondon (eds), *After Charlie Hebdo: Terror, Racism and Free Speech*. London: Zed.

Toscano, Alberto (2017) 'Notes on Late Fascism', *Historical Materialism*, 2 April. Available at www.historicalmaterialism.org/blog/notes-late-fascism (accessed 8 January 2019).

Traverso, Enzo and Marin, Grégory (2017) 'L'extrême droite reprend les codes de l'antisémitisme des années 1930', *L'Humanité* [online] 17 February. Available at www.humanite.fr/enzo-traverso-lextreme-droite-reprend-les-codes-de-lantisemitisme-des-annees-1930-632301 (accessed 8 January 2019).

Trilling, Daniel (2015) 'What To Do With the People Who Make It Across?', *London Review of Books* [online] 8 October. Available at www.lrb.co.uk/v37/n19/daniel-trilling/what-to-do-with-the-people-who-do-make-it-across (accessed 18 November 2018).

Trilling, Daniel (2018) *Lights in the Distance*. London: Pan Macmillan.

Tufekci, Zeynep (2013) 'Not this one': social movements, the attention economy, and microcelebrity networked activism, *American Behavioral Scientist, 57*(7): 848–70.

Tufekci, Zeynep (2018) 'YouTube, the Great Radicalizer', *New York Times* [online] 10 March. Available at www.nytimes.com/2018/03/10/opinion/sunday/youtube-politics-radical.html (accessed 25 November 2018).

Turner, Julia (2014) 'The Outrage Project', *Slate* [online] 17 December. Available at www.slate.com/articles/life/culturebox/2014/12/the_year_of_outrage_2014_everything_you_were_angry_about_on_social_media.html (accessed 8 January 2019).

Urry, John (2003) *Global Complexity*. Cambridge: Polity.

Vaccari, Christian, Chadwick, Andrew and O'Loughlin, Ben (2015) Dual screening the political: media events, social media, and citizen engagement, *Journal of Communication*, 65(6): 1041–61.

Vakil, Abdoolkarim (2010) 'Is the Islam in Islamophobia the Same as the Islam in Anti- Islam; Or When is it Islamophobia Time?', in S. Sayyid and Abdoolkarim Vakil (eds), *Thinking Through Islamophobia*. New York: Columbia University Press.

Valenta, Markha (2017) 'Symbolic Politics with Brutally Real Effects: When "Nobodies" Make History', in G. Titley, D. Freedman, A. Mondon and G. Khiabany (eds), *After Charlie Hebdo: Terror, Racism and Free Speech*. London: Zed. pp. 129–45.

Valluvan, Sivamohan (2017a) Racial entanglements and sociological confusions: repudiating the rehabilitation of integration, *British Journal of Sociology*, 69(2): 436–58.

Valluvan, Sivamohan (2017b) 'Defining and Challenging New Nationalism', *The Sociological Review* [online] 7 June. Available at www.thesociological-review.com/blog/defining-and-challenging-new-nationalism.html (accessed 19 November 2018).

Van Dijck, José (2013) *The Culture of Connectivity: A Critical History of Social Media*. Oxford: Oxford University Press.

Van Dijck, Teun (1995) 'A Proposal for Multicultural Media Monitoring in Europe', *The Electronic Journal of Communication*, 5(2/3). Available at http://www.cios.org/EJCPUBLIC/005/2/00529.html (accessed 23 January 2019).

Van Zoonen, Liesbet, Vis, Farida and Mihelj, Sabina (2010) Performing citizenship on YouTube: activism, satire and online debate around the anti-Islam video *Fitna*, *Critical Discourse Studies*, 7(4): 249–62.

Veilleux-Lepage, Yannick and Archambault, Emil (2017) 'Soldiers of Odin: The Global Diffusion of Vigilante Movements', Political Studies Association. Available at www.psa.ac.uk/sites/default/files/conference/papers/2017/Soldiers%20of%20Odin%20-The%20Global%20Diffusion%20of%20Vigilante%20Movements.pdf (accessed 8 January 2019).

Versi, Miqdaad (2016) 'What Do Muslims Really Think? This Skewed Poll Certainly Won't Tell Us', *The Guardian* [online] 12 April. Available at www.theguardian.com/commentisfree/2016/apr/12/what-do-muslims-think-skewed-poll-wont-tell-us (accessed 8 January 2019).

Virdee, Satnam (2014) *Racism, Class and the Racialized Outsider*. London: Macmillan.

Vis, Farida, Falukner, Simon, D'Orazio, Francesco and Prøitz, Lin (2015) *The Iconic Image on Social Media*, Visual Social Media Lab, Sheffield University. Available at http://visualsocialmedialab.org/projects/the-iconic-image-on-social-media (accessed 8 January 2019).

Volkmer, Ingrid (2014) *The Global Public Sphere*. Cambridge: Polity.

Wade, Peter (2010) The presence and absence of race, *Patterns of Prejudice*, *44*(1): 43–60.

Waldron, Jeremy (2012) *The Harm in Hate Speech*. Boston, MA: Harvard University Press.

Walters, William (2004) Secure borders, safe haven, domopolitics, *Citizenship Studies*, *8*(3): 237–60.

Warburton, Nigel (2009) *Free Speech: A Very Short Introduction*. New York: Oxford University Press.

Ward, Justin (2018) 'Wikipedia Wars: Inside the Fight Against Far-Right Editors, Vandals and Sock Pppets', *Southern Poverty Law Center* [online] 12 March. Available at www.splcenter.org/hatewatch/2018/03/12/ wikipedia-wars-inside-fight-against-far-right-editors-vandals-and-sock-puppets (accessed 25 November 2018).

Warner, Michael (2002) Publics and counterpublics, *Public Culture*, *14*(1): 49–90.

Wekker, Gloria (2016) *White Innocence: Paradoxes of Colonialism and Race*. Durham, NC and London: Duke University Press.

West, Caroline (2012) 'Words that Silence? Freedom of Expression and Racist Hate Speech', in Maitra I., M.K. McGowan (eds) *Speech & Harm: Controversies over Free Speech*. Oxford: Oxford University Press.

White, Aidan (2015) 'When It Comes to the Migration Story, Words Matter', *Open Democracy* [online] 31 August. Available at www.opendemocracy. net/aidan-white/when-it-comes-to-migration-story-words-matter (accessed 8 January 2019).

Wieviorka, Michel (2015) 'Is It So Difficult to be an Anti-Racist?', in P. Werbner and T. Modood (eds), *Debating Cultural Hybridity: Multicultural Identity and the Politics of Anti-Racism*. London: Zed.

Wilby, Peter (2015) 'Republish and Be Damned – What Should Our Newspapers Do With the Charlie Hebdo Cartoons?', *New Statesman* [online] 22 January. Available at www.newstatesman.com/politics/2015/01/republish-and-be-damned-what-should-our-newspapers-do-charlie-hebdo-cartoons (accessed 8 January 2019).

Williams, Apryl and Gonlin, Vanessa (2017) I got all my sisters with me (on Black Twitter): second screening of *How to Get Away with Murder* as a discourse on Black Womanhood, *Information, Communication & Society*, *20*(7): 984–1004.

Winter, Aaron (2017) 'Charlottesville, Far-Right Rallies, Racism and Relating to Power', *Open Democracy* [online] 17 August. Available at www.opende mocracy.net/aaron-winter/charlottesville-far-right-rallies-racism-and-relat ing-to-power (accessed 25 November 2018).

Wodak, Ruth (2013) 'Anything Goes!' – The Haiderization of Europe', in R. Wodak, M. KhosraviNik and B. Mral (eds), *Right-Wing Populism in Europe: Politics and Discourse*. London: Bloomsbury Academic. pp. 23–38.

Wodak, Ruth (2015) *The Politics of Fear: What Right-Wing Populist Discourses Mean*. London: Sage.

Wolfe, Patrick (2016) *Traces of History: Elementary Structures of Race*. London: Verso.

Wolff, Robert S. (2013) 'The Historian's Craft, Memory and Wikipedia', in J. Dougherty and K. Nawrotzki (eds), *Writing History in the Digital Age*. Ann Arbor, MI: University of Michigan Press.

Wolfreys, Jim (2015) 'After the Paris Attacks: An Islamophobic Spiral', *International Socialism*, *146*, [online] 11 April. Available at http://isj.org.uk/after-the-paris-attacks/ (accessed 25 November 2018).

Woodly, Deva (2016) 'Black Lives Matter: The Politics of Race and Movement in the 21st Century', *Public Seminar* [online] 18 January. Available at www.publicseminar.org/2016/01/black-lives-matter-the-politics-of-race-and-movement-in-the-21st-century/ (accessed 18 November 2018).

Yanay, Niza (2012) *The Ideology of Hatred: The Psychic Power of Discourse*. New York: Fordham University Press.

Yasseri, Taha, Spoerri, Anselm, Graham, Mark and Kertész, János (2014) '"The most Controversial Topics in Wikipedia": A Multilingual and Geographical Analysis', in P. Fichman and N. Hara (eds), *Global Wikipedia: International and Cross-Cultural Issues in Online Collaboration*. Lanham, MD: The Scarecrow Press.

Yilmaz, Ferruh (2016) *How the Workers Became Muslims: Immigration, Culture and Hegemonic Transformation in Europe*. Ann Arbor , MI: University of Michigan Press.

Yzola, Alana (2018) 'Hidden Meanings Behind Childish Gambino's "This is America"', *Business Insider* [online] 11 May. Available at www.businsinsider.com/hidden-meanings-behind-childish-gambino-s-this-is-america-2018-5?r=US&IR=T&IR=T (accessed 8 January 2018).

Zephaniah, Benjamin (2016) 'Foreword', in Hsiao-Hung Pai (ed.), *Angry White People: Coming Face-to-Face with the British Far Right*. London Zed.

Žižek, Slavoj (1997) Multiculturalism, or, the cultural logic of multinational capitalism, *New Left Review*, I/*225*: 28–51.

# Index

CPSIA information can be obtained
at www.ICGtesting.com
Printed in the USA
LVHW081848240919
632125LV00005B/375/P